Stop the Machines

To my parents

Stop the Machines
The Rise of Anti-Technology Extremism

Mauro Lubrano

polity

Copyright © Mauro Lubrano 2025

The right of Mauro Lubrano to be identified as Author of this Work has been asserted in accordance with the UK Copyright, Designs and Patents Act 1988.

First published in 2025 by Polity Press

Polity Press
65 Bridge Street
Cambridge CB2 1UR, UK

Polity Press
111 River Street
Hoboken, NJ 07030, USA

All rights reserved. Except for the quotation of short passages for the purpose of criticism and review, no part of this publication may be reproduced, stored in a retrieval system or transmitted, in any form or by any means, electronic, mechanical, photocopying, recording or otherwise, without the prior permission of the publisher.

ISBN-13: 978-1-5095-5573-4
ISBN-13: 978-1-5095-5574-1 (pb)

A catalogue record for this book is available from the British Library.

Library of Congress Control Number: 2024948637

Typeset in 10 on 13pt PSFournier Std
by Cheshire Typesetting Ltd, Cuddington, Cheshire
Printed and bound in Great Britain by CPI Group (UK) Ltd, Croydon

The publisher has used its best endeavours to ensure that the URLs for external websites referred to in this book are correct and active at the time of going to press. However, the publisher has no responsibility for the websites and can make no guarantee that a site will remain live or that the content is or will remain appropriate.

Every effort has been made to trace all copyright holders, but if any have been overlooked the publisher will be pleased to include any necessary credits in any subsequent reprint or edition.

For further information on Polity, visit our website:
politybooks.com

Contents

Acknowledgements vi

Introduction 1
1 Long Live King Ludd! 9
2 Smash the Prison-Society: Insurrectionary Anarchism 35
3 Nature Fights Back: Eco-Extremism 58
4 Anti-Tech to Accelerate: Eco-Fascism 81
5 The Fight to End Civilization 101
Conclusion 124

Notes 132
Selected Bibliography 180
Index 190

Acknowledgements

I began working on this book in 2021 as a PhD candidate at the University of St Andrews and I completed it as a lecturer at the University of Bath in 2024. This journey has been long and challenging, but thanks to the incredible friends and colleagues who have supported me, it has been an enjoyable and rewarding one. The list of people who deserve acknowledgement here is long, and I will do my best to recognize each one, knowing that their support has been instrumental.

I am deeply grateful to my editor, Louise Knight, copy-editor, Justin Dyer, and the exceptional team at Polity for their invaluable support and professionalism. My genuine thanks also go to Colin Clarke, who, after reading a journal article I published in 2021, recommended to Polity that I write this book, despite never having met me. I extend my sincere appreciation to the three anonymous reviewers who provided insightful and constructive comments on the early draft of this book. In addition, I would like to thank Sean Fleming. His work on the origins of anti-technology radicalism has been a great inspiration, and he's been a fantastic and encouraging colleague.

I would like to express my profound gratitude to the Department of Politics, Languages & International Studies at the University of Bath. Special thanks go to Peter Allen, Patrick Bury, Ivan Gololobov, Sophia Hatzisavvidou, Katka Vrablikova, David Moon, Peter Lambert, André Barrinha, Sophie Whiting, Maria Garcia, Brett Edwards, Benoît Dillet, Leslie Wehner, Brad Evans, Paul Higate, Mattia Cacciatori, David Galbreath, and Micha Germann. Their support, both in giving me a job and in providing a warm and stimulating environment in which to finish this book, has been invaluable.

I am also forever indebted to my PhD supervisors, Bernhard Blumenau and Kieran McConaghy, my PhD examiners, Richard English and Timothy Wilson, and colleagues such as Gary Ackerman and Yannick Veilleux-Lepage, whose guidance and support were instrumental in shaping this book and myself as a scholar. Special thanks also go to my PhD crew, particularly Aristidis Agoglossakis Foley, Sarah Gharib Seif, Sasha Clark, João Seixas, Kacper Terlecki, Kalyani Twyman, Andrea Gelardi, and Federico Solfrini, for the early conceptual discussions both in and out of the office and their friendship.

I can't go without mentioning my dear friends Lorenzo B., Matilde, Lorenzo F., Paolo, Riccardo, and Cody. Thank you for your curiosity, for reminding me not to take myself too seriously, and for our adventures together.

Then, huge thanks go to my partner Sammy for the long walks with scruffy Mabel, for the endless coffee, and for being by my side with her enthusiasm, softness, and strength.

Finally, I want to thank my parents, Mary Jo and Pasquale, and my brother Paolo. This project would have been impossible without their immense support, love, and care.

Introduction

It was 14 May 2019, Berlin, Germany. The U-Bahn stop at Görlitzer Bahnhof was only a few minutes from the anarchist social space I was headed to in the Kreuzberg neighbourhood. A few days earlier, I came across a leaflet about a meeting there. The topic of discussion was 'Fall of AI: A Call to Fight "Artificial Intelligence" as Part of the Technological Dominion'.[1] A year earlier, Google had planned to build one of its Google Campus start-up hubs in the same neighbourhood. Kreuzberg's response was strong – and unsurprising. After months of protests and demonstrations, Google backed down, renouncing its plans.[2]

In 2019, I was a first-year PhD student at the University of St Andrews in Scotland, specializing in political violence and terrorism.[3] I had followed the campaign against Google Campus and knew that anarchist groups had been at its forefront. More importantly, I knew that, in May 2019, Berlin would host the 2019 Rise of AI Conference.[4] The leaflet, with its headline mirroring the conference's title, naturally piqued my curiosity. I decided to attend the meeting. Of course, I never anticipated that it would end up motivating me to write this book!

The meeting wasn't exceptionally crowded – around a dozen people. And the first hour was, in all honesty, quite tedious. A few speakers went on about artificial intelligence, explaining what it is and how it works, and then discussed its potential moral and ethical issues. Halfway through, they switched from German to English following the request of a comrade whose German wasn't good enough to follow the discussion. I was relieved; I am fluent in German but more comfortable with English – especially when the discussion is quite technical, bordering on a computer science talk. But after this first endless hour, the topic changed. Echoing Lenin, the meeting moved to discuss *what is to be done* about AI. A few people asked to intervene. The first proposed a stable presence at the AI conference, distributing leaflets and trying to raise awareness about the potential risks of artificial intelligence. The second opted for the opposite approach: retreat to the countryside, form a commune, and renounce modern technology – a sort of anarchist Amish. The third, who had been quite vocal throughout the first session, clicked his tongue, pointing out how these paths had already been tried and had failed; there was no reason to believe they'd succeed now. The argument went like this: 'People won't change their mind because of a leaflet' and 'The consequences of AI and other emerging technologies will be too far-reaching to escape.' Encouraged to offer a solution, this third speaker admitted he had none but added that he couldn't exclude a near future when he'd punch someone in the face for wearing Google Glass. I couldn't tell how serious that comment was. But those words stuck with me for weeks, eventually prompting me to begin researching anti-technology politics as a side interest.

As a student of political violence and terrorism, I was already familiar with the story of Theodore J. Kaczynski, the Unabomber, who conducted a one-man war against technology in the United States from 1978 to 1995. But as I started reading more about this topic, it brought back snippets of related incidents I'd come across online or in the news but hadn't paid much attention to. I remembered sitting in my living room in Italy in 2012, reading about the CEO of a nuclear engineering group who had just been kneecapped by two insurrectionary anarchists from the Informal Anarchist Federation. What was the motive for such a heinous act? The two anarchists wanted to punish the CEO for pursuing and spreading nuclear technology around the world.[5] Additionally, I recalled hearing about another insurrectionary anarchist action against technology: an arson attack against the Italian Technology Institute on Christmas Eve in 2018.[6] These incidents no longer seemed like isolated events but rather part of a larger and more significant trend. However, despite sensing a bigger underlying phenomenon, I couldn't find any readings that fully satisfied my curiosity. Apart from books and articles on the Unabomber, most of what I found on the topic of political violence, terrorism, and technology focused on how violent extremists could adopt and exploit emerging technologies.[7] So I seized the nettle and took it upon myself to begin exploring this disturbing yet fascinating topic.

I will be honest: I did not find what I expected; I found much more. I embarked on this journey expecting to discover anti-technology extremism primarily directed against specific technologies, primarily emerging technology. After all, we live in an era of rapid technological advancement. The Fifth Industrial Revolution is on the horizon. It will see the convergence and integration of various technologies – such as artificial intelligence and machine learning – with humans, whereby the former will be given tasks and decision-making capabilities. The potential to bring about a paradigm shift in many sectors of society, from industry to public services, is enormous.[8] UK Research and Innovation (UKRI) – the public body of the UK government that directs research and innovation funding – published a report in December 2023 that compiled a list of the fifty emerging technologies that 'could change everything'.[9] From the Internet of Things, additive manufacturing, drones, biotechnology, neurotechnology, blockchain, and robotics to virtual and augmented reality, the world as we know it is changing. Yet for all the miracles and wonders these technologies herald, they also elicit anxiety, scepticism, and fear. I suspected anti-technology extremism would sit at the intersection of these feelings, motivated primarily by concerns such as exacerbating social and economic inequalities or privacy. Beyond this material realm, I also expected the unease about emerging technologies to stem from the emotional and psychological responses they provoke. For example, watching videos of humanoid robots performing complex tasks can evoke an 'uncanny valley' effect where the familiar and unfamiliar seem to merge. This discomfort can escalate into anxiety when people ponder the yet-unknown consequences of artificial intelligence and other emerging technologies. What exactly can AI do? What is machine learning? How far will they go? Will they surpass human intelligence? Such questions are loaded with uncertainty and can lead to broader apprehension about the direction in which our society is headed and the unknown ramifications that technology can bring. A recent poll, for example, found that 61% of Americans consider AI poses an existential risk to humanity's future, threatening civilization.[10] While the proportion of people who hold a similar belief is remarkably lower in the United Kingdom (18%), there is a generally pessimistic attitude towards artificial intelligence, with Britons lamenting a lack of confidence that AI can be developed or regulated responsibly.[11] Other recent technologies have similarly caused concern among the general public. For instance, 5G technologies have been associated with a series of harmful effects on human health.[12]

However, as I delved deeper, I soon realized there was much more to anti-technology extremism than this. Its roots run deeper and are far more complex than mere apprehension towards specific technological innovations. In other words, the resistance and unease I encountered were not just reactions to the latest gadgets or groundbreaking advancements. Sure, those do play a role in all this. The recent protests against 5G technology or mRNA vaccines can be seen as reactions to the above-mentioned concerns and to the disinformation, misinformation, and conspiracies that often come with them. But, beyond this, I found that anti-technology extremism constitutes a deep-seated response to the very essence of our modern existence – a reaction against our technological civilization. It is a multifaceted phenomenon; anti-technology extremism emerges as a cross-cutting ideological current found in different ideological milieus – defined as dynamic clusters of social actors that share some ideological traits, presenting both subcurrents and common beliefs. Indeed, while my first encounter with anti-technology extremism was within the anarchist realm, I soon discovered variations of these feelings within other ideologies. Ranging from radical environmentalism to the far right, I focused on the most extreme fringes of such movements to identify and explore the positions that advanced the most uncompromising and violent critique of technology. This exploration led me to different ideological milieus, namely insurrectionary anarchism, eco-extremism, and eco-fascism, which currently display the most marked forms of anti-technology extremism. Despite the many differences that set these milieus apart, they are united in their opposition to technology. This opposition is not, however, associated with one or more specific technologies but with technology as a whole – perceived as an entity that goes beyond the individual machines and takes on the characteristics of an all-encompassing mega-machine that enslaves both humans and nature. As such, this is not merely about a fear of the unknown or a reactionary resistance to change. To these extremists, the issue isn't just the dangers of artificial intelligence, the ethical dilemmas of biotechnology, or the environmental impact of industrial processes. These are merely symptoms of a more significant problem: the dominance of technology over human life and the subjugation of nature. In other words, technology has become an existential threat to humanity and the planet. In this sense, the stakes could not be higher.

All this entails the potential for escalation. From the perspective of anti-technology extremists, progress can't be halted, and the technological system can't be reformed. As the technological system is beyond reform and redemption, the only possible solution is to dismantle it. The only way to restore a genuine connection with nature and rediscover the true meaning of being human is to eradicate technology and do away with techno-industrial civilization (the stage of civilization that emerged following the Industrial Revolutions) before techno-industrial civilization does away with us. Combining an apocalyptic mindset beset by dystopian visions of the future with escalation-bent strategies like accelerationism offers an explosive mix for intensifying the struggle to stop the machines: anti-technology extremists aim to hasten the collapse of the system by pushing its internal contradictions to breaking point. This belief has real-world implications that could lead to a ramping-up of anti-tech activities, from sabotage to more direct forms of lethal violence. In other words, as I will argue throughout this book, anti-technology extremism can become a significant driver of political violence.

The book begins by retracing the historical evolution of anti-technology extremism over the last three centuries to show how it has developed from concerns over material security to viewing technology as an existential threat to humanity and the natural world. It then explores anti-technology extremism within three distinct milieus: insurrectionary anarchism, eco-extremism, and eco-fascism. Each chapter retraces the emergence of anti-technology extremism in these contexts, examining the ideological justifications for rejecting technology and analysing the strategies and tactics to stop the machines. Insurrectionary anarchists intertwine the fight against technology with the class struggle, viewing technology as a manifestation of power structures and the cornerstone of a dystopian 'prison-society' where individual freedom and the environment are both endangered. Eco-extremists consider technology as nature's arch-nemesis – the ultimate adversary of all that is not wild. Driven by nihilistic and misanthropic beliefs, eco-extremists do not fight for a better future but solely to defend and avenge nature. Eco-fascists, a growing fringe group within the far right, perceive technology as a force of modernity that disconnects humanity from nature, threatening racial purity and societal stability. They engage in attacks on technological infrastructure to provoke societal collapse and ignite a race war. The final chapter synthesizes these movements, arguing that anti-technology extremism has emerged as a reaction to the Anthropocene, an attempt to undo the epoch of human domination, and exploring its potential for escalation.

On 'Extremism', 'Radicalism', and 'Terrorism'

The focus of this book – anti-technology extremism – represents a particularly insidious and rising form of violent extremism. But what is extremism? In this context, it refers to an anti-establishment force that views politics as a struggle for supremacy rather than peaceful competition between parties seeking support for advancing the common good. Usually found at the periphery of society, extremists seek to conquer the centre by employing a stark Manichaean 'us vs them' framework that considers political and social struggles as zero-sum games. In doing so, extremist movements tend towards authoritarianism and totalitarianism, glorify violence as a conflict resolution mechanism, and are unwilling to compromise.[13] A cognate term, radicalism, similarly refers to the desire for sweeping political change as a form of hostility against the status quo. Yet, although following ideals that can sometimes contain utopian elements, radical political parties or movements seek to restructure or overthrow outdated political structures without glorifying or necessarily resorting to violence. As anti-technology extremists seek to eradicate technology rather than reform it – or change our approach to it – they display a staunch, uncompromising position that legitimizes the use of violence against technology and those who represent it. Therefore, while this book does include reflections on forms of anti-technology radicalism, the label 'extremism' more accurately describes the anti-technology politics on which it squarely focuses.[14]

When extremists believe their cause justifies violence, they may turn to different forms of political violence – 'a genuinely multifaceted and varied phenomenon' that includes a vast range of activities, from street protest to genocide.[15] In particular, some anti-technology extremists turn to terrorism. In this book, I define terrorism as a form of political violence directed against victims selected for their symbolic value, with the intent of sending a message to a broader target audience and thereby manipulating its perception and behaviour.[16] The defining relationship is not between the perpetrator and the victim but between the perpetrator and the target audience. Hence, victims are not selected for who they are but for what they represent. The goal is to instil fear or provoke a reaction that furthers the perpetrators' cause among a sympathizing audience.[17] This underscores the severity of anti-technology extremism, where political violence and terrorism have become the tools to target technology and its proponents, aiming to dismantle technological civilization. Yet, to fully grasp this phenomenon, we must first understand what we mean when we talk about technology and civilization.

On Technology and Civilization

Technology is a complex term. Curiously, a word so familiar and inherently intertwined with virtually every aspect of life and society can be challenging to capture. What is technology? Is it the keyboard I am using to type these words, the process that went into producing the keyboard itself, or the knowledge necessary to create that process in the first place? We might instinctively link it to devices or science, but technology is more than that. Although I am more interested in how anti-technology extremists define technology, I still need to explain what I mean by the term. We can think of technology within a four-dimensional framework and distinguish it as: (a) an artefact – that is, tools and manufactured objects; (b) knowledge – whether in terms of 'how-to', engineering, or insights from the social and physical sciences; (c) a process – namely, problem-solving, research and development, invention, and innovation; and (d) volition – meaning technology as a social force and a social construct.[18]

Technology is, then, intrinsically linked to the concept of civilization. First used in 1756, this term has many definitions.[19] Wolf Schäfer gives one that is particularly suited for this project. Distinguishing between culture and civilization, he argues that we can 'define the social construction of meaning as the work of culture and the technoscientific handling of nature [...] as the work of civilization'.[20] Whereas history has witnessed the rise and fall of different civilizations at the local level, the contemporary world has many local cultures but a single global civilization spanning the entire planet. Such a civilization 'has no fixed territory; to find its backbone, one has to look for the worldwide matrix of technoscientific networks. This essential constituent defines the civilization of our time as a *deterritorialized ensemble of networked technoscientific practices with global reach.*'[21] This definition allows us to emphasize the link between technology and civilization – a link that anti-technology extremists themselves decry. Therefore, I will use the terms 'technology' and 'techno-industrial civilization' interchangeably throughout the book. Doing so highlights one crucial aspect that will emerge from the following pages: for anti-tech extremists, attacking technology is attacking the civilization it supports and enables. To eradicate one is to tear down the other.

Ultimately, the pages that follow will present a compelling argument about the potential for anti-technology extremism to become a significant driver of political violence in the years ahead. It is crucial to understand the motives, worldviews, and strategies driving this phenomenon if we are to address the challenge effectively. As such, I hope this book serves as the first comprehensive exploration of this emerging trend, providing an in-depth understanding of the movements and groups aiming to eliminate technology.

1
Long Live King Ludd!

It is hard – if not impossible – to overstate the role of technology in the history of humanity. From the discovery and mastery of fire to the promise of nuclear fusion, technology has undeniably altered and improved how we live, work, and interact. Deprivation, hunger, and diseases still haunt many parts of the globe. Still, people are nowadays globally better fed and clothed than they were just a mere hundred years ago when leading causes of death were infectious diseases that can now be easily treated with over-the-counter drugs. Of course, technological progress did not just afford us abundant food and effective therapies. It would be difficult to find any area of human activity that hasn't been affected by technology. Technological change has not, however, maintained the same pace throughout history. In his *The Power of the Machine*, Robert Buchanan argues that technological change is as old as technology itself – in other words, as old as the human species.[1] Yet, while progress has always accompanied humanity in its journey, the last three centuries have witnessed an unprecedented and continuous series of technological revolutions. This process has inevitably resulted in a cascading effect whereby every aspect of human life has been profoundly affected and reshaped at the individual, societal, and global levels.

Our economic structures have been dramatically altered throughout the four Industrial Revolutions of the last three centuries.[2] This, in turn, has had profound repercussions on social structures, labour dynamics, and cultural norms. The world is nowadays caught in an intricate web of connectivity that enables us to create, exchange, and receive information instantaneously. Besides making the world more interconnected and globalized, this has also contributed, for example, to empowering social movements and activists and to improving education standards. Travelling at a slower pace than information, news, instant messaging, and financial operations, but still much faster than their obsolete counterparts, modern means of transportation allow for goods and people to be taken quickly and safely between different places on the globe. Technology has played a significant, if not essential, role in shaping the world we know today and ourselves as humans. In this regard, Gilbert Ramsay is not wrong when he argues that '[w]e forget that technology doesn't just help us to get more of what we want. It changes what we want, and how we understand our very existence.'[3]

However, not all these changes have had a positive impact. There is, in other words, a darker side to technological progress. While technologies have afforded us tools that have substantially enhanced our lives, they have also given us the means to destroy each other. From the rudimentary hunting tools our ancestors fashioned from sticks and rocks to the discovery of nuclear fission, history brims with examples of technologies that threaten to end, rather than improve, life. Nuclear and chemical weapons are arguably the most notorious examples, but the case of dynamite is perhaps the most paradigmatic. In the mid-nineteenth century, explosives were widely used in the mining, construction, and transportation industries. However, many such explosives were highly unstable, posing considerable safety risks until 1867, when the Swedish chemist, engineer, and inventor Alfred Nobel patented the safer and more stable dynamite. Nobel saw dynamite's potential to revolutionize mining and other industries but was not blind to its danger if it were to fall into the wrong hands – which it did. Amidst the societal and technological changes of this period, anarchists were waging their struggle against the state, authority, and capitalism. Trapped as they were in a dramatic asymmetric conflict, they welcomed Nobel's invention as the gift that would help them wage their 'propaganda of the deed'.[4] The adoption of dynamite, along with other explosive devices – for example, the Orsini bomb[5] – resulted in a series of bloody bombings, such as the 1886 Haymarket Massacre,[6] that claimed several innocent lives and injured many others.[7] It is easy to imagine why dynamite appealed to those interested in creating chaos and destruction. In 1605, when conspirators of the Gunpowder Plot sought to blow up the House of Lords during the State Opening of Parliament in London, they amassed thirty-six barrels of gunpowder. Two hundred and fifty years later, anarchists could theoretically afford a similar result with a few easily concealable sticks of dynamite.[8]

Besides giving us the means to kill each other, the ever-increasing pace of technological development has contributed to environmental challenges such as climate change. Discussions on the long-lasting consequences of climate change are now part of everyday public debate, with the majority of the scientific community pointing its finger at pollution and resource depletion as consequences of industrialization and technological progress.[9]

Moreover, technology has been identified as a source of insecurity concerning individual liberties. In particular, the digital age has raised significant concerns about privacy and surveillance, sparking debates over civil liberties, security, and individual rights. In our contemporary hyper-capitalist society, we are constantly bombarded with targeted ads – suggestions for products, travel, entertainment, or investments based on our online activities, location, or demographic profile. The fear that our smartphones and similar devices might be 'listening' to us to feed us with ads for products that match our interests has become the source of much speculation and concern.[10] Overall, human behaviour has become a valuable data source that can be used to maximize profit. In this regard, in *The Age of Surveillance Capitalism*, Shoshana Zuboff maintains that human experiences have been claimed as free raw material for translation into behavioural data. Fed into machine learning, the data gathered by global tech companies such as Google and Facebook can be used to predict our behaviour but also to influence and modify it, which, Zuboff argues, has had catastrophic consequences for democracy and freedom.[11] This represents a prime example of how technology can shape economic structures. After all, technological developments have often created new opportunities. However, in doing so, they have also contributed to exacerbating social disparities, leaving many sectors struggling to adapt to a rapidly changing labour market. Recent examples include the many debates about the impact that automation or artificial intelligence might have on people's jobs and lives. Following the release of ChatGPT on 30 November 2022, for example, specialized outlets frantically rushed to compile lists of jobs that might face extinction because of the chatbot.[12] Even industries like Hollywood have not been spared and have witnessed strikes and protests over the use of AI.[13] When considering this darker side of technology, it is thus not surprising that, throughout history, many have raised concerns or expressed scepticism about the role of technology. While such critics often neither reject technology outright nor condone the use of violence against it, certain individuals and groups have resolved to adopt more radical and extremist goals and means. This chapter retraces the modern history of the critique of technology, seeking to understand the emergence and evolution of contemporary forms of anti-technology extremism in the last three centuries – the centuries of unprecedented technological development, as per Buchanan – and it does so by starting with what constitutes perhaps the most misunderstood example of a critique of technology: the nineteenth-century Luddite movement.

Machine-Breaking

The legacy of the Luddite movement does not do justice to its struggle to improve labour conditions in early nineteenth-century England. This is because the term 'Luddite' is nowadays often used as a synonym for 'deluded technophobe' or 'anti-technology'.[14] In everyday parlance, we might use this term to tease the one friend who's particularly inept with technologies, prefers traditional methods and techniques, or is hesitant about adopting the latest gadgets. But this label has also been used as an insult, with the term 'Luddite' taking on a pejorative meaning to suggest a 'mindless, reactionary opposition to technological improvement, an ignorant impulse to destroy or resist the inevitable march of mechanized progress'.[15] 'Luddite' has become a convenient and effective way to dismiss anyone who raises concerns or criticisms about the role and impact of technology, even when those concerns are valid and well founded.[16] This was the case, for example, for the anti-globalization movement that gained momentum in the 1990s, even though it must be said that its followers were 'defiantly proud of their Luddism'.[17] On other occasions, the term has been used in a hyperbolic and grossly misleading manner to revile al-Qaeda following the 9/11 attacks. George Gilder – co-founder of the Discovery Institute and Senior Fellow of the Center on Wealth & Poverty – coined the term 'Osama bin Luddites' to depict al-Qaeda and Osama bin Laden as some backward individuals who were after US technology.[18] Therefore, considering the connotations that the terms 'Luddism' and 'Luddite' have acquired, it appears Gavin Mueller is right when he argues in *Breaking Things at Work* that history has not been entirely kind to the Luddites.[19]

Who, then, were the Luddites, and what was their struggle about? The original Luddites were a movement of machine-breakers and social activists primarily active in the early nineteenth century in the counties of Nottinghamshire and Yorkshire – although other counties, such as Lancashire, also witnessed Luddite activity. At that time, the English economy was gradually escaping the Malthusian trap.[20] This sustained economic growth was mainly due to technological progress and the introduction of labour-saving, automated devices – such as the stocking frame, the gag mill, and the shearing frame – that promised to revolutionize the production process.[21] Thanks to these new devices, cloth could now be produced using a fraction of the labour times and skills that were previously required. A profession once dominated by highly skilled and well-remunerated artisans now opened up to cheap, unskilled workers – including, sometimes, children.[22] As such, productivity increased while the quality of life lagged behind.

Against this backdrop, the Luddites emerged as a movement of skilled labourers – mostly weavers and textile workers – who took direct action against the disruption of their trade and traditional ways of life. This was by no means the first time that workers had rioted against new machinery. Stocking frames, for example, had already been targeted towards the end of the seventeenth century. Karl Marx even noted hostility to wind- and waterpower stretching back to at least the 1630s.[23] Similarly, cases of machine-breaking were reported across England in the seventeenth and eighteenth centuries.[24] According to Joel Mokyr, machine-breaking was a less frequent phenomenon during the Middle Ages because the various guilds and trade associations were sufficiently powerful and effective in preventing the introduction of those technologies that could have jeopardized their importance in the production process and the economy.[25] By contrast, the early phases of the industrialization process in England witnessed numerous cases of machine-breaking riots, which gained momentum in the nineteenth century with the emergence of the Luddites. England was not an exception here. Similar machine-breaking events had occurred in other countries before the Luddites and would also occur after their demise.[26] None of these incidents, however, matched the legendary aura that the Luddites implanted in the collective imagination and persists to this day.

The term 'Luddites' came from their alleged leader, the almost mythical figure of Ned Ludd. Historians have not conclusively established the origins of 'King Ludd'. Some argue that Ludd was a young man with a cognitive disorder who may have misunderstood an order and accidentally destroyed his framing machine. Others maintain he did so out of anger.[27] Be that as it may, the legend of King Ludd reverberated across the movement, 'a potent collective fiction' that named and united its followers and was believed to be real by some government officials at the time.[28]

The movement emerged in the spring of 1811 as Luddites protested in Nottinghamshire. Armed with sledgehammers and other rudimentary tools, they assaulted factories, smashing framing machines.[29] The first three months of the protest resulted in the destruction of almost a thousand knitting frames.[30] The following months saw the protests and sabotage spreading and escalating, prompting the authorities to dispatch twelve thousand British troops to quell the machine-breakers. With Parliament making it a capital offence to destroy industrial machinery, several Luddites were hanged, with many others ending up in the penal colony of Australia.[31] The demise of the Luddites did not represent the end of machine-breaking in England. The years 1816 and 1826 witnessed Luddite revivals, while, in 1830, agricultural workers launched a large-scale machine-breaking offensive – known as the Swing Riots – in southern and eastern England.[32] After that, while persisting on a smaller scale,[33] machine-breaking declined, not least because other forms of collective action were becoming available to workers, thanks to the legalization of trade unions in 1824.[34]

What emerges here is that the Luddites' opposition to technology was not quite an expression of technophobia. These machine-breakers were not against technological progress or the integration of machinery in the production process. After all, the machines that the Luddites sought to destroy had already been available for two centuries in England and elsewhere.[35] As historian Eric Hobsbawm argued, this wasn't a 'question of hostility to machines as such. Wrecking was simply a technique of trade unionism' at a time when organized unions hardly existed. Therefore, through this form of 'collective bargaining by riot'[36] the Luddites composed themselves as a class during a period when workers had individualized rapports with bosses.[37] The objective was to demand fair wages and control over their trade.[38] Violence was not the first answer. As previous attempts had successfully protected their livelihoods from technology, the Luddites had initially tried to present a petition to Parliament. However, preoccupied with the conflict against Napoleon, the authorities had little time for craftsmen and artisans, so their demands went almost unnoticed, prompting the resort to violence.[39] Whether this was a wise choice has been the subject of lengthy scholarly debates. Indeed, scholars have historically held radically different positions regarding the effectiveness of the Luddites' campaigns in halting or delaying the diffusion of the new machines to minimize the possible negative consequences of the transformation of the production process. Some, like Shaun Bythell, argue that the Luddites' impact was minimal, whereas Malcolm Ian Thomis maintains that the riots did not delay the diffusion process. Others, like John Rule and Adrian Randall, assert that, in some cases, the diffusion of new technology was delayed. For example, the dissemination of the threshing machine was postponed by almost two decades following the 1830 Swing Riots.[40]

Regardless of whether the Luddites were successful, their legend lived on, serving as a poignant example of the enduring tension between progress and its social consequences. As we transition to the twentieth century, we shall delve into movements and figures grappling with technology's impact in their respective eras. Throughout this journey, we will see how a group of technology critics enthusiastically adopted the term 'Luddite', now often used pejoratively. In doing so, however, these critics signalled a fundamental difference between them and the original Luddites. The latter opposed technology because of its unmitigated impact on their profession and livelihood. As the next section will show, the neo-Luddites were, instead, primarily concerned with the pervasive nature and influence of technologies in contemporary societies and their potential for harming humans and degrading social relations.

Towards the Twentieth Century

Once the march of progress defeated the Luddites and the rioters who followed in the first half of the nineteenth century, the following decades saw – in particular in Western countries – a period of significant technological advancements and industrialization: the Second Industrial Revolution (1870–1930), a process even more transformative than the First Industrial Revolution in England.[41] Concurrently, the world entered the so-called 'first wave of globalization', an era of increased interconnectedness and integration among economies and societies across the globe.[42] Undoubtedly, technology played a crucial role in connecting the world. The construction of railways, the expansion of steamship routes, and the telegraph were among the developments that enabled goods, people, and information to move more swiftly and efficiently across different regions.[43] Not all nations entered this period of intense globalization willingly. Pursuing new markets, European powers aggressively expanded their empires, bringing vast parts of Africa, Asia, and the Pacific under colonial rule. In some cases, Western technology was targeted with violence as it represented a symbol of Western encroachment. For example, the Yihetuan Movement – also known as the Boxer Movement – destroyed telegraph poles and other symbolic Western technology during the uprising at the turn of the twentieth century.[44] Similarly, George Wong argues that certain movements emerged in China during the late Ming and early Qing dynasties to free 'Chinese society from the possibility of complete Western technological domination'.[45] In an analogous attempt to fight Western political and military domination, railways became targets of political resistance and protest in India.⁴⁶ Clearly, these are not examples of movements that sought to eradicate technology as such, but rather instances of symbolic violence against devices that represented the colonial domination of the West.

Meanwhile, positivism emerged as a philosophical and intellectual movement that embraced the scientific method as the ultimate means to understand and perfect society. It was argued that empirical observation, experimentation, and rationality could solve social problems and that progress could be pursued indefinitely.⁴⁷ In this period, technology started being systematically and wrongly collapsed into science as if the two terms denoted an identical notion.⁴⁸ The spirit of this era is encapsulated in the series of world expositions in major cities around the globe at the turn of the twentieth century. Particularly iconic are the 1889 and 1900 *Expositions Universelles* in Paris. These expositions epitomized positivist ideals, showcasing the achievements of various nations in science, technology, and industry and celebrating human progress and technological innovations as the key to continuous progress. There was a widespread belief that a better future for humanity was possible thanks to knowledge and reason. It is tragically ironic how this period of intense optimism ended with the world plunging into the catastrophe of World War I. The same science, technology, and industry that – coupled with 'reason' – were supposed to afford humanity a brighter future delivered, instead, the bloodiest conflict the world had ever experienced.

While this period did not witness any Luddite-like mass movement of resistance to technological innovations, a few voices began expressing concerns about the scale, magnitude, and consequences of technological progress and industrialization. One such voice was that of that of Thomas Carlyle, a Scottish historian. A staunch critic of industrialism, Carlyle defined his period as the 'Age of Machinery' – a world where nothing is 'done directly, or by hand; all is by rule and calculated contrivance'.⁴⁹ In his famous 1829 essay 'Signs of the Times', he identified pervasive materialism as a pernicious characteristic of this era, calling – at the same time – 'for a reformation not of society or the economy, but rather of the inner self'.⁵⁰ Another important figure of this period was John Ruskin, an English writer and polymath and a close friend of Carlyle.[51] Ruskin was not anti-technology, welcoming technological innovation where this was useful and life-enhancing.[52] Nonetheless, he lamented a dissatisfaction with modernity and the industrial age. In his writings, Ruskin expressed support for improving the condition of the poor while also arguing against the increasing mechanization and division of labour, which he considered dehumanizing.[53] In February 1884, Ruskin delivered a series of two lectures titled *The Storm-Cloud of the Nineteenth Century* at the London Institution, in which he identified industrialism as the cause of air pollution and the degradation of the environment.[54] Both Ruskin and Carlyle would eventually become influential in the development of anti-urban and anti-industrial feelings.[55] A similar call to abandon the industrialized world and return to the countryside was championed by Edward Carpenter – an English writer, poet, and activist who refused the industrial civilization of his time, portraying and idealizing nature as its 'grand alternative'.[56] Carpenter's argument, emphasizing the return to a nature that is fundamentally interconnected with humanity, parallels the message of a short dystopian story by one of his close friends, E.M. Forster.

First published in 1909, Forster's 'The Machine Stops' is set in a future where people live underground, relying entirely on an all-encompassing computer-like Machine that tends to their every need and with minimal interactions with other humans. The narrative follows Vashti, a fervent follower of the Machine, and her son Kuno, who, instead, questions the Machine and sets out to explore the outside world. Throughout the story, the Machine shows signs of decay, eventually leading to a total system breakdown. 'The Machine Stops' offers a powerful reflection on the consequences of technology and the importance of human connection and the natural world. Despite being over a century old, it raises several thought-provoking questions about our relationship with contemporary technology. It highlights several parallels that can be drawn between the world that Forster depicts and our contemporary society. So, as we can see, antagonism and scepticism towards technologies may not have given rise to protest movements or machine-breaking riots, but critical, intellectual voices were getting louder at the turn of the century. Such voices found an almost natural outlet in the dystopian literature to which Forster's story belongs. To name two, works like Yevgeny Zamyatin's *We* or Aldous Huxley's *Brave New World*, published respectively in 1924 and 1932, depict future technology-based dystopian worlds.[57] Arts and literature, especially the techno-dystopian science fiction genre, have always provided a powerful counterpoint to the utopias promised by scientists and techno-optimists.[58] Scholars equally engaged with critiques of technology.

Perhaps the most poignant example of this period is Lewis Mumford's *Technics and Civilization*. First published in 1934, this work retraces the history of technology and its relationship with civilization, arguing that our resort to technology should not come at the expense of physical and spiritual well-being, thereby paving the way to alienation from nature and other people.[59] Throughout the rest of his career, Mumford authored several other works on technology, providing substantial contributions to the critical study of technology and influencing not only various authors, including Jacques Ellul and Murray Bookchin, but also anti-technology extremists. The following chapters will discuss how segments of contemporary anti-technology extremism have embraced some of the concepts Mumford put forward. One such concept is the 'mega-machine', an entity that dehumanizes and enslaves people, 'the disciplined cohesive organization of man and machine controlled by absolute power for productive – and sometimes destructive – purpose'.[60]

So, overall, the turn of the century and the interwar period were marked by a series of intellectual and cultural contributions that highlighted, decried, or conceptualized the dangers posed by technologies but did not witness the emergence of a proper mass anti-technology movement. A similar trend characterized the immediate post-World War II period. The fresh horrors of World War II brought renewed anxiety about what technology could do to humanity, with the destructive power of the atomic bombs epitomizing its existential threat. Meanwhile, George Orwell's *1984* provided a powerful illustration of potential misuses and abuses of advanced technology in the hands of powerful, totalitarian, and repressive elites. This creeping anxiety ripened throughout the 1950s, becoming a constitutive element of the general rebellion against authorities in the 1960s and fuelling the paranoid belief that a 'shadowy, generalized technology lies behind many, if not most, of the modern evils of society'.[61] Concerns about surveillance and widespread technology-based conspiracies are evident in the famous speech that Mario Savio, leader of the Berkeley Free Speech Movement, gave on 2 December 1964 on the steps of Sproul Hall at the University of California, Berkeley:

> There's a time when the operation of the machine becomes so odious, makes you so sick at heart that you can't take part! You can't even passively take part! And you've got to put your bodies upon the gears and upon the wheels, upon the levers, upon all the apparatus – and you've got to make it stop! And you've got to indicate to the people who run it, to the people who own it – that unless you're free the machine will be prevented from working at all![62]

The 'machine' for Savio was the apparatus of the state and its technology.[63] The Berkeley Free Speech Movement, a student protest movement active between 1964 and 1965, was not an anti-technology movement, but it was critical of the role of technology in society. We can then see how, where technology constituted an element in the production process that threatened the Luddites' material security in the nineteenth century, it now takes on a new, menacing form: that of a ubiquitous, protean, omnipresent, and oppressive apparatus. This idea of technology as much more than a mere collection of tools, but rather a complex, pervasive, and autonomous system exerting profound influence on human behaviour, culture, and values was championed and popularized by Jacques Ellul in his 1954 *The Technological Society*.[64] Ellul and other authors such as Paul Goodman, Martin Heidegger, Neil Postman, and Lewis Mumford became highly influential figures for the anti-technology sentiments circulating within segments of the counterculture movement that emerged in the 1960s.

The 1970s consolidated these trends but introduced a crucial variant: active resistance to the techno-industrial civilization. This resistance developed along two main – and often interconnected – trajectories: radical environmentalism and anarchism. The radical environmentalist strand gained momentum as the critique of technology intertwined with advocacies of environmental issues and the emergent deep ecology philosophy. Coined in 1973 by Arne Næss, deep ecology is an environmental philosophy that takes a biocentric perspective, positing that human beings are part of a wider community of living beings that all have equal worth regardless of whether they are helpful or not to humans.[65] However, the growing human population and its related activities endanger biodiversity on earth. As such, some proponents of deep ecology – such as Dave Foreman and Christopher Manes – argue in favour of a gradual decrease in human population.[66] More often than not, deep ecology promoted a rollback of civilization to allow wilderness to restore an ecological balance that would suit all living creatures.[67]

While fundamentally opposed to targeting or harming humans, this philosophy inspired many activists to act against the assets that threatened to harm nature. For example, the Sea Shepherd Conservation Society – an offshoot of Greenpeace established by Paul Watson in 1977 in the United States – maintained that animal lives take precedence over machinery and private property. Watson argued that any human achievement or creation was 'vanity' and 'worthless to the Earth when compared to any one species of bird, or insect, or plant'.[68] Another organization that emerged in this period was the Animal Liberation Front (ALF). Originating in the United Kingdom in 1976 after it splintered from the less radical Hunt Saboteurs Association, the ALF is a leaderless movement of like-minded activists who further the cause of animal liberation and condone the use of vandalism and other violent means – provided that the necessary precautions not to harm humans are taken.[69]

While one would expect radical environmentalists and animal rights activists to agree on their core principles, this was not entirely the case. Despite a general common understanding that humans are not the most important beings in the world, they disagreed on a crucial issue. Radical environmentalists were more broadly focused on entire species and ecosystems rather than just sentient beings; they had little concern for individual animal rights. As Keith Makoto Woodhouse argues, radical environmentalists found that the underlying principle of animal liberationists put them 'in line with modern liberal thought and its focus on individual liberties and protections'.[70] As such, radical environmentalists distanced themselves from animal liberationists. Both were, however, part of a burgeoning trend that led to a proliferation of radical environmentalist and animal rights movements and groups. One such group was created in 1980: Earth First! (EF!). A movement that promotes radical, direct actions to advance the environmental cause, EF! neither condones nor condemns illegal acts of property destruction.[71] Twelve years later, the Earth Liberation Front emerged as an offshoot of Earth First! promoting underground, clandestine activities to halt the destruction of the environment.[72]

These are just a few prominent examples of the movements and organizations that mushroomed in this period. Central to all these groups were a few tenets derived straight from deep ecology, including the idea that human society must return to a pre-industrial state where centralized bureaucratic authority and advanced technology are banished.[73] An aspect explored in more detail in Chapter 3, the critique of technology is thus central to deep ecology.

In one way or another, these movements engaged in acts of sabotage. In this regard, Edward Abbey's 1975 satirical novel *The Monkey Wrench Gang* provided a fundamental inspiration.[74] A work of fiction telling the story of a group of eco-activists in the American Southwest who take direct action to protest environmental degradation due to industrial development, this novel gained a substantial following among the adherents of deep ecology, inspiring campaigns of eco-sabotage that included property destruction, arson, blockades, and tree-spiking to halt the destruction of the environment. Ten years after the publication of *The Monkey Wrench Gang*, Dave Foreman – co-founder of Earth First! – co-edited *Ecodefense: A Field Guide to Monkeywrenching*, a volume that owed much to Abbey's work. Much of the content of this book came from the *Earth First! Journal* and, in particular, from one of its columns called 'Dear Ned Ludd'.[75] In this column, Earth First! offered 'nuts-and-bolts, how-to advice on eco-sabotage'.[76] Naming the column after Ned Ludd was a straightforward attempt to give the twentieth-century eco-activists an explicit anti-technology dimension and link their struggle to the original Luddites.

They were not alone in this regard. In 1990, author and activist Chellis Glendinning published 'Notes Toward a Neo-Luddite Manifesto'. In this manifesto, Glendinning sought to re-evaluate the experience of the nineteenth-century Luddites, who were, as discussed, primarily viewed as 'reckless machine-smashers', while also dramatically denouncing that

> [t]he technology created and disseminated by modern Western societies are out of control and desecrating the fragile fabric of life on Earth. Like the early Luddites, we too are a desperate people seeking to protect the livelihoods, communities, and families we love, which lie on the verge of destruction.[77]

Glendinning's manifesto mounts a powerful critique against the worldview that sees technology, material acquisition, and technological development as the keys to human potential, fulfilment, and social progress. In doing so, it denounces the political nature that underlies all technologies, whereby technologies created by the technological society will inevitably favour and serve the perpetuation of the same kind of society. As harmful devices increasingly populate the world, Glendinning's programme for the future, as outlined in the manifesto, entailed dismantling certain destructive technologies, including television, chemical, genetic, engineering, electromagnetic, computer, and nuclear technologies. In particular, nuclear technology had already been targeted throughout the 1970s and 1980s by different, non-violent movements.[78]

A few years later, Kirkpatrick Sale published *Rebels Against the Future*. This book – another seminal work of the neo-Luddite movement – attacked what Sale considered the cornerstone of global capitalism: the ideology of technological progress.[79] *Rebels Against the Future* soon became a significant source of inspiration for 1990s neo-Luddism, not least because of the author's theatrical attitude. In his public readings and lectures in support of his books, Sale used to smash a personal computer with a giant sledgehammer.[80] Needless to say, the sledgehammer was an evident and explicit reference to the original Luddites. Other neo-Luddites such as Sven Birkerts, David Noble, Clifford Stoll, and Theodore Roszak, shared, to varying degrees, the message of both Glendinning and Sale.[81]

Championing the anarchist strand, a profoundly influential figure of the 1990s neo-Luddite movement is undoubtedly John Zerzan. A prolific author, Zerzan outlined his anarcho-primitivist ideas in a few seminal writings, including *Future Primitive and Other Essays*, published in 1994.[82] Essentially, Zerzan argued that many of the problems that afflict contemporary society directly result from the adoption of technology. Unlike Glendinning, who advocated dismantling certain harmful technologies, Zerzan promoted the dismantlement of civilization itself, as the pre-civilized life of the hunter-gatherer societies allowed greater individual freedom and a more harmonious relationship with the natural world.[83] John Filiss heralded an analogous position. Like Zerzan,[84] Filiss defined technology as 'tool manufacture and utilization that has become sufficiently complex to require specialization, implying both a separation and eventual stratification among individuals in the community, along with the rise of toil in the form of specialized, repetitive tasks'. Primitivism offers a solution in the form of a 'pursuit of ways of life running counter to the development of technology, its alienating antecedents, and the ensemble of changes wrought by both'.[85]

Many of these different neo-Luddite ideas were discussed at the Second Luddite Congress, which took place in Barnesville, Ohio, in April 1996. Here, 350 delegates gathered for three days 'to write a declaration of independence from the modern world'.[86] The decision to baptize the congress as the 'second' was yet another attempt to link the neo-Luddite movement to the nineteenth-century one and a supposed 'first' meeting that most likely never took place – at least not in the sense that the neo-Luddites ascribe to it. Kirkpatrick Sale delivered the keynote speech at the congress, from which neo-Luddism emerged as a 'leaderless movement of passive resistance to consumerism and the increasingly bizarre and frightening technologies of the Computer Age'.[87]

However, not all those who opposed technology in the second half of the 1990s did so on non-violent terms. We previously mentioned the acts of sabotage perpetrated by groups like Earth First!, the Animal Liberation Front, and the Earth Liberation Front. Yet these organizations considered violence against people a threshold they would not cross. In their worldview, humans might be inadvertently harmed in defending nature, but their purposeful targeting was out of the question. Active between 1980 and 1983 in France, the anarchist organization CLODO (Committee for Liquidation or Subversion of Computers – *Comité Liquidant pour Détournant les Ordinateurs*) similarly targeted technology without harming people. Located mainly in Toulouse, CLODO's attacks targeted companies like CII Honeywell Bull, ICL, and other firms related to computer technology. Overall, CLODO remains a nebulous instance of anti-technology extremism. None of its members have ever been apprehended or identified, and except for a few communiqués published by the organization and a recently published documentary,[88] we do not know much about them. A different opinion on whether humans could be targeted was championed by the individual who represents perhaps the 'father' of contemporary anti-technology extremism – or at least its most emblematic figure: Theodore John Kaczynski, aka the 'Unabomber.'

The Unabomber

Born on 22 May 1942 in Chicago, 'Ted' Kaczynski pursued an academic career as a mathematician before embarking on his one-man war against technology and civilization. After earning his PhD in mathematics from the University of Michigan in 1967, he was appointed assistant professor at the University of California, Berkeley.[89] Kaczynski appeared to have what it takes to aim for a brilliant academic career. In the words of many of his former professors, he had an exceptionally bright mind capable of solving mathematical problems so tricky that renowned scholars could not figure them out. Professor George Piranian, for example, commented on Kaczynski's skills, declaring, 'It is not enough to say he was smart.'[90] Similar praise came from his supervisor, Professor Allen Shields. When evaluating Ted's PhD thesis, *Boundary Functions*, Shields used words that every PhD student dreams of hearing, but few get a chance to: 'This thesis is the best I have ever directed.'[91] Yet Kaczynski's mathematical talent remained largely unexpressed. Without any explanation, he resigned on 30 June 1969.

After resigning, Kaczynski moved back to his parents' home in Illinois for a couple of years before relocating again to just outside of Lincoln, Montana. Here, he pursued a primitive lifestyle in a small, remote cabin he had built that had no access to amenities such as electricity or running water, with occasional jobs and support from his family being the primary sources of his subsistence. Over the next few years, he became increasingly isolated and alienated from society, spending much of his time writing and reading numerous authors, including Jacques Ellul, British zoologist Desmond Morris, and American psychologist Martin Seligman.[92] An introvert and shy person, Kaczynski held a deep-seated and increasingly extreme opposition to modern industrial society and technology. There has been much speculation about episodes in his life that might or might not have contributed to this increasing hostility. From being bullied in school and participating in a particularly abusive psychology study led by Henry Murray in 1962 to allegedly experiencing episodes of gender dysphoria throughout the 1960s, a complex psychological profile emerges.[93] However, while Kaczynski suffered from depression, anxiety, and insomnia, there is little evidence that he experienced delusions, psychosis, or was 'insane'.[94]

His opposition to technology became more pro-active as the years went by. In 1975, he started performing small acts of sabotage against developments near his cabin, thereby joining the larger family of activists who were 'monkeywrenching'. Ecological sabotage was not enough for Kaczynski, however, and so, in 1978, he carried out the first of a long series of terrorist attacks. His first two bombs targeted universities – respectively, the University of Illinois-Chicago and Northwestern University – whereas the third one struck American Airlines flight 444. These first three instances went relatively unnoticed, and it took the fourth attack – which hit and injured the President of United Airlines, Percy Woods – for the authorities to realize that these incidents were the work of a single person. Interestingly, this early targeting pattern gave Kaczynski his title, with the media taking 'Unabomber' from

UNABOM (University and Airline Bomber), the identifier the FBI used when they started working on the case.

The Unabomber's campaign against technology lasted nearly seventeen years – from 1978 to 1995. In all, he placed or mailed sixteen bombs that he fabricated in his cabin, resulting in the deaths of three people and injuries to an additional twenty-three. The FBI's search for the Unabomber was the United States' longest and most expensive manhunt for a serial killer – a testament to Kaczynski's skills and acumen.[95] He was finally apprehended in 1996 after his brother, David Kaczynski, recognized his sibling's writing style and ideas in the manifesto published in the *Washington Post* and the *New York Times*. Famously titled *Industrial Society and Its Future*, the manifesto was published on 19 September 1995. In this work, the Unabomber exposed his worldview. As Sean Fleming aptly summarizes, Kaczynski argued that modern technology constitutes a unified, self-perpetuating 'System', in which all parts depend on one another, and which is beyond human control. Human beings are biologically, but also psychologically, maladapted to live in a technological society. Therefore, the continued development of technologies will eventually lead to catastrophic events, such as the destruction of humanity or its subordination to the System. According to the Unabomber, an anti-technology revolution is the only hope to overthrow the System and avoid these scenarios. Moreover, Kaczynski despised left-wing politics and its reformist attempts, considering them forms of pseudo-rebellion that essentially divert the focus from technologies and allow the reproduction and survival of the System.[96] Crucially, he believed that the technological System cannot be reformed and must, therefore, be destroyed. Only the eradication of technologies and the collapse of techno-industrial civilization can save humanity. Eradicating technology is thus essential for Kaczynski. So long as there will be technologies, the techno-industrial civilization will survive. This is because the defining characteristic of technology is that it 'seeks to expand indefinitely the power of the system' into nature – which is then logically identified with 'that which is outside of the system'.[97]

There is, however, a kind of technology that even the Unabomber was willing to tolerate. He called it 'small-scale technology'. Unlike 'organization-dependent technology' that depends on large-scale societies, communities can use small-scale technologies without outside assistance. In other words, small-scale technologies are simple, hand-held tools that can accomplish specific tasks more efficiently or effectively – for example, a hammer or a saw. They are extensions of human beings rather than extensions of the System since they do not require or involve complex industrial processes in their production or use. It is the kind of technology that does not depend on the survival of the techno-industrial society. Once civilization collapses, small-scale technology will still be around. Conversely, any organization-dependent technology – the Unabomber gives the example of the refrigerator – cannot be built or operated without relying on a series of other technologies, for example food processing or electrical power, and with tragic consequences for individual freedom. Therefore, the Unabomber's war was against those technologies that depend on the System and seek to expand it at the expense of the environment and, most importantly, humans.[98]

Different reactions came from the neo-Luddite ranks following the publication of the manifesto and Kaczynski's arrest. Understandably, the jailing of the Unabomber channelled media attention towards the neo-Luddites, who were, coincidentally, holding the Second Luddite Congress in the same month as Kaczynski's arrest: April 1996. The association between neo-Luddites and the Unabomber wasn't welcomed by the former. Similarly, Earth First! and the Earth Liberation Front were suspected of harbouring sympathies or having direct connections with Kaczynski. While there were cases of support for his message among these groups, actual ties have never existed.[99] Likewise, the resort to violence was condemned, with Earth First! spokesperson Judy Bari going as far as labelling the Unabomber a sociopath and declaring that there was no space for violence within the radical environmentalist movement.[100] Yet the outer fringes were drawn to Kaczynski. Among them was John Zerzan, who corresponded with him and attended his trial. The two were on amicable terms for some time until they fell out because of a fundamental disagreement about the role of technology. Whereas Zerzan sees technology as one of many facets of civilization alongside patriarchy, racism, and exploitation of the environment, 'Kaczynski's opposition to technology is stubbornly single-minded'.[101] In addition to such disagreements, Zerzan accused Kaczynski of having been dishonest when critiquing his work in a treatise that the latter wrote in prison in 2008.[102]

Despite sitting in jail – where he spent the rest of his life until he passed away on 10 June 2023 – Kaczynski was indeed a prolific writer and authored several pieces, including a few books. Crucially, he had hoped to inspire a new generation of anti-technology warriors, a generation that would move beyond the moderate nature of the neo-Luddites, thereby committing to eradicating technologies. He largely failed, however, in kickstarting an anti-technology revolution in the mid-1990s. Indeed, in 2016, he himself admitted that up until 2011, he did not have a substantial following.[103] Nevertheless, his story was captivating enough to inspire TV series, podcasts, and documentaries. In some cases, these inadvertently popularized his worldview and message.[104] Then, some twenty-five years after the publication of *Industrial Society and Its Future*, the anti-technology extremism Kaczynski championed began to take hold. One group among his followers is the *indomitistas*.[105] Led by his Spanish correspondent Último Reducto, the *indomitistas* are Kaczynski's 'apostles' and are mainly preoccupied with translating and analysing his writings. As Fleming points out, they represent the Unabomber's inner circle and also used to conduct research for him and manage his publisher, Fitch & Madison.[106] But the Unabomber has been gaining consensus in at least three other milieus of violent extremists, that is, insurrectionary anarchism, eco-extremism, and eco-fascism.[107] Ironically, Kaczynski hadn't kind words for most of his current followers. If anything, his comments about these three milieus were quite harsh.[108] Whether or not they enjoyed the sympathy of the late Unabomber, however, these milieus are the protagonists of contemporary anti-technology extremism. Yet before turning to their analysis in the following chapters, we should take stock of what this journey from the nineteenth-century Luddites to the Unabomber has taught us.

Technology as an Existential Threat

As this brief overview shows, concerns regarding the impact of technology on society, culture, the environment, and humans' very existence have been recurrent over the last three centuries. Yet the recurrence of such concerns doesn't mean that the opposition to technology has been homogeneous or that its expressions, scopes, and practices have been consistent. Challenging the narrative of progress, these critiques come from various ideological backgrounds. They can be rooted in concerns about labour and employment, environmentalism, philosophical critiques of industrial society, and even radical political ideologies. As discussed in the first part of the chapter, the Luddites were primarily concerned about their livelihood and ways of life. The unmitigated introduction of new technologies jeopardized their position within the production process, thereby fundamentally undermining their material security. Their objective was thus to secure their position within the production process along with more favourable working conditions, not to halt progress, eradicate technology, or dismantle civilization.

By contrast, the critique of technology that emerged in the last decades of the nineteenth century and the first sixty years of the twentieth century revolved mainly around the potential harm that technology could do to the environment but also to humans, society, and culture. Edward Tenner aptly summarized this transition, arguing that 'the indignation of nineteenth-century producers has yielded to the irritation of late-twentieth-century consumers'.[109] As such, this critique reflected worries about the impact of technology on human connections and the natural world. Technology's pervasive and increasingly autonomous nature became an oppressive force challenging or undermining people's ontological security: the sense of order and continuity in their individual experiences, sense of self, and societal values.[110]

The second half of the twentieth century saw the neo-Luddites' progressive emergence. Despite their attempts to link their opposition to technology to that of the original Luddites, the so-called neo-Luddites had, objectively and with all due respect for Kirkpatrick Sale and his sledgehammer, little in common with the nineteenth-century machine-breakers. Crucially, their anti-technology stance expressed concern about what certain technologies (e.g. nuclear but also communication and computer technology) were doing to humans and the environment. This opposition thus manifested itself in the demand to halt these harmful technologies, calling, at the same time, for a paradigm shift in the way we use and live with technology. If there is one aspect that many neo-Luddites shared with the original Luddites, it is that, albeit with entirely different motivations, they opposed *specific* technologies rather than technology as such. Whereas the Luddites poured their frustration and anger onto the power cotton looms and wool shearing machines, the neo-Luddites came up with the list of harmful technologies included in Glendinning's 'Notes Toward a Neo-Luddite Manifesto'.

Admittedly, some of the more radical fringes pursued a more ambitious agenda. Championed by figures like John Zerzan, a more radical interpretation of neo-Luddism regarded the dismantlement of civilization – of which technology constitutes a cornerstone – as the sole panacea against the collapse of the environment, the erosion of individual freedom, and the other dangers posed by technological progress. For Zerzan and other primitivists, there is no distinction between good and bad technology. This is because technology is 'the ensemble of division of labor/production/industrialism and its impact on us and on nature'. It 'is the sum of mediations between us and the natural world and the sum of those separations mediating us from each other'.[111] As such, it is part and parcel of civilization. Even if we eradicated a few noxious technologies, the alienation and degradation that civilization brings with it would persist. Hence, the anarcho-primitivist argument that the only solution must involve dismantling civilization itself.

Thus, there is tension within the neo-Luddite movement regarding the extent and focus of their opposition to technology. In some cases, neo-Luddism can take a rather selective approach and identify specific harmful technologies, whereas, in other cases, it argues that technology as such is the problem. Such a stance reflects a duality mirrored in the scholarly critique of technology. As Andrew Feenberg argues in *Transforming Technology: A Critical*

Theory Revisited, we can identify two schools of thought regarding technology: instrumentalism and substantivism. According to the former, technology is entirely neutral, whereas the latter reflects a position that sees technology as an essence that subjugates humanity and nature.[112] Naturally, with different diagnoses come different treatments, which range from the eradication of harmful machines to the dismantlement of civilization. Therefore, neo-Luddism presents itself as a spectrum where opposition to technology can be more or less absolute. Despite such differences, what defines neo-Luddism is a deep concern about the nefarious consequences that technology will have on human lives and the planet. If left unchecked and unbalanced, technology can constitute an existential threat: that is, technology poses long-term risks that threaten humanity's existence.

Theodore Kaczynski did not fundamentally disagree with these concerns. As he argued in 1995, the Industrial Revolution and its consequences had already been 'a disaster for the human race', and the 'continued development of technology will worsen the situation'. This doesn't necessarily mean that humans will be extinguished. But, even if they survived, they would be reduced – along with other living organisms – to 'engineered products and mere cogs in the social machine'.[113] While technically alive, they would have lost what makes them humans. Hence, technology constitutes an existential threat for Kaczynski as well. Yet, unlike the neo-Luddites, he doesn't just consider it one of the cornerstones of civilization. Instead, he sees it as the single greatest component of the techno-industrial civilization, and he is willing to strike both technology and those who represent and promote it to bring it down.

His willingness to resort to violence against property and people and to wage war against techno-industrial society stands out and allows us to draw a line that separates contemporary anti-technology extremism even further from neo-Luddism.[114] While both anti-technology extremism and neo-Luddism consider technology an existential threat, the latter does not necessarily condone or advocate the resort to violence – especially against people. In contrast, Kaczynski's unrestrained violence and mission to topple the techno-industrial society assume the characteristics of a cosmic war against technology. Therefore, neo-Luddism constitutes a radical opposition to specific technologies, or civilization as such, that advocates for a paradigm shift in how we interact with the environment and technology. While occasionally resorting to violence, it doesn't consider it as an essential means. Conversely, anti-technology extremism represents an ideological current that pursues the violent eradication of technology and the collapse of techno-industrial civilization, thus sanctioning and justifying the use of violence to achieve this objective.

What emerges here is that the critique of technology has experienced a progressive, although not necessarily linear, development through the nineteenth, twentieth, and twenty-first centuries: from technology as first a threat to material security, then a threat to ontological security, and finally an existential threat. This progression does not imply that previous forms of critique had to make way for anti-technology extremism to advance. These perspectives – the material, the ontological, and the existential – can coexist in the same epoch. In other words, critiques of technology and technological progress still exist that are primarily, if not entirely, based on concerns of a material or ontological nature or on perspectives that view only specific technology as potentially harmful. For example, apprehensions about the impact of AI on society are sometimes linked to its consequences on job opportunities and how fairly people will be treated in society.[115] At the same time, 5G technology has also become the subject of intense debate, with non-violent movements undertaking legal campaigns to regulate it.[116] Despite the persistence of such radical positions, anti-technology offshoots have embraced more extremist positions, pursuing the violent eradication of techno-industrial civilization.

In his 2018 book *The Darkest Sides of Politics*, Jeffrey Bale argues that all political ideologies, extremist or otherwise, claim to provide the answers to three fundamental and interrelated questions: (a) 'What is wrong with the world?'; (b) 'Who is responsible for those wrongs?'; and (c) 'What needs to be done to correct those wrongs?'[117] The above discussion gives us insights into the evolution of the critique of technology, thus answering the first two questions. Interestingly, the shift from material and ontological security to existential threat is mirrored by a similar progression regarding the crucial question of 'what is to be done'. The Luddites' contention with technology as a threat to their livelihood was expressed through actions that aimed to secure their position in production. Practically, this translated into machine-breaking. In the twentieth century, by contrast, the neo-Luddite praxis turned to dismantling those technologies that were harmful to nature and human connection, thereby promoting a rollback of technological progress. Finally, the emergence of anti-technology extremism sanctioned the beginning of the war on civilization; techno-industrial society's dismantlement was deemed the only viable solution to save humanity from the harmful consequences of technology. Who has joined the war on technology? Who are the anti-tech extremists who seek to bring about the collapse of techno-industrial civilization? The following chapters will now discuss the individuals, groups, and movements that have set out to stop the machines.

2

Smash the Prison-Society

Insurrectionary Anarchism

It was 5 March 2024, Grünheide, Germany. In the quiet early hours of a Tuesday morning, at approximately 4:50 a.m., an electricity pylon in the German state of Brandenburg was suddenly engulfed in flames. The eerie fire cast its light on a pile of old tyres stacked at the base, suggesting the deliberate nature of the arson. Moments later, the power supply to the nearby villages ceased. The blackout extended to Tesla's Gigafactory in Grünheide. A factory designed to produce 750 electric cars each day was suddenly halted, prompting the evacuation of its 12,000 workers. Announcing that production would not resume within the week, Tesla estimated the damage to be several hundred million euros – a substantial blow.[1] Later in the day, a group called *Vulkangruppe Tesla abschalten* (Volcano Group Shutting Down Tesla) published a communiqué on the internet claiming responsibility for the attack. 'We sabotaged Tesla today,' the document began. The *Vulkangruppe* framed the attack as part of a larger resistance against technological totalitarianism. It claimed that Tesla vehicles contribute to surveillance and militarizing public spaces with their high-resolution cameras, autonomous driving, and smart technology. At the same time, they denounced the Gigafactory as a form of 'green capitalism' that perpetuated environmental degradation and colonialism because of lithium mining and collusion in geopolitical and human rights abuses in Bolivia and China. Finally, as the attack occurred close to International Women's Day, *Vulkangruppe* positioned it also as part of a broader struggle against patriarchy.[2] Commenting on the event, Elon Musk said, 'These are either the dumbest eco-terrorists on Earth or they're puppets of those who don't have good environmental goals.'[3] But the 'Technoking' of Tesla was wrong. These were neither the dumbest eco-terrorists nor puppets. These were insurrectionary anarchists, and this act of sabotage was a perfect example of their fight to stop the machines, one that blends social and ecological issues with concerns about the rise of a new form of oppression: the totalitarianism of the machines.

There is a certain degree of irony here. When Nobel's invention of dynamite began spreading in the nineteenth century, anarchists were quite enthusiastic about adopting this then-emerging technology in the hope that it would further their revolutionary aspirations. Now, some a hundred and fifty years later, segments of insurrectionary anarchists are at the forefront of the struggle against technology. How did it come to this? Why do some insurrectionary anarchists reject modern technology? How do they fight against techno-industrial civilization? To answer these questions, we must first paint a nuanced picture of insurrectionary anarchism, retracing the milieu's history and the emergence of its animus towards technology.

Defining anarchism is not easy. Emerging during the 'Age of Ideologies'[4] in the nineteenth century amidst profound societal changes, it represents a complex and multifaceted political philosophy. Pre-dating the emergence of the movement, the term 'anarchist' was initially used pejoratively during the English and French revolutions of the seventeenth and eighteenth centuries to indicate people who wanted anarchy in the sense of chaos and confusion. Starting from the 1840s, however, anarchists adopted the term to signal their opposition to government and authorities. Originating from the Greek ἀναρχία, the word 'anarchy' carried both these meanings. Naturally, anarchists prefer the latter one.[5]

Although its intellectual roots trace back to the eighteenth century, a distinct anarchist movement did not materialize until 1864.[6] This year marked the First International – also known as the International Workingmen's Association – in London in September. As Robert Graham argues, certain individuals identified as anarchists before this date, but there was no movement as such.[7] This is not to suggest that, once it started, the movement was cohesive or monolithic. Quite the contrary, Murray Bookchin reminds us that anarchism encompasses various theories and movements. Its historical roots are rich, and the various forms of anarchism are deeply embedded in distinct social and historical contexts.[8]

Following its inception, anarchism quickly became the main revolutionary force of the nineteenth century.[9] Throughout the period between 1864 and the outbreak of World War I, anarchists carried out numerous bombing campaigns and assassinations targeting monarchs, heads of state, and heads of government. So many were the rulers who fell at the hands of anarchists that this era earned the label 'Golden Age of Assassination'.[10] However, anarchism's momentum waned with the rise of nationalism during and after World War I, thereby losing its primacy as the most momentous revolutionary ideology. Then, Marxism-Leninism, spearheading the New Left in the 1960s and 1970s, relegated anarchism to a marginal role among the revolutionary movements. While the 1968 protests espoused many anarchist ideas, the anarchist movement itself was in disarray.[11]

Yet anarchism did not disappear, and its flame was rekindled in the late twentieth century. The demise of the Soviet Union and the disillusionment with the communist ideal played a significant role in dismantling the myth of the Marxist-Leninist vanguard. Simultaneously, this period saw a resurgence in the popularity of anarchism among far-left circles.[12] By the end of the millennium, the world heard once more about anarchism, as hordes of 'black blocs' took to the streets of Seattle in a series of anti-globalization protests during the 1999 World Trade Organization Ministerial Conference.[13] After that, anarchism continued to gain prominence, with the number of anarchist organizations growing from 808 in 1997 to 2,171 in 2005 in sixty-three countries worldwide.[14] The diverse purposes and characters of these organizations underscore the heterogeneous nature of anarchism. The fundamental question then naturally emerges: what do anarchists want?

At its core, anarchism is rooted in rejecting the state and other authoritative forms of government – a notion based on the idea that no one should be in power.[15] Possessing 'a unique combination of values and goals', anarchism is intricate and multifaceted.[16] As succinctly expressed by Bob Black, an American anarchist:

> To call yourself an anarchist is to invite identification with an unpredictable array of associations, an ensemble which is unlikely to mean the same thing to any two people, including

any two anarchists. (The most predictable is the least accurate: the bomb-thrower. But anarchists have thrown bombs and some still do.)[17]

In this quote, Black powerfully and effectively captures the diverse nature of anarchism, its many nuances, and its divisive issues – not least the issue of violence, to which we will return shortly. Disagreements are prevalent, with anarchists being 'at odds over work, industrialism, unionism, urbanism, science, sexual freedom, religion and much more which is more important, especially when taken together, than anything that unites them'.[18] Anarchism can thus be viewed as 'a set of overlapping and sometimes competing traditions or aspects rather than a general theory or coherent ideology'.[19] This explains the proliferation of different strands of anarchism, each with its peculiar characteristics. These strands include anarcho-individualism, anarcho-communism, anarcha-feminism, anarcho-syndicalism, anarcho-primitivism (mentioned in the previous chapter), and insurrectionary anarchism. Historically, anarchists have, regardless of their respective strands, rallied behind issues such as anti-militarism, opposition to state repression and the prison system, the environment, support for immigrants, and the fight against far-right political parties and organizations.[20]

Despite their disagreements, anarchists share a few universal principles. One such principle is the rejection of coercive relationships of power, advocating for a society without rulers and exploitation of the subaltern classes.[21] Hailing from this opposition to rulers and authorities, another common characteristic of anarchism is 'horizontalism', emphasizing decentralization of decision-making and power.[22] At an organizational level, this translates into adopting leaderless resistance. Embraced by both violent and non-violent actors, leaderless resistance is based on the absence of a single central authority. As such, it reflects the anarchist understanding that an egalitarian society is more likely to emerge from movements that are not leader-driven or hierarchical.[23] When facilitating the resort to violence, the leaderless approach constitutes a 'strategy of opposition that allows for and encourages individuals or small cells to carry out acts of violence or sabotage entirely independent of any hierarchy of leadership or network of support'.[24] It is important to note that the leaderless nature of a movement doesn't necessarily lead to the complete disappearance of leadership figures. Informal leaders and opinion leaders can, indeed, emerge even within leaderless movements, providing inspiration and/or operational guidance on when, where, and how to conduct attacks.[25] Two additional, interrelated notions are intimately related to the leaderless nature of anarchism: affinity groups and direct action. Affinity groups, representing the essential building block of anarchist organization,[26] consist of autonomous militant units 'who share a sense of the cause worth defending and of the types of action they prefer to engage in'.[27] The affinity group's lack of formal chain of command-and-control does not imply the absence of coordination. While lacking 'the formality and authority which separate organisers and organised',[28] informal organizations emerge to coordinate the affinity groups into effective campaigns.

Organized into affinity groups, anarchists engage in direct actions. This term reflects a do-it-yourself approach that fundamentally consists of a series of practices of resistance against structures, individuals, and positions of power.[29] In other words, direct actions are unmediated actions that oppressed individuals or groups undertake to overturn or destroy that which oppresses them.[30] These may range from boycotts to assault and other tactics.[31] At the violent end of the spectrum, direct actions are associated with the concept of 'propaganda of the deed', the idea, which emerged in the nineteenth century, that violent actions will awaken and alert the masses to their predicament, paving the way to the revolution.[32] The issue of violence is, however, somewhat controversial, with the majority of the anarchist movement subscribing to non-violent resistance and pacifism.[33]

The minority who condone the resort to violence take two main stances. The first, exemplified by anarchists like Mikhail Bakunin, accepts violence against property.[34] The second stance – advocated by anarchists like Errico Malatesta – supports violence against both property and people. Malatesta argued that, while anarchism was essentially opposed to violence, resorting to physical violence was inevitable to counter the 'legions of soldiers and police [. . .] ready to massacre and imprison anyone who will not meekly submit to the laws which a handful of privileged persons have made in their own interests'.[35] Hence, the violence of the oppressed is necessary to fight and defeat the violence of the oppressors. This minority view, emphasizing violence against property and people as an integral part of the revolutionary process, constitutes the basis of insurrectionary anarchism – an 'extremist tendency within the anarchist movement which emphasizes the practice of revolutionary "insurrection" through illegal and violent actions'.[36] Unlike their nineteenth-century ancestors, contemporary insurrectionary anarchists tend to prioritize non-lethal violence, even though their attacks do occasionally result in casualties.[37] Despite this tendency to shy away from lethal violence, the 'illegalist-infused insurrectionary approach' has become progressively more nihilistic and individualistic over the years – characteristics that are somewhat at odds with the collectivist and more utopian precepts of most strands of anarchism.[38] In the words of a nihilist insurrectionary anarchist:

> By anarchism, I mean the will to live anarchy now, right away, leaving aside expectations of a future revolution. [. . .] It is in this nihilism that my anarchy is being fulfilled, true, real, today, now. A nihilist destroys, he doesn't build anything because there is nothing he wants to build. A revolution would inevitably create more chains, new authority, new technology, new civilization. An anti-civ[ilization] anarchist can only be a nihilist, for it is in the destruction of society that this new anarchy is being fulfilled.[39]

As such, contemporary insurrectionary anarchists represent a violent and pessimistic departure from what is otherwise 'the most utopian of ideologies'.[40] This is a crucial aspect, and, indeed, one should remember it when reading the following pages: the anti-technology anarchism described here refers to fringe movements and networks that have broken with more 'mainstream' versions of anarchism.

Spearheads of the Movement

Insurrectionary anarchism thus emerges as the most violent and extremist galaxy within the broader anarchist universe. Like other strands of anarchism, insurrectionary anarchists organize in affinity groups, with informal organizations emerging to coordinate their efforts around a shared purpose and campaign. It must be noted that not all insurrectionary anarchists embrace the concept of informal organization, revealing a chasm between those who prioritize anonymity over acronyms and those who, instead, argue against any 'dogmatic cult of "anonymity"'.[41] Essentially, proponents of anonymity say that the informal organization can become a means for self-centred individuals to 'impose a hegemony on a movement' and 'to play the vanguard', thus betraying the very essence of anarchism.[42] Nonetheless, many of the insurrectionary anarchist activities of the last two decades have centred on the informal organization model.[43]

One notable example is the Informal Anarchist Federation – International Revolutionary Front (FAI-FRI, *Federazione Anarchica Informale – Fronte Rivoluzionario Internazionale*). Originating in Italy in 2003, the FAI has grown into what is arguably the world's largest insurrectionary anarchist network, boasting an incredibly high number of claimed attacks. According to a study from the Radicalization Awareness Network, there were 414 left-wing and anarchist terrorist (failed, foiled, or completed) attacks in Europe between 2006 and 2020, with the FAI being responsible for many of these, including some that resulted in several injuries.[44] Eight years after its establishment, the FAI launched the International Revolutionary Front (FRI), beginning an important internationalization process. From now on, militants of the Federation adopted the acronym FAI-FRI when claiming attacks. Overall, the FAI-FRI has claimed responsibility for attacks across various countries, including Italy, Greece, Spain, Germany, the United Kingdom, Indonesia, Chile, Brazil, and Mexico.[45]

Another noteworthy anarchist organization is the Conspiracy of Cells of Fire (CCF, Συνωμοσία Πυρήνων της Φωτιάς – also translated as Conspiracy of the Fire Nuclei). Founded in Greece in 2008, the CCF gained notoriety for the 2010 series of parcel bombs targeting European political leaders and foreign embassies, as well as numerous other actions involving bombings and incendiary devices against government buildings, representatives, law enforcement, and banks. Some of these attacks resulted in casualties beyond property damage. The CCF actively supported the inception of the FRI and is generally believed to entertain a special relationship with the FAI.[46] Other Greek groups include Rouvikonas (*Ρουβίκωνας*), the Sect of Revolutionaries (*Σέχτα των Επαναστατών*), and the Organization for Revolutionary Self-Defence (*Οργανισμός Επαναστατικής Αυτοάμυνας*), and we could also mention Brazil's Nucleus of Opposition to the System (*Núcleo de Oposição ao Sistema*), Chile's Antagonic Nuclei of the New Urban Guerrilla (*Núcleos Antagónicos de la Nueva Guerrilla Urbana*), and the International Revolutionary People's Guerrilla Forces. This list is not exhaustive and encompasses only major networks and organizations. When carrying out attacks, smaller cells typically claim affiliation with larger ones, particularly the FAI-FRI and CCF.

Within these networks, the issue of technology has become increasingly predominant. Many anti-tech anarchists use the FAI-FRI or the CCF acronym when striking technology. Equally, others have formed *ad hoc* cells, such as the above-mentioned *Vulkangruppe* in Germany or ACRATES (Coordinated Associations for the Anti-Tech Revolt and Eco-Sabotage) in France.[47]

Consistent with the precepts of leaderless resistance and the clandestine nature of these networks, militants are not known – often not even to each other. As mentioned, this doesn't prevent a few individuals from rising as prominent figures. Usually, this occurs once their identity is revealed following their arrest. One such figure is Alfredo Cospito, who has recently become quite influential despite sitting in jail since 2012, the year he kneecapped Roberto Adinolfi, the CEO of the nuclear engineering group Ansaldo Nucleare. Writing from jail, his documents have circulated among insurrectionary anarchists and have contributed to debates surrounding, among others, the issue of technology.[48] His increasing influence did not go unnoticed, and so the Italian authorities decided to transfer him to a special prison regime. This regime system, known as 41-bis, allows prison authorities to suspend certain prison regulations to avoid contact with the outside world. It is typically enforced against people imprisoned for Mafia-related crimes, terrorism, or attempts to subvert the constitutional system when there is a reasonable suspicion that those inmates can still direct their respective organizations from behind bars, thereby constituting a risk even from within the prison. This turned out to be a counterproductive move. Though an influential figure, Cospito is not a conventional leader within the FAI-FRI and doesn't issue orders. Protesting against the hard prison regime, he launched a hunger strike that lasted from October 2022 to April 2023. The anarchist movement rallied behind Cospito in solidarity with his strike. This resulted in violent public demonstrations and clandestine attacks that swept several countries, including Italy, Bolivia, Chile, Argentina, Brazil, Greece, Spain, Germany, and Switzerland.[49] Another influential figure within anti-tech insurrectionary anarchism is Toby Shone. A UK anarchist apprehended on charges of terrorism (which were subsequently dropped in favour of minor drug charges),[50] Shone was accused of being an administrator of the 325.nostate.net. This now defunct website published several documents denouncing technology. Commenting on his judicial adventures, Shone argued that his imprisonment provides further evidence of the ever-expanding surveillance projects of the techno-elites and their efforts to eradicate any opposition; as 'a resurgence of anarchist, anti-civilization and anti-capitalist action is taking place', the state is seeking 'to cut any wild roses before they bud'.[51]

It must be reiterated that not all those anarchists opposing technologies do so through violent means. As mentioned in the previous chapter, some branches of anarchism (e.g. anarcho-primitivism) display marked neo-Luddite features, rejecting technology without endorsing violence. Other examples include the Anti-Tech Collective, a collaborative network that advocates 'for the legal dismantlement of the Global Technological System'.[52] Crucially, it is at the intersection of insurrectionary anarchism and anti-technology sentiments that the struggle against machines develops. The remainder of this chapter lingers on anarchist violence against technology, trying to understand both the rationale of such violence and the strategies employed in the war against civilization. Given that the analysis predominantly centres on insurrectionary anarchism, the terms 'anarchism' and 'insurrectionary anarchism' will be used interchangeably unless otherwise specified.

Against the Prison-Society and the Totalitarianism of the Machines

Not all anarchists hate technology. In fact, they entertain a 'complex love–hate relationship' with it.[53] Their anti-technology agenda has gained prominence since the early 2010s, although its roots extend back to the 1970s and 1980s. During this period, the Detroit-based anarchist periodical *Fifth Estate* (*FE*) began to examine the role of technology in society critically. Influenced by the writings of Karl Marx, Jacques Ellul, and Lewis Mumford, several issues of *FE* expressed growing discomfort with techno-industrial society.[54] As Steve Millett argues, the anti-technology arguments put forward in *FE* can be organized into seven distinct areas. First, technology is viewed as an integral part of the capitalist socioeconomic system, as it 'interlinks and interacts with the economic processes of capitalism to create a new social form, a "megamachine" which integrates not only capitalism and technology but also the State, bureaucracy and military'.[55] Second, technology does not adapt to its users; instead, humans must conform to the implicit laws of the technology itself. Third, technology contributes to forming an authoritarian and hierarchical society through the division of labour and political structures. Fourth, technology engenders dependence, making humans reliant on its systems and the experts who develop and run them. Fifth, techno-industrial society is deemed harmful to the environment owing to the unforeseeable consequences of industrial technologies, their inability to solve all problems, potential mechanical or human error resulting in catastrophes, and inevitable environmental contamination. Sixth, humans' perception of the world adapts to technology, making us think and act within the frameworks and conditions of the mega-machine. Finally, computers and information technology represent crucial aspects of domination, allowing the control and channelling of information to suit capitalist interests.[56]

It is interesting to observe how some aspects of the anti-technology message in *FE* resemble the Unabomber's manifesto – published years later and discussed in the previous chapter.[57] Both sources emphasize the division of labour and the consequences of technology on humans and the environment. Similarly, *FE* endorses the distinction between 'tools' and 'technologies'. The former are small or simple enough to be implemented and integrated into a small community. In contrast, the latter constitute part and parcel of the systems of domination.[58] Yet, unlike the Unabomber, *FE* provides neither a blueprint for action nor an image of an alternative society. In the words of one of its prominent contributors, T. Fulano (the pen name of David Watson), what *FE* intended to promote was

> nothing less than the radical deconstruction of society, but this cannot come about through a political and technological program with its blueprints and its agendas, for that would be more of the same. We can only attend to first things first: and that is to begin by refusing to accept the idiom of technology, and to look at the world once more with the eyes of human beings and to articulate its promise in human terms.[59]

Therefore, *FE* did not contemplate resorting to violence to solve the technology issue. This is not to say that this earlier stage of anti-technology anarchism did not feature more antagonistic, violence-prone stances. Pierleone Porcu, for example, promoted a 'perspective based on the need to completely destroy technology'.[60]

Despite the varying positions on the use of violence, a significant continuity exists between the anti-technology stance of contemporary anarchists and the early writings of *FE*. An analysis of the current anarchist critique reveals that insurrectionary anarchists' concerns are traced back to the seven areas of anti-technology critique discussed above. However, a crucial qualitative difference is that contemporary anti-technology anarchists actively seek to eradicate technology, aiming to bring about the collapse of techno-industrial civilization through violence. To fully grasp this qualitative leap, we must first understand how contemporary anarchists define technology and civilization. Through this understanding, we can unravel the motivations behind their intent to fight techno-industrial society.

Anarchists view technology as 'more than wires, silicon, plastic, and steel'.[61] Instead, it is envisioned as a complex system entailing division of labour, resource extraction, and exploitation, benefiting those overseeing its process. Technology is therefore regarded as the 'sum of mediations' between us and the natural world, embodying the cumulative effect of separations that mediate individuals from one other.[62] It is not merely individual machines but the entire technological system.[63] To view technology as physical, separate entities is to ignore a more subtle – but no less oppressing – dimension: 'machines are not units; they are all part of the megamachine'.[64] As such, technology encompasses the bureaucratic processes, the military and police techniques, the scientific research, and all those other aspects serving as vectors for dominion.[65] Lewis Mumford's concept of the mega-machine is dear to anarchists, suggesting that civilization itself constitutes 'a huge machine which gains its own momentum and becomes beyond the control of even its supposed rulers'.[66] In other words, civilization encompasses 'the logic, institutions, and physical apparatus of domestication, control, and domination'.[67] Emerging from this conception of technology are several themes that have come to shape the anarchist critique of technology.

First, in alignment with *FE*, insurrectionary anarchists adopt the Kaczynskian distinction between tools and technologies. Unlike tools, technology involves complex systems that introduce a level of separation, thereby creating an unhealthy and mediated experience for the user. This separation 'leads to various forms of authority',[68] highlighting a critical distinction between the immediate, straightforward utility of tools and the intricate, potentially alienating nature of technology. What follows from this is that technology cannot be neutral. Even just the idea of a neutral technology is 'patently ridiculous'.[69] This is because the 'values and goals of those who produce and control technology are always embedded within it'.[70] Essentially, the instruments created by the powers that be are necessarily bound to serve their interests and aims 'no matter who uses them and in spite of any apparent advantages they might bring to society'.[71] Yet the non-neutrality of technology is not solely a reflection of the agenda and interests of its developers and controllers. It also arises from the intrinsic nature of technology itself. As Fulano argued in 1981, technology is not neutral because it 'tolerates no judgment from without and accepts no limitation', bringing its own 'method of being used'.[72] Technology has thus become an entity that, propelled by its own momentum, seems to have an existence independent from humanity.[73] As such, technology is not neutral because it serves the interests of those who control it *and* because it constitutes an essence which leads to the subjugation of humanity and nature.

Yet it is also undeniable that 'those who produce and control technology' benefit from their privileged position. Such 'techno-elites' constitute an amalgamation of the traditional economic and political elites (i.e. the dominant class) with scientists and researchers, who form 'the new intermediate class produced by the technological revolution'.[74] This argument contends that science, just like technology, is not neutral; instead, it is 'loaded with motives and assumptions that come out of, and reinforce, the catastrophe of dissociation, disempowerment, and consuming deadness that we call "civilization"'.[75] The same can be said for research as well as the researcher, who supplies technological society with the technical means to achieve its dire ambitions, being therefore directly responsible for the devaluation of 'human labor through simplification and automation [. . .], colonization and disfigurement of everyday life by technological merchandise, the improvement of military and police techniques, the depletion of our environment and the extinction of species'.[76] Ultimately, technology cannot be neutral because it inevitably constitutes 'the texture and the form' of domination.[77] This idea of domination and control underlies the second theme emerging from the anarchist critique of technology.

Indeed, central to anarchist beliefs is the view that technology embodies a unified scheme orchestrated by the techno-elites. The ultimate goal is the establishment of a 'prison-society'; a dystopian vision of a pending totalitarian regime where humans dominate each other through technological means.[78] In the prison-society, technology will allow the techno-elites to 'good-naturedly do what yesterday's fascists and secret services wanted to impose brutally'.[79] This will occur in two subsequent stages: repression and prevention. The first stage of repression revolves around the ideas of surveillance and regulation.[80] In this sense, technology will allow the techno-elites to perfect the means and techniques of surveillance:

> The prison-society is not just the regime of 'intelligent' surveillance cameras, databases, police-stations and prisons, it is urban planning, biometrics, contactless smart chips, electronic tagging and pattern recognition. It is satellite mapping, private security armies, automated drones and unmanned border planes. It is universalisation of social welfare systems, banking and corporate services. It is telephone voice analysis, high-definition CCTV, facial-recognition systems, 'X-Ray' microwave scanners, covert units of police for breaking and entry, bugging and tailing, and the global surveillance network, Echelon.[81]

These means of mass surveillance will ensure compliance on a 'scale hitherto unimaginable'.[82] However, once the new totalitarianism of the prison-society is fully implemented, surveillance and regulation won't be necessary, as repression will move on to prevention.[83] Since technologies deeply influence people's perspectives and expectations, even ideas that may seem rebellious or subversive are easily assimilated or co-opted within the overarching system created by technology. As a result, it becomes challenging for individuals to truly envision or believe in the potential for transcending or fundamentally changing this societal structure.[84] Accelerating this process, emerging technologies such as robotics, artificial intelligence, and nanotechnology are believed to be playing a crucial role in controlling people's desires, infantilizing them and making them more and more dependent on machines, thereby preparing them for the post-human: the integration of technology into human bodies.[85] Transhumanism is considered the arrival point of technological development, a process that will biologically modify humans to create 'artificial slaves for the elite to profit from'.[86] The ontological transformation of humans will lead to an 'anthropotechnical cyborg concept, where the human being is undetermined, and co-builds himself with technology, an indetermination which is technical hybridisation, where the very nature of human, his biological existence, is technological'.[87] This process will turn the human body into a technological artefact by destroying the border between the living and the machine.

The totalitarianism of the machines will thus work subtly. It won't implement a pyramidal form of domination but rather a horizontal system of oppression so pervasive that eventually we will align 'with the Dominant System before we are even born'.[88] From this perspective, the evolution of the mega-machine is inevitably linked to the evolution of domination; the prison-society will lead to the implementation of a new form of totalitarianism where 'domination by men is replaced by domination by machines'.[89] The last few years have witnessed an intensification of this narrative. The COVID-19 pandemic has indeed given anarchists renewed strength whereby the virus was considered an excuse to strengthen social control, presenting the techno-elites with the most incredible opportunity to test and implement the prison-society: physical isolation, total dependence on technology for communication, and the use of technology for mass surveillance and compliance.[90]

Related to the topic of the pandemic, an additional theme emerging from the anarchist anti-technology narrative is that of the natural world and the environment.[91] However, more often than not, this focus on nature is grounded in something other than the principles of deep ecology. When contemplating the consequences of technology on the natural world, anarchists adopt a marked anthropocentric perspective. This is not to dismiss their environmental concerns and the influence of deep ecology, which can be rather central in the context of certain branches, such as green anarchism and anarcho-primitivism, but also insurrectionary anarchism. As the next chapter will also discuss, there exists, indeed, a profound relationship between anarchists and radical environmentalists. Keeping faith with this tradition, the contemporary insurrectionary anarchist movement holds its environmentalist concerns dear, with the central idea being that humans have 'ceased to have any connection to nature, freedom and the free wildernesses a long time ago'.[92] This decoupling has led to environmental disasters, ecological collapse, and the artificialization of nature. Like humans, nature becomes an artefact organized by computers, commodified, and exploited.[93] Yet the human dimension, with its power relationships between the oppressed and the oppressors, appears to remain the primary concern. Much like Kaczynski himself, insurrectionary anarchists decry the degradation of nature and environmental collapse, but they are primarily worried about the prison-society, where the totalitarianism of the machines will deprive them of what freedom they have left.[94]

Summing up, the narrative unfolds through the lens of domination, portraying technology not merely as a tool but also as a facilitator of a 'prison-society', where surveillance, control, and prevention of dissent are the norm, inevitably leading society towards the new totalitarianism of the machines. This vision extends to transhumanism, portraying the integration of technology into human bodies as a journey towards creating 'artificial slaves for the elite'. Recent events, notably the COVID-19 pandemic, intensify these concerns, as anarchists see it as an opportune moment for techno-elites to test and implement their societal control mechanisms. The environmental dimension adds another layer, with an anthropocentric perspective lamenting the disconnection between humanity and the natural world and blaming technology for ecological collapse and the artificialization of nature. In essence, the anarchist perspective on technology reveals a profound scepticism, emphasizing its non-neutrality, the role of the techno-elites, and the potential threats it poses to individual autonomy and freedom.

This, in turn, reveals a dichotomy in the conception of technology. Anarchists tend to view technology as an essence in itself but also as the means of the techno-elites. Such a stance reflects a duality mirrored in the scholarly critique of technology: the instrumentalist and substantivist approaches discussed in the previous chapter. As proponents of substantivism like Jacques Ellul and Lewis Mumford exert considerable influence on anarchists, it is not surprising that the anarchist critique of technology revolves around the idea that technology has become an enslaving essence. Yet, at the same time, anarchists contend that technologies allow the techno-elites to execute their plans, thereby establishing the prison-society. This assumption implies that technologies might be used differently under an alternative ruling class. Therefore, there appears to be an unresolved tension hiding in the anarchist critique: an understanding that oscillates between viewing technology as an essence and as the means in the hands of individuals with agency. In the anarchist critique, these two perspectives are not mutually exclusive, and they both concur in establishing the prison-society.

This dystopian world will not fully emerge until society reaches the Singularity. This term – popularized by Vernon Vinge, professor of mathematics and science fiction writer – indicates the convergence of different fields of high technology and represents the moment at which machine intelligence surpasses human intelligence; 'an age of massively intelligent machines, conscious, sentient, creative and a trillion times more powerful than their primitive human creators'.[95] Predicted to occur around the year 2045, anarchists believe that the Singularity will lead to a conflict between those who support and those who oppose technology, a conflict that will evolve into 'the longest and fiercest war that humanity has ever faced, a struggle against a dystopian future of technological control that seeks to impose unending oppression through scientific advances'.[96] This war will be for 'survival against the techno-system'.[97] Crucially, some anarchists believe this war has already started, as 'Ted Kaczynski began it way back in 1978'.[98]

What emerges here, then, is a palpable apocalyptical element. The looming Singularity is portrayed as a momentous juncture instigating a protracted and intense conflict between advocates and adversaries of technology. The anticipation of this struggle for survival against a dystopian future of unyielding technological control resonates with an apocalyptic narrative, underscored by a pervasive sense of urgency among anti-tech insurrectionary anarchists. The belief that this war has potentially already commenced further accentuates the apocalyptic undertones within the anarchist discourse on technology. The question then arises: if this war has begun, how are anarchists fighting it?

An Anti-Civilization Fight

'As the new technologies change our social systems, we are looking now at a permanent universal asymmetrical urban war to the end.'[99] The anarchist anti-technology strategy is fundamentally centred on the evergreen principle of propaganda of the deed: that is, attacks that strike the centre of power and domination and 'make the fear change side'.[100] The ultimate objective is to overthrow and destroy the mega-machine and, therefore, techno-industrial civilization. To do so, the anarchist strategy aims at identifying and pushing up through the cracks and fissures in the system to hasten its demise.[101] The impending ecological collapse offers an opportunity in this regard 'to create contagious breakdowns and attacks on the techno-industrial system during the chaos'.[102] This element of accelerationism – that is, using violence to exacerbate social and structural tensions, thereby hastening societal breakdown – appears intrinsic to the anarchist strategy. The best course of action, then, is to identify the system's vulnerabilities and ruthlessly attack them to accelerate the demise of civilization. In this regard, anarchists align themselves with the Unabomber, who similarly argued that anti-tech revolutionaries should hasten the onset of the system breakdown.[103]

At an operational level, this strategy develops along two trajectories. First, the growth of the mega-machine and the 'becoming One of all machines and devices'[104] entails a huge risk for techno-industrial civilization: a malfunctioning part may compromise the whole entity. Just like in Forster's 'The Machine Stops', where the malfunctioning Mending Apparatus brings down the whole Machine, a blow to the system's Achilles' heel will bring down techno-industrial civilization. Therefore, a clever anti-technology strategy should aim to target the weak links of the mega-machine, that is, the critical infrastructure on which the system depends. One such infrastructure is the electrical grid, with anarchists openly calling for attacks.[105] As long as the mega-machine depends on centralized electrical power, the 'edifice of Power' will rely on cables, connective coupling, antennas, and relays. Such constitutive elements of the '*network* of domination can not all be protected, weak points will exist', and it 'is only a matter of researching the methods, applying them, replicating and evolving the techniques of sabotage and attack'.[106]

Understanding the interlocking nature of the components of the mega-machine is thus a prerequisite for the war on technology. Anti-technology revolutionaries should, therefore, commit themselves to studying technology and keeping up with its development. Such knowledge is part and parcel of rebelling against technology: if you know how it works, you can destroy it.[107] This alone provides a sufficient rationale for the anarchists' seemingly hypocritical resort to technology. Anarchists give additional justifications. The system will use any means to expand and destroy those who dare to rebel, so it is legitimate to use any means to oppose it. Yet the choice of such means is limited, with anarchists describing their situation as that of 'prisoners planning the collapse of the concentration camp with the tools that are in the same camp'.[108] As such, while some are said to adopt rudimentary methods and avoid computers or telephones deliberately, insurrectionary anarchists accept the use of technology to destroy technology and resort to explosives, firearms, as well as the internet for awareness-raising and encrypted applications for communication.[109]

Moving to the tactical level, the assault against the weak links of the system translates into campaigns against power grids, repeaters, cell towers, 5G antennas, and, interestingly, 'green' energy sources.[110] These campaigns include a repertoire of tactics that range from sabotage to arson and bombing. Attacks are carried out using rudimentary means such as improvised explosive devices and improvised incendiary devices.[111] On the internet, anarchists circulate detailed instructions on how to attack targets such as cell towers and 5G antennas, a *vade mecum* for those who want to join the war on the machines.[112] Occasionally, specific cells might display a more sophisticated *modus operandi*, but these remain the exception.[113] Consistent with the anarchist tradition, attacks rarely result in casualties as they are primarily intended to take down infrastructure and damage property.[114]

Examples include the forty-six attacks that targeted infrastructure in France in the first ten months of 2022. One such attack resulted in a massive internet sabotage, affecting 100,000 individuals and 2,000 businesses in the Reims region in April that year.[115]

More recently, on 26 July 2024, a cell called An Unexpected Delegation targeted train infrastructure by placing incendiary devices at four locations along high-speed railways in France. This caused travel chaos just hours before the opening ceremony of the Paris 2024 Olympic Games. The group claimed responsibility for the attack and denounced high-speed railroads and infrastructure as tools of colonialism, devastation, and state control. In addition, they criticized the role of various private companies in the destruction of the environment.[116] France also experienced attacks against electrical transformers in May 2020, with the perpetrators – a cell named Offspring of Disaster – releasing the following statement:

> We attacked the electricity network because today, without it, this civilization would collapse. We don't desire to return to some time in the past. We have no illusions about the fact that some civilizations were built without electricity. All we know is that this one relies on it so much as to be unable to do without it. And that this is one of its weak points.[117]

In the same year, the Chilean cell Autonomous Revolutionary Squads similarly attacked the electrical grid in the Atacama region,[118] while, in 2014, the International Conspiracy for Revenge – FAI-FRI attacked three power plants in Indonesia.[119] At the same time, anarchist attacks against telecommunication infrastructure, including 5G cell towers and repeaters, have multiplied over the last few years in several countries, from Sweden to Italy and the United Kingdom.[120]

Recently, the COVID-19 pandemic has reinforced these patterns. While the virus was considered an excuse to strengthen social control and hasten the establishment of the new totalitarianism, anarchists have established links between technology and the pandemic. One leitmotif, for example, is that 5G antennas weaken people's immune systems.[121] Unsurprisingly, the COVID-19 vaccination campaign has similarly come under fire. At the Fifth International Meeting 'Three Days Against Techno-Sciences' – a non-violent initiative to discuss the nefarious nature of technology – held in Italy at the end of July 2023, vaccines were indeed associated with cancer, genetic engineering, and infertility.¹²² The vaccination campaign is therefore considered part and parcel of the elites' project of domination, and it stems from the same logic 'that declared "war on terror" to justify bombings'.¹²³ Therefore, anti-technology anarchism displays a tendency for conspiracy thinking – a common trend among extremists.¹²⁴ This has led to a widening of the front against technology, with medicine now representing the latest addition among the many columns 'upon which [. . .] techno-industrial capitalist system is founded'.¹²⁵ Vaccination centres and research laboratories have thus been legitimized as targets of anarchist violence.¹²⁶

This leads us to the second trajectory of the anarchist anti-technology strategy: attacks on research centres, laboratories, companies specializing in technology, and those representing techno-industrial civilization.¹²⁷ The rationale for striking such targets is straightforward: these attacks will delay or destroy ongoing research while also sending out shock waves in the scientific community.¹²⁸ A noteworthy attack of this sort occurred a little more than a decade ago as Nicola Gai and Alfredo Cospito – militants of the Olga Nucleus of the FAI-FRI – kneecapped Roberto Adinolfi in 2012. The broader insurrectionary anarchist movement rejoiced, with the Greek CCF praising their FAI-FRI comrades for this attack against a 'high priest of the new totalitarianism of science and technology imperatives'.¹²⁹ While this is perhaps the most spectacular attack that anarchists have carried out against representatives of technology, it also constitutes an anomaly in their *modus operandi*. Typically, anarchists tend to prioritize attacks on property and infrastructure over striking people. Then, when they do target individuals, they seldom use firearms or intend to kill or injure seriously.¹³⁰ Roughly a year before the Adinolfi attack, the FAI-FRI had already claimed responsibility for a parcel bomb sent to Swissnuclear in Olten, Switzerland.¹³¹ Both these attacks were part of an anti-nuclear campaign that emerged following the 2011 Fukushima disaster.¹³² In 2010, instead, anarchists attempted to bomb IBM's nanotechnology laboratory in Zurich.¹³³ A similar trend underlies the attack on the Italian Institute of Technology and its robotics research programme on 24 December 2018 and the fire against a techno-scientific research laboratory in Gières, France, on 23 February 2020.¹³⁴ These instances represent only a fraction of the violence unleashed by anarchists. Yet this second trajectory of the anarchist strategy appears to be less substantial than the first one, as most anarchist attacks seem to target infrastructure. An accurate count is, however, elusive given both the ambiguous anarchist stance towards claiming attacks and an objective lack of scholarly engagement with the topic.[135]

The anarchist war on civilization is thus characterized by a strategic blend of targeting vulnerabilities within the system and striking at the symbolic pillars of technological dominance. The ultimate objective remains the overthrow and destruction of the mega-machine, driven by a belief that accelerating its demise is the most effective means of ushering in a new era free from the shackles of techno-industrial civilization.

Looking to the future, the trajectory of anarchist anti-technology could result in a progressive escalation in violence. The COVID-19 pandemic has introduced new dimensions, intertwining public health measures with anti-technology sentiments. Conspiracy thinking has seeped into the discourse, linking the pandemic to technology and framing the vaccination campaign as part of the elites' project of domination. Also, several anarchist foreign fighters are now present in conflict zones such as Ukraine and Syria.[136] Upon their return, the future anarchist ranks could be filled with battle-hardened militants whose expertise could enhance anarchist capabilities. In this regard, it is worth noticing that initiatives to deradicalize and disengage anarchist extremists are 'virtually non-existent'.[137] While law enforcement agencies diligently monitor anarchist activities, the lack of such initiatives and scholarly engagement with this issue arguably creates a blind spot in this area.

Adding to this, more extremist nihilist positions are advancing among the fringe extremist anarchist ranks; a belief that nihilism is the culmination of anarchism and the essence of what it means to fight civilization – 'for it is in the destruction of society that this new anarchy is being fulfilled', as Cospito put it.[138] Such a nihilist stance has been accompanied by a rethinking of the long-standing anarchist reticence towards striking people and resorting to lethal violence. Calls for the resort to more destructive or lethal violence are multiplying, with members of law enforcement noticing that anarchists have been adopting a more unscrupulous use of force over the last twenty years.[139] This development is in line with the anarchist narrative. In the war against the machines, anarchists encourage each other to strike 'without scruples' and overcome their 'deep-rooted and indestructible repugnance for any bloody act' – an aversion to lethal violence which, some anarchists argue, 'doesn't help us at all'.[140]

As technological landscapes continue to evolve and technologies become more and more integrated into our everyday lives, we might, therefore, witness an increase in anarchist anti-technology violence. The decentralized, leaderless nature of the anarchist threat will probably prevent the movement from carrying out spectacular, coordinated attacks – and this organizational principle is unlikely to change; if it did, anarchists would cease to be anarchists. Nonetheless, the possibility of escalation does exist, influenced by the ongoing dance between technological advancements and the ideological fervour of those committed to the war against the machines. Although even the most sophisticated anarchist campaign would, arguably, have little chance of bringing about the collapse of civilization, if the current escalatory trend were to persist, it could bring further financial damage, disruption, and – potentially – the loss of human lives.

3
Nature Fights Back
Eco-Extremism

It was 13 January 2017, Santiago, Chile. A young woman delivered a parcel wrapped as a gift to a residence in Santiago's La Reina neighbourhood, the name of a professor of mining engineering at the University of Chile listed as the sender. The residence belonged to Óscar Landerretche Moreno, CEO of the state-owned mining *Corporación Nacional del Cobre* (Codelco) – the largest copper mining company in the world. The parcel was an improvised explosive device, a bomb. It went off; luckily, Landerretche – along with his daughter and his maid – suffered only superficial injuries.[1] An online document published by the local cell of a transnational network calling itself *Individualistas Tendiendo a lo Salvaje* (ITS – Individualists Tending Towards the Wild) claimed responsibility for the attack, justifying the strike against Landerretche because of his role 'at the head of the major project of devastation of all that is beautiful on Earth'.[2] In the document, the attackers identified themselves as a '[h]orde of eco-extremist savages, nihilists and egoists' who 'shit on [. . .] the people who are accomplices to the techno-industrial system'.[3] With this attack, they wanted to seek vengeance for the Earth, moribund because of technological progress. For his role as chief of a 'megaproject devastating all the beauty of Earth', ITS proclaimed that the 'pretentious Landerretche deserved to die for his offenses' against the planet.[4] Two years later, a 29-year-old man called Camilo Eduardo Gajardo Escalona was arrested. In addition to the Landerretche bomb, he was accused of at least six further bombings that he conducted in the name of ITS. In October 2022, Gajardo was convicted and sentenced to forty-five years' imprisonment.[5]

This wasn't the first time the Individualists' fury had struck Chile. The forefront of a phenomenon known as eco-extremism, ITS has haunted South America since 2011, later spreading to Europe.[6] Deeply entrenched in its disdain for technology, the eco-extremist movement has joined the fight against techno-industrial civilization. Despite its recent emergence, it traces its lineage to the latter half of the twentieth century, with its genesis being closely related to three phenomena, namely insurrectionary anarchism, Theodore J. Kaczynski's war against technology, and the radical environmentalist movement birthed in the post-World War II period. As both the Unabomber and anarchism have already been discussed in the previous chapters, to understand where contemporary eco-extremism comes from and what it is seeking to achieve, we first need to turn to the late 1950s, a decade that witnessed the dawn of radical environmentalism in the United States and the United Kingdom. Back then, stalwart activists embarked on a crusade to stem the tide of civilization, attempting to halt the degradation of the planet and the exploitation of animals. Those early forays manifested in rudimentary acts of sabotage where anti-hunt advocates obstructed roads or laid false scents to mislead hunters' hounds.[7] While such endeavour persisted throughout the 1960s, the advent of the 1970s saw the blossoming of a robust movement that fervently set out to defend Earth and all its denizens. Central to the rise of this movement was the emergence of ecotage, a tactical recourse whereby environmental activists would sabotage to thwart ecological desecration, safeguarding both ecosystems and animals. Bron Taylor argues that ecotage was instrumental to the birth of radical environmentalism.[8] Without it, this movement might not have emerged at all. Ecotage served a dual purpose: garnering media attention, thus generating public awareness and sympathy, while inflicting substantial financial repercussions on corporations, driving up costs beyond profitability, and forcing them to halt their operations.[9]

Concurrently, the concept of deep ecology – developed by Arne Næss in 1973[10] – provided the movement with a coherent philosophical and ideological underpinning.[11] Rejecting anthropocentrism and adopting a biocentric perspective, deep ecology advocates a belief that all living creatures are of equal worth.[12] Inherent in its precepts, there is a call for a rollback of civilization – an inescapable precondition to allow for the restoration of wilderness.[13] As such, deep ecology entails a strong prescriptive element. Emboldened by this ideology, various groups emerged in the 1970s, including the Band of Mercy – a revival of a group of activists that sought to thwart fox hunting in England in the nineteenth century – and the Animal Liberation Front (ALF).[14] Although animal rights activists and radical environmentalists are here discussed together, it is important to remember that, as noted in Chapter 1, the relationship between them was not always a harmonious one, with radical environmentalists prioritizing entire species and ecosystems over individual animals.[15]

The next two decades saw the rise of Earth First! (EF! – 1980), the Animal Rights Militia (ARM – 1986), the Earth Liberation Front (ELF – 1992), and the Justice Department (JD – 1993), each contributing to the mosaic of radical environmentalist and animal rights activist movements.[16] These groups usually displayed anarchist influences in their ideologies and *modus operandi*, from the rejection of authoritarianism to the adoption of direct actions and affinity groups.[17] Yet, in contrast to the societal concerns that predominated in anarchism, radical environmentalism focused on the ecological issue. Moreover, a marked apocalyptic millenarian mindset characterized these groups: a belief that humanity is close to the point of no return and that radical – and sometimes violent – actions are necessary and justified to hasten the collapse of techno-industrial civilization, thus saving the planet by realizing a better world where humans live in harmony with nature.[18] There were, of course, also groups that advocated a purely non-violent approach to save the environment, such as Greenpeace.

Whereas the conceptualization of deep ecology furnished the movement with an ideological framework, the publication of Edward Abbey's *The Monkey Wrench Gang* in 1975 and, perhaps more importantly, of Bill Haywood and Dave Foreman's *Ecodefense: A Field Guide to Monkeywrenching* in 1985 provided radical environmentalists with a practical blueprint for action.[19] So inspired, radical environmentalists embarked on a broad campaign of ecotage, ranging from tree-spiking (to thwart loggers) to arson, boycotts, strikes, animal liberation, and vandalism.[20] These actions left a wake of financial upheaval in their trail: for example, the ALF caused more than £250,000 worth of damage in 1980, its first year of operation.[21] However, while targeting property, humans were largely spared. Indeed, radical environmentalists have traditionally shied away from targeting or harming humans. Taylor argues that the belief that all life is sacred created a barrier against harming people among radical environmentalists.[22] That doesn't mean that certain more radical factions haven't sought to harm or kill people. Betraying the sanctity of life they professed, groups like the Animal Rights Militia and the Justice Department targeted fellow humans.[23] Curiously, statistical findings show that animal rights activists are more than five times more likely to target people than are environmental activists.[24] This also reminds us of the tensions between deep ecology and animal rights activism discussed in Chapter 1. Yet, despite the slightly more aggressive nature of animal rights activists, Michael Loadenthal's exhaustive inquiry spanning 11,562 illegal incidents associated with the environmental and animal rights movements from 1973 through to 2010 found a mere four fatal attacks – and three of these were perpetrated by the same person, Theodore Kaczynski, who was anyway hardly an eco-radical or an animal liberationist, but rather an anti-technology extremist, and should have perhaps not been included at all in this dataset.[25] Similarly, another study found that, of the actions carried out by environmental and animal activists between 1970 and 2008, only 17% can be considered terrorist attacks.[26] What follows is that the radical environmentalist movement is a 'broad and loosely organized amalgam of individuals, groups and organizations that condone radical (i.e., non-legal) actions to realize a world in which both animals and the environment are fully respected'.[27] The technology issue looms large within radical environmentalism, casting a long shadow over the movement. At its core, many radical environmentalists are unhappy with technology's dominant role in society and our daily lives, perceiving it as humanity's attempt to subjugate and control nature.[28] After all, one of the central tenets of deep ecology is that human society must return to a pre-industrial state where all advanced technologies are banished.[29] Essentially, radical environmentalists' antipathy towards technology stems from ecological concerns.[30]

Despite their criminal activity and the resort to violence against (mostly) non-human targets, the application of the term 'terrorism' appears both misguided and harmful. Many scholars have argued that 'ecoterrorism' – a term popularized by Ron Arnold in 1983[31] – constitutes a dangerous misnomer.[32] Nonetheless, in the post-9/11 era, radical environmental groups found themselves castigated, as countries like the United States elected them to the status of the predominant domestic terrorist threat – an emblematic case of the fraught relationship between activism and security in the context of the Global War on Terror.[33] More recently, a plethora of non-violent radical environmentalist movements has emerged. Unfortunately, groups like Just Stop Oil, Extinction Rebellion, Fridays for Future, and Last Generation might suffer a similar fate considering the growing number of activists who have recently been associated with violent extremism, offering yet another powerful reminder of the often-misplaced connection between radical environmentalism, activism, and terrorism.[34]

Spearheads of the Movement

Along with these groups of activists, a new strand of radical environmentalists surfaced at the dawn of the 2010s. Marking a discernible shift in the movement's most radical fringes, technology assumed a more prominent role. Organizations like Deep Green Resistance (DGR) – based on the eponymous book published in 2011 – epitomize this trend.[35] Arguing that 'the only level of technology that is sustainable is the Stone Age', Derrick Jensen – one of DGR's founders – maintained that any technology developed since the First Agricultural Revolution, which started around 10,000 BCE, will inevitably destroy Earth and life.[36] To avoid this, DGR proposes a radical approach: 'We just have to bring down industrial civilization first.'[37] The organization employs a dual-fronted strategy, comprising an above-ground movement that promotes alternatives to techno-industrial civilization and an underground wing committed to 'strategically dismantling the institutions killing the world'.[38] While DGR has justified the resort to lethal violence to prevent ecological collapse, it has yet to substantiate such claims – if it ever will.[39]

This period also witnessed the emergence of additional radical and non-violent movements, such as the Dark Mountain Project, challenging the myth of progress, the separation of humans from nature, and the myth of civilization.[40] Similarly, websites advocating for the eradication of technology, such as Wilderness Front, For Wild Nature and Against Industrial Society – often featuring the writings of Theodore Kaczynski – or *Resistanze al Nanomondo* (Resistance Against the Nanoworld) mushroomed in the last decade.[41] The growing relevance of technology within radical environmentalism paralleled the increasing following that Kaczynski gained throughout the 2010s. As John Jacobi – a prominent anti-technology activist – delineated, Kaczynski's followers could be grouped into different categories. First, there was a group of 'puritans', the *indomitistas*, led by Último Reducto (UR), who adopted a rigid 'Kaczynskianism' and worked closely with the Unabomber himself up to his death in June 2023, contributing to a formalization of his ideology.[42] Then, within radical environmentalism, Kaczynski's followers coalesced into two factions: the Wildists and the eco-extremists. Jacobi championed the Wildist faction. Initially closer to the positions of the *indomitistas*, he distanced himself because of their strict adherence to Kaczynski's worldview and refusal to acknowledge the necessity of a multifaceted approach and a coalition of anti-civilization radicals in the fight against technology.[43] Upon breaking away from the *indomitistas*, Jacobi founded and ran a conservation magazine called *The Wildernist* from 2014 to 2016. After that, he established the Wildist Institute, which managed *Hunther/Gatherer* – a publication 'intended to be a forum for wildists'.[44] The Wildist Institute published a few issues of *Hunter/Gatherer* before it was rebranded Wild Will.[45] Since October 2019, the Wild Will website has been offline, with Jacobi's works being reposted on different platforms, including For Wild Nature and Against Industrial Society or Wild Will's Facebook page, which is still active but, as of October 2024, hasn't posted anything since December 2021.[46]

In essence, Wildism is an ethical philosophy that stresses the importance of wildness in conserving and restoring nature.[47] It has three core elements. The first is a belief in the material world and the use of reason to understand it, with life sciences replacing physics as the defining science of our culture. This materialist philosophy implies a form of nihilism: 'the understanding that there is no objective value in the world, and thus that all value is "imbued" by a valuer'.[48] Second, Wildists critique the 'myth of progress' as the idea that humans artificially modify Nature to improve the world and the human condition.[49] Third, Wildists profess the imperative to rewild.[50] This practice involves actions in favour of Wild Nature, aiming to preserve the natural environment and spread it into urban space.[51] Importantly, the objective of such actions is not to regress or 'return' to some past or primitive state. Jacobi contends that the primitive hasn't been lost to us; humans are civilized but not domesticated. Therefore, reviving the wild within us necessitates 'repenting' to the primitive.[52]

Wildism operates on the premise that the 'biggest problems of the twenty-first century are and will be technological problems'. The emergence and rapid spread of diseases, mass surveillance, mass extinction, and climate change are irrefutable evidence of this. And yet, despite these pressing issues, 'scientists, governments, and corporations push for even more invasive and destabilizing technologies like nanotechnology, genetic engineering, and advanced artificial intelligence'. Wildism asserts that the only solution to this is the collapse of civilization, as industry and technology are fundamentally incompatible with rewilding. Partial reforms or eliminating certain harmful technologies will not suffice because 'you cannot separate the good parts of technology from the bad' – technology constitutes a system so complex that 'you either take all of its central aspects or you take none'.[53] Nature is also a system, but unlike technology, it arose spontaneously, created us, and will keep ensuring our survival if we do not sacrifice it at the altar of technological progress. However, since 'a technological system has to regulate humans and nature in order to function',[54] technology will never be compatible with the survival of nature – and, therefore, humans. As such, in Wildism, technology ceases to exist as an instrument or tool and emerges as an all-encompassing essence that enslaves nature and humanity – a trend that will only worsen. We may eventually need to be technologically augmented to be compatible with techno-industrial civilization, a transhumanist process that will ultimately destroy human nature,[55] which 'consists of those parts of the human being that are not influenced by man or his technics'.[56] Yet eradicating technology won't mean the end of human-made tools. Indeed, Jacobi accepts Kaczynski's distinction between small-scale technology (any technology created and maintained by small communities) and organization-dependent technology (technology that requires large-scale organization, specialization, and division of labour), identifying the latter as the most pernicious.[57]

Thus, Wildism opposes technology as the leading cause of destruction in the natural world. In doing so, it maintains that the system won't collapse 'unless a group of dedicated people placed firmly on the side of wild nature decides to take action'.[58] In other words, Wildism promotes the establishment of a vanguardist anti-tech movement firmly convinced that the collapse of techno-industrial civilization is both a desirable and an achievable outcome.[59] Yet, despite acknowledging its engagement in a protracted war against techno-industrial civilization, Wildism is 'not interested in bombs and terrorism' and operates mostly above ground.[60] Unlike the Unabomber, who also advocated for a group of anti-technology revolutionaries, Wildists do not condone or advocate violence – or, at least, not unless forced to resort to it as a means of last resort. Instead, the Wildist strategy involves conservation work to enhance and spread wildlife, journalistic endeavour to advocate for the Wildist cause, academic engagement to explore the rewilding of the planet, and, only if necessary, illegal activities such as monkeywrenching.[61] As of 2016, Wildism was – according to Jacobi – present in the United States, Germany, and the United Kingdom, though this information can hardly be verified. While the end goal remains the collapse of techno-industrial civilization, its short-term goals centre on globalizing the Wildist ideology, linking the various groups, and contributing to destabilization and tension within the system.[62]

The growth of Wildism is, however, not unchallenged. As Jacobi himself admitted, a major obstacle lies in the expansion of eco-extremist thought. Writing in the mid-2010s, he acknowledged a certain impact in the eco-extremists' narrative and methods, going as far as saying that, so long as the eco-extremists continued on their then-current path, they might come to define radical environmentalism in the twenty-first century.[63] So, what exactly is eco-extremism?

The spectre of eco-extremism materialized as a virulent fringe within the radical environmentalist and animal rights activist movement around 2011 in Mexico. Influenced by insurrectionary anarchism and the writings of the Unabomber, a 'group of young people [...] began to move away from militant animal rights and vegan ideologies' to develop a position where violent confrontation takes precedence.[64] The main moniker around which these 'young people' have organized is Individualists Tending Towards the Wild (*Individualidades Tendiendo a lo Salvaje* – ITS).[65] Emerging in the spring of 2011, ITS describes itself as an 'anti-industrial, anti-technological, and anti-civilization group formed by radical environmentalists'.[66] This self-identification with radical environmentalism should not mislead one into thinking that there is a somewhat continuous spectrum from radical environmentalism and animal liberationism to the violent misanthropic eco-extremism that ITS champions. On the contrary, it is important to distinguish eco-extremism from them. While it may have originated from local radical environmentalist fringes, the following pages will clarify how ITS soon evolved into a distinct phenomenon that has distanced itself from radical environmentalism and animal liberationism to move closer to far-right extremism. In this sense, while 'eco-terrorism' has become a pejorative label assigned to several environmentalists by law enforcement, it is more accurately exemplified by the tendency of ITS to target human life in pursuit of ecological regress.[67]

However, adopting tactics that 'have at times resembled the insurrectionary methods of clandestine attack', ITS has often been associated with insurrectionary anarchism.[68] The fact that its communiqués circulated through the same channels as anarchists' has reinforced such speculations. The truth is that ITS had originally expressed some interest in the FAI – the Informal Anarchist Federation that sprang up in Italy in 2003 before spreading to other countries in 2011. Yet the two ended up parting ways, with ITS criticizing the FAI for deviating from its original promotion of indiscriminate violence in favour of a less extremist approach perceived as a mere 'pretext for some to raise the most putrid, sterile, and aberrant flags of the social anarchists' in the name of 'oppressed people'.[69] Similarly, eco-extremists have expressed their disdain for the FAI's cousin, the Greek Conspiracy of Cells of Fire.[70] The contempt is largely mutual, as most anarchists, with the occasional exception,[71] have condemned the fury of the eco-extremists. ITS, in turn, has vehemently rejected the allegations of any association or collusion with the anarchist universe.[72]

Upon entering the stage in 2011, ITS embarked on a series of bombings against universities and research centres, particularly those specializing in nanotechnology.[73] A few months later, it claimed its first lethal operation, as it allegedly murdered a researcher at the Biotechnology Institute of the National Autonomous University of Mexico (UNAM).[74] The 'Tendency' launched by the Individualists in 2011 spread across Mexico in the following years. In 2014, ITS claimed to have merged with other groups – including the Informal Anti-Civilization Group, the Obsidian Point Circle of Attack, the Uncivilized Autonomous, the Wild Indomitables, the Terrorist Cells for the Direct Attack, and the Luddites Against the Domestication of Wild Nature – forming a new network of eco-extremists called Wild Reaction (*Reacción Salvaje* – RS).[75]

Wild Reaction experienced a brief but intense period of activity before eventually burning out. After just one year, the project dissolved, paving the way for the resurgence of the ITS in 2016. In its first post-RS communiqué, ITS declared itself 'the continuation of the eco-terrorist project begun in the year 2011'.[76] It is noteworthy how ITS accepts – or even appropriates – the label of 'terrorist', a term violent non-state actors normally reject. Following the dissolution of RS, several new groups emerged, including the Pagan Sect of the Mountain, the Eco-Extremist Circle of Terrorism and Sabotage, the Indiscriminate Faction, Kaos ITS, and the Ouroboros Nihilista. These groups spread across Mexico, South America (Peru, Chile, Argentina, and Brazil), and Europe (Greece, Spain, Italy, and Scotland).[77] All these entities formed what ITS referred to as the 'eco-extremist Mafia'.[78] Evidence of such expansion into Europe was recently substantiated when, in March 2022, the Italian police arrested Federico Buono during Operation Misanthropy (*Operazione Misantropia*). Buono, known to the authorities for his previous anarchist militancy, appeared to have adhered to the eco-extremist Tendency. Charged with planning to carry out terrorist attacks, he was also found to be one of five individuals managing the main eco-extremist website related to ITS, www.maldicionecoestremista.altervista.org, which was subsequently closed down by the authorities.[79]

Avenging Nature

Thus, the Tendency that emerged in 2011 eventually morphed into a loose international network: the eco-extremist Mafia. Central to eco-extremism is a radical critique of technology. This, in turn, is based on five main pillars. First, eco-extremists promote the concept of Wild Nature as the 'primary agent of the struggle against civilization and the ultimate beneficiary of civilization's demise'.[80] Wild Nature encompasses all that eludes the process of domestication and subjugation that civilization imposed on nature. It is the antithesis of artificiality – from micro-organisms to celestial bodies, it is all that which resides outside of technology.[81] Second, eco-extremists resort to 'individualism' as an 'important tactical choice within mass society'.[82] This concept is akin to leaderless resistance. Eco-extremist groups embrace it as it offers tactical advantages, ensuring anonymity while making it harder for authorities to detect them.[83]

Third, eco-extremists staunchly advocate for 'indiscriminate violence'. To attack indiscriminately – they argue – is 'to strike a target without regard for so-called innocent bystanders or collateral damage'.[84] Such practice has attracted much criticism, particularly from anarchist ranks and more moderate radical environmentalist fringes.[85] However, eco-extremists easily brush off such criticisms, labelling them as the civilized heritage of the Christian golden rule, 'do unto others as you would have them do unto you'.[86] They further justify their stance on indiscriminate violence by asserting their identification with Wild Nature. In their view, their attacks echo the inherent violence and lack of discrimination observed in nature, drawing parallels with natural disasters: 'Tsunamis don't suddenly stop when they reach poor neighborhoods, alligators don't distinguish between the innocent and the guilty in their nocturnal hunts, and hurricanes don't attack people according to race.'[87] If Wild Nature 'destroys everything in its path without consideration for morality' and eco-extremists personify it, then why should they stop at all in front of bystanders?[88] If this wasn't enough, eco-extremists also argue that the concept of 'innocence' holds little significance. They reject the notion that anyone can be considered innocent in a society that perpetuates and benefits from technology. To them, those who do not heed the eco-extremist call are complicit in the destruction of Wild Nature.[89] By extension, they view bystanders as active participants in the demise of nature and, as such, legitimate targets.

Fourth, eco-extremism is marked by a deepening nihilism. Whereas a more optimistic attitude permeated nihilism in the Wildist endeavour, the eco-extremist nihilistic outlook represents a stark departure from this and assumes defeatist connotations regarding the possibility of overthrowing techno-industrial civilization. Eco-extremists harbour no illusions about the futility of a revolution against such a formidable system. Despite this grim outlook, they side with nature, preferring 'to be defeated in a war against total domination than to remain inert, waiting, passive, or as part of all this'.[90] Their goal is not to destroy techno-industrial civilization; instead, they seek to disrupt the relentless march of technology.[91] Over the years, this position has become increasingly more extreme. While the pre-RS ITS opposed revolutions mostly out of defeatism, RS and the post-2016 ITS built on this position, arguing that revolutions are not only impossible but also undesirable 'aberrations of modernity'.[92] Distancing themselves from Kaczynski's revolutionary ideals, eco-extremists argue that any revolution would still be carrying some of the values of the very system it intends to bring down – the values of civilization. Therefore, it would inevitably end in different forms of domination while also 'falling into a religious dogmatism' typical of leftists and their 'blind confidence they have that someday the "revolution" will come'.[93] It is crucial to note that eco-extremists anticipate the eventual collapse of techno-industrial civilization. Yet they do not think they have an active role to play in it. The demise of civilization will stem either from its self-destructive tendencies or from the forces of Wild Nature.[94] Recently, ITS rejoiced in the COVID-19 pandemic, stating that this was 'a scenario that we prefer infinitely many times before returning to the normality of the mundane life of the civilized'.⁹⁵ Considering it a watershed in the history of techno-industrial civilization, ITS argued that the pandemic revealed fractures within the system. While maintaining that a revolution would be impossible and undesirable, it saw these cracks as weaknesses that they should exploit to hasten the 'Days of Chaos'.⁹⁶

This underlying pessimism reflects the profound nihilist stance characterizing eco-extremism; a nihilism that constitutes a 'refusal of the future'.⁹⁷ Eco-extremists are not fighting for a 'better tomorrow', nor do they believe in any utopia: 'We don't want to solve any problems here, we aren't proposing anything to anyone. We aren't trying to change the world, and we don't want the masses to join us. [. . .] Enough with the thinking that we can have a better world!'⁹⁸ As such, eco-extremist nihilism differs substantially from the Wildist interpretation. Where Wildists considered nihilism a philosophical position that rejects any objectivity of values and morality, eco-extremists interpret it as a disbelief in revolution.⁹⁹ Remarkably, their objectives lack tangible endpoints; the attack against the system becomes its own end. The violence they unleash against technology springs from atavistic and primal impulses, an instinct to defend Nature and 'to avenge the devastation of the earth, to return even minimally the damage that modern humans have done to natural environments'.¹⁰⁰ In essence, eco-extremists view their violence as a natural reaction. A 'violent resistance that mimics the reflexive reaction of Wild Nature itself against what seeks to alienate and enslave all living and inanimate things'.¹⁰¹ A further divergence from Kaczynski emerged following the birth of Wild Reaction. The original, pre-RS ITS was more indebted to the Unabomber, whereas now RS distanced itself from him. A change in vocabulary also accompanied this. Kaczynskian terms, such as 'power process', were replaced by concepts like 'hyper-civilized' or 'hyper-artificial', distinguishing eco-extremists from the *indomitistas* or the Unabomber.¹⁰² Overall, eco-extremists' relationship with Kaczynski is troubled: the Unabomber is someone eco-extremists admit they learned a great deal from, yet they fundamentally disagree with him regarding overthrowing the system.¹⁰³

Finally, eco-extremism is based on pagan animism. Again, it is necessary to distinguish the pre-RS ITS from Wild Reaction and the post-2016 ITS. With the establishment of Wild Reaction in 2014, eco-extremists disposed of the last remnants of 'scientific humanist thought'.[104] Moving away from their initial materialistic interpretation of eco-extremism, they embraced ancestral religious beliefs, marking a revivalist turn in their ideology.[105] Aiming 'to revive the worship of the spirits of the Earth and to offer sacrifices to them', this ideological turn also exacerbated the eco-extremist practice of indiscriminate attack.[106] Overall, this resurgence of animism serves a dual purpose: to reclaim indigenous beliefs and to break free from the perceived moral shackles imposed by Christianity.[107] Christianity and the Church are, indeed, perceived as tools of civilization, utilized to subdue and domesticate humans 'through the spread of morality and fear of God'.[108] At the same time, animism also represents an opposition to the philosophy of secular scientism, a crucial pillar of techno-industrial civilization but also – interestingly – of those anarchists who, in eco-exremists' view, futilely and foolishly oppose technology without relinquishing its constitutive paradigms.[109] While acknowledging that they owe much to anarchism as a long-standing philosophical tradition, eco-extremists reject its humanistic secularism, clinging 'to the historical pagan gods and spirits of the lands where they inhabit' and 'reclaiming their peoples' gods with a war-like ethos'.[110]

As such, the notion of the native holds significant importance within eco-extremism. The reappropriation of indigenous beliefs among eco-extremists in Mexico and other parts of South America serves as a means to resist the injustices of (Western) technological civilization. The past plays a crucial role, inspiring the struggle against technology. Eco-extremists see themselves as 'a group of modern humans possessed by the primitive warriors of the past'.[111] They look at the wars their ancestors fought against the very same enemy – for example, the Mixton Rebellion and the Chichimeca War that swept much of Mexico in the sixteenth century – drawing lessons from them.[112] This is also reflected in the *noms de guerre* that eco-extremists often adopt to celebrate and connect to their ancestors. Some prominent examples include MictlanTepetli, Xale, or Chahta-Ima, with the last one considered by some fellow extremists 'to be the most important eco-extremist theorist in this newest cycle'.[113]

This appreciation for bygone days comes, however, with two caveats. First, there is no desire to 'restore the past' – not least because of eco-extremists' pessimistic and nihilistic stance about the future.[114] As the past and the future disappear, 'the present is all that we have'.[115] Second, eco-extremists do not idealize the past. If anything, they are critical of the portrayal of primitive life by green anarchists and anarcho-primitivists as idyllic and joyful. According to eco-extremists, primitive life involved a great deal of hardship and suffering. Violence was also widespread, if not universal, with no trace of the perfect egalitarianism that anarchists usually ascribe to the primitive.[116] Thus, the eco-extremist vision of the primitive serves as a wellspring of inspiration rather than a blueprint for the future.

It is remarkable how, in this context, terminology related to to colonialism or imperialism is conspicuously absent. If one were to make an educated guess, this is likely due to eco-extremists' 'rejection of all that encompasses leftism'.[117] This extends to other leftist principles and causes, including gender equality. While eco-extremists recognize patriarchy as a system of domination, they view the concept of gender equality as a dangerous tool of civilization to enforce and perpetuate its control, arguing that those women who fight for equality don't realize that it is 'precisely what the system wants: to make all equal so that everyone can serve the same system and perpetuate it, regardless of gender, race, economic condition, language, etc.'.[118] Instead, they embrace gender differences, rejecting queerness in favour of a perceived 'natural' division between men and women. Like their male counterparts, eco-extremist women are seen as having a role to play in the war against technology.[119]

Another principle adamantly opposed by eco-extremists is veganism, which they perceive as a myth of techno-industrial society. They argue that vegan food is not genuinely vegan due to its reliance on practices that harm ecosystems. They also contend that vegan food production requires modern industrial agriculture to deforest large tracts of fertile land. This process involves displacing, domesticating, and even extinguishing various animal species within these ecosystems.[120] As such, the production and distribution of vegan food depend heavily on technological interventions. Put differently, the 'self-called "vegans" depend on the modern Techno-Industrial Society to carry out their diet'. In contrast, eco-extremists believe that in Wild Nature, dietary habits are determined by the environment rather than individual preferences. As such, vegans, or vegetarians for that matter, would struggle to survive outside of techno-industrial civilization.[121]

As it emerges from this background picture, eco-extremists consider technology the central issue plaguing the planet. Their critique of technology encompasses several interrelated points, including the domestication and subjugation of nature, the artificialization of humanity, and surveillance. Although certain technologies (e.g. nanotechnologies[122]) elicit more hostility, the broader concern lies with the entire techno-industrial civilization and the mega-machine that sustains it. Techno-industrial civilization is thus seen as

> the conjunction of physical components as well as conceptual ones (values) that include complex Technology, science, industry, Civilization and artificiality. The Techno-industrial System is the target to strike because from it (and its population [the Techno-industrial Society]) emanates the functioning, improvement and perpetuation of the megamachine called Civilization.[123]

In this view, technology is an 'immense barrier between ourselves and the natural world'.[124] Ultimately, this leads to Wild Nature's total domestication and subjugation.[125] Technology's advance is irresistible and threatens both the environment and human beings, propelling us all towards a catastrophe where 'all that is wild and natural is destroyed' in the name of progress and techno-industrial civilization.[126] Parallel to the tenets of Wildism, the eco-extremist critique regards technology as an all-encompassing force that enslaves and destroys Wild Nature, along with humanity. Indeed, since humans have become dependent on technology, they have transformed, losing their inherent natural qualities and evolving into artificial beings that eco-extremists term the 'hyper-civilized'.[127] This renders humans not only responsible for the destruction of Wild Nature wrought by technology but also active contributors to its subjugation.[128] The artificialization of humans extends beyond the metaphysical and moral realms and is anticipated to manifest physically with the advancement of transhumanism.[129] Consequently, humans are far from innocent bystanders and can be legitimate targets in the war against civilization.

To oppose techno-industrial civilization is to resist its domestication project, the very idea of modernity, progress, and science.[130] All this constitutes a process akin to Wildist rewilding, although eco-extremists approach this as an individual endeavour to reclaim a feral existence. This takes two primary forms. First, individualist eco-extremists may embrace a nomadic lifestyle in Wild Nature, periodically returning to civilized areas to enact attacks against the system. Alternatively, there are the 'city eco-extremists'. For the city eco-extremist to rewild, they need

> to know how to wage war, how to attack, ambush, evade authorities, mug, use firearms, and savor the last breath when taking the life of an enemy. All of this is also re-wilding: to return to the primitive in a conflict inherited from our ancestors. [. . .] To re-wild ourselves is to know how to move about like hunters, to learn to stalk the enemy, to hate him, to spill his blood, to scalp him and offer the scalp to the dead. But it is also to know wild nature, to lose oneself in the wilderness, to be in contact with the cycle of the seasons; to know it, breathe it in, and love it.[131]

For those who remain indifferent to the call of Wild Nature and refuse to rewild, eco-extremists see little hope. They argue that '[t]hrough a multiplicity of tools, techno-industrial civilization has overridden the capacity for criticism in the minds of the hypercivilized'.[132] People have become akin to 'automatons', navigating daily routines without questioning their destructive impact on Wild Nature. Confronted with this apathy, eco-extremists ask: 'They don't care at all about any of it. So then, why should we care at all about their pathetic lives?'[133] Among the arsenal of tools employed to suppress dissent, surveillance technology – the 'artificial eyes' of the system – plays a crucial role, vigilantly '[g]uarding the centers of domination and domestication'.[134] These centres – deemed the 'incubators of progress' – serve as hubs for the 'development of the technological, scientific, and industrial system'. They encompass universities, academic institutions, research centres, and high schools, where young minds are 'blinded by modernity' and rendered 'complicit in the destruction of Wild Nature'.[135] Expressing their disdain for scientists and researchers, eco-extremists would 'prefer to see them dead or mutilated rather than continuing to contribute with their scientific knowledge to all this shit, to continue feeding the Domination System'.[136] In this regard, their 'objectives are very clear: injure or kill scientists and researchers (by the means of whatever violent act) who ensure the Technoindustrial System continues its course'.[137]

However, the system stifles dissent and actively suppresses it should it arise. Eco-extremists are acutely aware that the pervasive surveillance culture of the system has also made anonymity rather tricky. Adopting an individualist (i.e. leaderless) approach stems also from such considerations. Eco-extremists understand the imperative of taking every precaution to evade detection, particularly when handling electronic devices such as cell phones.[138] This doesn't preclude them from using technology to destroy technology. Here again, the lesson of the past is crucial: 'What would have happened if these natives had rejected the weapons of the white people and clung instead to their old implements for hunting and fighting?' They argue that confining themselves 'to the old weaponry just because we criticize the technological system' would be unwise. Instead, they advocate to 'use the weapons of the system against itself. Just as the Native American participants did not hesitate to use those repeating firearms, we are not going to hesitate to use any modern weapon that might cause the enemy casualties.'[139]

The War on the Nerves

So, how exactly do eco-extremists wage their war against techno-industrial civilization? The eco-extremist Mafia employ a strategy they call the 'War on the Nerves'. This involves tactics ranging 'from the sharp criticism to the destructive bomb', constituting a form of 'total war' against techno-industrial civilization.[140] A war 'carried out by individualists who truly hate to the death all human progress', the eco-extremist assault is direct against the nerve centres of progress.[141] 'Universities, educational centers, academic institutions, etc. are the places where they prepare present and future progressivists (that is, those who believe in progress). Thus, they are an immovable target for eco-extremist attacks.'[142] While eco-extremists do not aim at triggering an anti-technology revolution and argue that they have no part to play in bringing about the demise of techno-industrial civilization, an accelerationist argument is nonetheless present in their strategy. Indeed, as noted above, ITS argued that the recent COVID-19 pandemic presented eco-extremists with the opportunity to strike at the system's vulnerabilities to hasten the 'Days of Chaos'.

Over the years, eco-extremists have given substance to the War on the Nerves and have carried out attacks on various university campuses and research institutions, including the Institute of Nuclear Science UNAM, the National Technological University in Buenos Aires, Argentina, the New School of Technology in the municipality of Coacalco, Mexico State, and the Centre for Computing Research at the National Polytechnic Institute in Mexico City.[143] However, their offensive extends beyond educational institutions, including targets such as banks, shopping centres, public transport, car dealers, and large public events like the 2016 Olympic Games in Brazil.[144] These targets are seen as embodiments of techno-industrial civilization and symbolize the artificiality that threatens Wild Nature.

When attacking the system, '[e]co-extremists act on their own at the chosen time and according to the best method for their circumstances'. An 'Eco-Extremist Rule Book dictating when and how to attack doesn't exist, and neither does an eco-extremist rule of life'.[145] As such, the eco-extremist War on the Nerves represents a flexible framework within which the anti-technology fight can be furthered. If there is anything resembling an absolute rule, it is that even though victory against civilization is impossible, the war against the technological system should nonetheless be approached with tactics and intelligence to ensure the capacity 'to deal blows to the mega-machine to the best of our abilities'.[146]

The War on the Nerves has faced criticism from different milieus. For one, critics have accused ITS and its fellow eco-extremists of being 'murderous psychopaths'[147] who promote misogyny and rape culture. ITS has taken these criticisms light-heartedly, dismissing them with disarming nonchalance. It has argued that it does not discriminate against women in its hatred towards humanity and cannot, therefore, be accused of misogyny. It has also made it clear, however, that it doesn't care if people rape or commit other heinous crimes.[148] At the same time, ITS has been accused of falsely claiming attacks 'to get a free ride on the coattails of a tragedy' and garner the 'attention they so desperately seek'.[149] For example, in May 2017, it claimed responsibility for the murder of Lesvy Berlín Rivera Osorio, a student at UNAM, adding further confusion to an already troubled case.[150] Indeed, the public prosecutor ruled that Rivera, who was found dead with a telephone cord around her neck, killed herself, while evidence seemed to point at her partner as the culprit. This ruling caused much outrage, with activists launching a campaign demanding justice for Rivera and, more generally, for the issue of violence against women in Mexico.[151] It is unclear why ITS claimed responsibility for Rivera's death. The most logical explanation seems to suggest that the group was, as indicated above, only trying to get some attention. On other occasions, by contrast, ITS rushed to deny its involvement in attacks that were attributed to the eco-extremist Mafia.[152]

Even Kaczynski criticized eco-extremists. In his opinion, besides having utterly misinterpreted his work, they had an understanding of revolution that was 'at a kindergarten level'. However, above all, the Unabomber could not absolve the eco-extremist 'attitude of hopelessness about the possibility of eliminating the technological system'.[153] His words were echoed by his disciple Último Reducto.[154] In addition, anarchists like Scott Campbell have labelled ITS as an eco-fascist organization,[155] and similar condemnations have also come from insurrectionary ranks.[156] Nonetheless, ITS has remained unfazed by any criticism, whether it comes from the 'deluded romanticist Zerzan', the 'deluded radical Kaczynski', or the 'disgusting Leftists'.[157] Interestingly, ITS reacted with less vehemence to allegations of having allied with right-wing, fascist, and Satanist movements, such as Tempel ov Blood or the Order of Nine Angles (O9A). ITS denied such allegations but stated there are lessons to be learned from such groups.¹⁵⁸ While contending that eco-fascists 'do not have a real critique of the Techno-industrial System and they adopt recycled and useless ideologies',¹⁵⁹ it acknowledged having 'taken some organizational experiences' from these groups without paying attention to their political orientation.¹⁶⁰ Essentially, eco-extremists reject eco-fascism because of the latter's inherent forward-looking, progressist nature, whereas '[w]e, in opposition to eco-fascism, are not moved by cravings of willing to live better in the future, the present is what we have, and that's that'.¹⁶¹ Nonetheless, despite its alleged roots in the insurrectionary anarchist milieu and the radical environmentalist milieu, it can't be denied that eco-extremists feel a certain attraction for neo-fascist, neo-Nazi, and Satanist networks. As Loadenthal argues, the inclusion of O9A imagery within eco-extremist online channels provides further evidence for this. In other words, although ITS's origins may be rooted in insurrectionary anarchism and radical environmentalism, the Tendency eventually disowned these legacies, modelling itself on hyper-violent far-right networks.¹⁶²

Finally, the War on the Nerves has faced criticism from within the broader militant milieu, with some pointing out its apparent failure: 'Civilization still exists, the universities still exist, the papers, the environmental groups, even nanotechnology still exists. Worse off, they are expanding.'¹⁶³ In all fairness, whoever made this comment wasn't paying particular attention: ITS clarified on many occasions that it isn't trying to bring civilization down. It is not a futile task, however, to make an overall assessment of the War on the Nerves and the eco-extremist trajectory thus far. This is a tricky task. Developing a detailed, accurate, and comprehensive record of eco-extremist attacks is not easy, as with all under-researched topics. This is even more the case when eco-extremists themselves keep claiming responsibility for attacks they haven't carried out. To give an idea of the complexity of this endeavour, the Global Terrorist Database attributes fifteen attacks to ITS. One such attack, an explosion at Mexico oil firm Pemex, occurred on 31 January 2013, and resulted in the death of thirty-seven people.¹⁶⁴ Yet subsequent investigations evidenced the non-criminal nature of the explosion.¹⁶⁵ Similarly, ITS has probably carried out more than fifteen attacks if one considers that between 2011 and 2013 alone it reportedly carried out thirteen.[166] As such, traditional databases are not helpful when trying to determine the extent and scale of the eco-extremist War on the Nerves. Triangulating between the groups' claims and external sources such as scholarly works, newspaper articles, law enforcement reports, and databases, it seems plausible to assert that, since the early 2010s, eco-extremists have carried out more or less a hundred actions that could be considered terrorist attacks. Consistent with the insurrectionary style of their attacks and with the limits imposed by operating in decentralized networks, the War on the Nerves has thus luckily wreaked less destruction than it promised.[167]

Recently, the fury of the eco-extremists seems to have ebbed. Between 2014 and 2018, the landscape was dotted with attacks claimed by, or attributed to, eco-extremists, yet this trend appears to have tapered off in recent years. Interestingly, this was discussed during ITS's ninth interview, during which Xale – self-appointed leader of ITS-Mexico – acknowledged a decline in operations. Xale characterized this downturn as akin to a natural process: 'Just as the flower has its time to bloom, so we have our time to carry out public terrorist activities.' However, Xale clarifies that this hiatus does not mean 'that we have stopped. There has to be a lapse of time for the improvement of acts, caution and planning.'[168]

This decrease in operational activity corresponded to a series of false claims and arrests. In one of the last posts featured in maldicionecoestremista.altervista.org before it was taken down, ITS claimed responsibility for the murder of Tushar Atre and Eric Valenti – CEOs of tech companies in California.[169] Yet subsequent investigations have cast doubts on ITS's involvement, leading to speculation that the group may have falsely claimed responsibility for the murder.[170] As mentioned, this isn't the first time ITS has made false claims. Combined with its decreased operational activity and a string of arrests in various countries, it suggests a downward trajectory for the Tendency. One such arrest took place in 2019 when Camilo Eduardo Gajardo Escalona – the Landerretche bomber – was charged with association with ITS and, as mentioned, at least six additional bombings.[171] Additionally, Federico Buono was arrested in Italy earlier that year. As part of Operation

Misanthropy, the Italian Police alerted their Argentinian counterparts, which led to the apprehension of two individuals in the Villa Urquiza neighbourhood of Buenos Aires.[172]

Furthermore, eco-extremists' online activities experienced a downgrade quantitatively – with the closure of maldicionecoestremista.altervista.org playing a significant role – but also qualitatively. The fiery rhetoric that characterized the apex of eco-extremism in the mid-2010s has softened somewhat. For example, Communiqué 94 was devoted to a moment of 'self-criticism, reflection and analysis' addressing different issues, including the rumours about ITS being a false group or even accusations of it being a government front.[173] Other documents, by contrast, discussed the above-mentioned alleged alliance between ITS and right-wing, fascist, and Satanist movements, such as Tempel ov Blood or O9A.

Despite the apparent downturn in eco-extremists' activities, it would be premature to dismiss this phenomenon entirely. While they may be experiencing setbacks, the ingredients for their potential resurgence remain present. History has shown that extremist underground movements often undergo cycles of dormancy and resurgence, adapting to changing circumstances and evolving strategies. The IRA appeared to have been almost finished by the second half of the 1960s, and we all know what a formidable and lethal organization it became in the following decades. In this regard, it is also important to note that groups like ITS are not akin to centralized, hierarchical organizations such as the IRA, ETA, or al-Qaeda. Being decentralized and leaderless, they are inherently more resilient to organizational degradation. The underlying ideological motivations driving eco-extremism – a vigorous opposition to technology and its role in the degradation and subjugation of Wild Nature – still resonate with extremist fringes and groupuscules. Therefore, while eco-extremists may currently be at a low ebb, it would be prudent to remain vigilant, as they may yet stage a comeback to exact their revenge on techno-industrial civilization.

4
Anti-Tech to Accelerate
Eco-Fascism

It was 3 August 2019, El Paso, Texas. Patrick Wood Crusius walked into a Walmart store in El Paso, Texas. Bracing a WASR-10 rifle, the 21-year-old killed twenty-three people while injuring an additional twenty-three. Once the lead stopped pouring, Crusius fled the scene. Soon after that, he was intercepted by the authorities and surrendered. Eleven months later, he was sentenced to ninety consecutive life sentences. As a sort of macabre ritual typical of far-right terrorists, Crusius had posted a manifesto, titled 'The Inconvenient Truth', on the online message board 8chan shortly before the shooting. This five-page document presented the attack as a response to an alleged 'Hispanic Invasion' of Texas. Tapping into a conspiracy theory known as the 'Great Replacement',[1] Crusius argued that the growing number of non-white immigrants was threatening the cultural and ethnic survival of the United States. At the same time, he expressed concerns for the ongoing destruction of the environment. Yet his short manifesto insisted on another point: automation. Crusius didn't leave any room for doubt, clearly stating how he considered this to be 'one of the biggest issues of our time'. Because of automation – the increasing use of technology and robotics to perform tasks that humans previously did – half of the jobs in the United States will be lost within two decades, Crusius argued. To make things worse, the interplay between continued immigration and automation will exacerbate the ontological and material security of the 'native' (i.e. white man). While analyses of Crusius's manifesto typically – and correctly – emphasize his anti-immigration and environmental theses, the relevance of the automation discourse should not be discarded. After all, Crusius himself reminds us of its importance. When lamenting the lack of prospects in his life, one of the main points he makes, along with his anti-immigrant argument, is that his whole life, he had 'been preparing for a future that currently doesn't exist. The job of my dreams will likely be automated.'[2]

Crusius's attack was not an isolated event. Between 2007 and 2017, far-right extremism rose dramatically in different countries, with the United States alone suffering a 1,450% increase in attacks.[3] Western Europe did not fare much better. A 2020 report by the UN Counter-Terrorism Committee Executive Directorate reported a 320% increase in far-right attacks over the previous five years. Most such attacks occurred in Europe.[4] Yet this transnational wave of far-right attacks stretched beyond Europe and North America to reach Australia and New Zealand. In March 2019, a few months before Crusius went on his killing spree in El Paso, a 29-year-old Australian citizen, Brenton Tarrant, killed fifty-one people at two mosques in Christchurch, New Zealand. There is a thread linking the El Paso and the Christchurch attacks. For one, Crusius expressed his support for Tarrant.[5] Moreover, in his manifesto – a seventy-five-page-long document titled 'The Great Replacement' after the conspiracy theory – Tarrant similarly pointed his finger at the degradation of the environment and the threat of immigration.[6] Both Tarrant and Crusius identified as 'eco-fascist'. A fringe phenomenon gaining a spotlight in recent years, eco-fascism has become a significant hub of anti-technology feelings within the disparate and conflicting projects that characterize the contemporary far right. To understand the emergence and characteristics of anti-technology extremism within this ideological milieu and the broader far right, we need to start with a historical overview to grasp the processes of change and continuity that have led to the current scenario.

Adopting Kristy Campion's definition, eco-fascism represents 'a *reactionary* and *revolutionary* ideology that champions the *regeneration* of an *imagined community* through a return to a romanticised, ethnopluralist vision of the natural order'. Drawing on this, we can thus understand eco-fascism as a sub-form of fascism rather than the fusion of fascism and ecologism.[7] It is, however, worth acknowledging that the literature is divided regarding the status of eco-fascism as an ideology. While some subscribe to this view, others downgrade it to the status of 'state of mind' or 'system of belief'.[8] This chapter will consider eco-fascism an ideological current within the broader far-right movements. It is essential, however, to note that eco-fascism is not the only strand concerned with the environment within the far right. In this regard, Balša Lubarda argues that 'contemporary far-right ecological values are too complex and elusive to be reduced to (neo)fascism'. Instead, the broader term 'far-right ecologism' might be more appropriate to capture this complexity.[9] The intricacy of such values reflects the multifaceted nature of the contemporary far right; eco-fascism represents but one of its many ideological currents and trends, each displaying its unique characteristics. However, there are overlapping themes, too. As Chetan Bhatt maintains, a core ideological element shared by all the far-right strands is the theme of 'white extinction' or 'white genocide'[10] – terms also common in attackers' manifestos.[11] This notion aligns with other organizing principles to shape far-right extremism in the individual strands, including the European New Right, the alt-right, the alt-lite, the 'manosphere', white supremacy and accelerationism, the anti-Muslim movement, and eco-fascism. As I will discuss later in the chapter, these strands can overlap substantially where, for example, a white supremacist can hold accelerationist but also eco-fascist and anti-Muslim views. Moreover, a further prominent feature of the contemporary far right is the ubiquity of conspiracy theories, ranging from the Zionist Occupation Government to QAnon and the Great Replacement.[12] This phenomenon has gained prominence in the last few years. To give a sense of its growth, terrorist attacks committed by individuals motivated by conspiracy theories rose from six to 116 between 2019 and 2020 – an increase of 1,833%.[13]

Back to eco-fascism, we can then think of this phenomenon as a fringe but increasingly popular strand within the contemporary far right. Romanticizing a mystical past of ecological harmony, eco-fascists decry the forces of modernity – such as industrialization, urbanization, materialism, and individualism – blaming them for severing the connection between nature and humanity, resulting in modern society's weakening and corruption.[14] Moreover, in eco-fascist thought, there is an identity between nature and fascism. In this view, nature is fascist, as it has a strict hierarchy – one where Aryans (should) comfortably sit at the top.[15] Ultimately, eco-fascists strive to recover this lost state of harmony by returning to an idealized 'natural order', which will, in turn, lead to the rebirth and re-creation of their imagined community of nativists. To do so – to safeguard nature and promote the white race – they are ready and willing to justify the use of violence. It is perhaps surprising, but certainly ironic, that such a nativist argument can emerge among people with quite a long history of colonialism on their shoulders. To obviate this apparent contradiction, eco-fascists make the convenient argument that aspiring nativists can also appear in settler societies. In this context, eco-fascism provides a mechanism 'through which a select community can lay privileged claims on territory, often in conjunction with broader constructs of racial homogeneity, to reject other settlers'.[16] This explains the seemingly contradictory nativist claims of eco-fascists in settler societies, such as the United States or Australia.

While gaining notoriety following the 2019 attacks, eco-fascism has a much longer history – longer, indeed, than the term itself, which emerged only in the 1960s.[17] In fact, eco-fascist ideas can be traced back to the mid-1800s. A time of intense industrialization, urbanization, and socio-political changes in Western Europe, this period saw social forces within society opposing these dynamics. In Germany, these entities coalesced, forming the *völkisch* movement. The *völkisch* ideology 'affirmed the intimacy of entire people (albeit still strictly constrained in their classes), or "Völker" with their lands, a natural condition imperilled by modernity'.[18] Essentially, it constituted a rejection of the Enlightenment and Marxism and their tendencies to objectify nature or perceive it as an instrument.[19] Instead, the *völkisch* movement championed an anti-modern, idyllic return to a romanticized notion of nature. In a nutshell, the idea was that there is an intimate connection between the nation and its environment whereby the latter shapes and determines the former. As nature embodied the Germanic spirit, the *völkisch* movement advocated the return to the land to rediscover its links with nature, rejecting industrialization and modernity.[20] Thus, this idea developed in the context of German Romanticism, from which the infamous slogan 'Blood and Soil' (Blut und Boden) sprang, an expression which epitomized the profound spiritual relationship that the *völkisch* movement ascribed to nature and nation.[21] Unsurprisingly, such notions were also intimately related to ideas of racial superiority. After all, as Janet Biehl and Peter Staudenmaier argue in one of the first works on this topic, *völkisch* thought was heavily influenced by prominent natural scientists and authors, such as Ernst Haeckel, who, besides being credited with having established the field of ecology as a scientific discipline, was a staunch believer in Nordic racial superiority and eugenics.[22] Surviving the turn of the century and World War I, several aspects of *völkisch* ideology were eventually incorporated into the green wing of the German Nazi party. Richard Walter Darré, Reich Minister for Food and Agriculture, was a central figure here. Besides popularizing the slogan 'Blood and Soil', Darré was a strong proponent of the expansionist *Lebensraum* (living space) project.[23]

A special relationship with nature was also central to Italian fascist ideology. Yet there was a crucial difference: whereas Nazism emphasized the mystic ties between racially pure populations and their environment, Italian fascism saw nature as something to be conquered, 'a wild and powerful force that needed to be tamed and controlled by humanity'.[24] Controlling and ultimately changing the natural landscape was crucial for the regime's goal of regenerating the Italian nation.[25] We can, then, see two approaches to the relationship between nation and nature in the pre-World War II era. As Campion argues, they reflect different branches of eco-fascism. On the one hand, the Italian fascist idea was that an exclusive relationship between land and nation could be created by conquering nature. This 'conqueror' branch of eco-fascism is therefore associated with a rather anthropocentric perspective. On the other hand, German Nazism saw nature as something to be conserved for its intrinsic value. According to this eco-centric 'custodian' branch, only native people can protect and preserve nature.[26]

The defeat of the Axis powers during World War II did not, unfortunately, relegate fascism or Nazism to history. As Europe began to recover from the destruction brought by the conflict, a proliferation of small groups kept the neo-fascist and neo-Nazi flame alive. Hampered by divisive ideological conflicts and personal disputes between competing *Führers* at the domestic level, several of these groups sought ties with counterparts in other countries, thereby forming neo-Nazi and neo-fascist 'internationals' – such as the New European Order or the *Organisation de l'Armée Secrète* (Secret Army Organization).[27] Among these international networks was a figure who played a crucial role in sowing the seeds of what was to become contemporary eco-fascist thought, Savitri Devi. Born Maximiani Julia Portas, Devi was a French-born Greek and an admirer of Adolf Hitler who oscillated between India and Europe. Her main contribution to Nazi ideology consisted of 'Esoteric Hitlerism', a subculture that merged elements of Hinduism and Nazism, worshipping Hitler as the reincarnation of the Hindu god Vishnu.[28] In her 1959 book *Impeachment of Man*, Devi criticized human-centred societies and their exploitative attitudes towards nature and animals. Blaming Judaism for the shift from a traditional, nature-centred society to a modern human-centred civilization, she denounced the separation between humanity and nature. This idea was naturally intimately related to constructs of race; Aryans alone possessed the virtues of being custodians of nature.[29] Adopting a bio-centric perspective, Devi's anti-civilizational worldview also promoted the depopulation of Earth. As the 'root of much human misery – and in particular of many wars – seems to lie in the steadily increasing number of human beings in the world', Devi argued it was therefore crucial to 'stop the indiscriminate production of babies [. . .], *unless of course these be of exceptionally fine racial stock*'.[30] Many such arguments have been adopted decades later by contemporary eco-fascists.

In addition to Devi, Graham Macklin argues that there are two other central figures in eco-fascism: Pentti Linkola and the omnipresent Theodore J. Kaczynski.[31] A prominent Finnish deep ecologist and philosopher, Linkola espoused misanthropic and anti-democratic views and advocated extreme means to address the problems of overpopulation and environmental degradation. To give a measure of his character, he went as far as praising mass murder and genocides, considering these as blessings to the ecosphere.[32] Now, Linkola believed that drastic population measures had to be adopted to deal with the impending ecological doom. Yet he maintained that democracies would never be able to do what had to be done to save the environment. As such, the only hope, according to Linkola, lay in small vanguards pursuing eco-fascist goals.[33] Crucially, the issue of overpopulation is intimately related to technology. Linkola considered technology as 'the foundation of the most anti-intellectual and religious culture Western civilisation, or indeed the world, has ever known' – a religion which is inherently 'aggressive and destructive'.[34] The disastrous consequences of technology are manifold, according to Linkola. For one, technology is directly responsible for the unbearable overpopulation plaguing the environment.[35] At the same time, technology deprives life of its true meaning. In Linkola's words: 'Through all his technical inventions and celebrated innovations, man has made himself useless. In recent years technological progress has been explosive: humanity has been successful in obliterating the roles of producer, refiner, transporter, distributor and serviceman.'[36] Linkola argues that we will eventually get rid of the role of the consumer, and then 'everything will be over. A clanking of robots for some time; then, only deep silence.'[37] So, along with depopulation, Linkola promoted the destruction of 'everything we have developed over the last 100 years'.[38]

As previously discussed, a similar radical anti-technology stance was at the heart of Kaczynski's worldview. There are a few reasons why the Unabomber has become such an influential figure within eco-fascist subcultures and the wider far right. First, Kaczynski's anti-technology ideas resonate well with the anti-modernism underlying large segments of the far right. Then, Kaczynski also gained respect as a symbol of resistance against modern society. His primitive lifestyle in his self-made cabin in Montana set a model for breaking away from society. Besides, the Unabomber's distaste for 'leftism' made his ideas more palatable for the far right.[39] This admiration was not mutual, however. On 29 September 2020, Kaczynski wrote a short article titled 'Ecofascism: An Aberrant Branch of Leftism', in which he denounces eco-fascists' moderate anti-technology stance and their fixation on race, urging them to reread his works carefully.[40] Despite this non-reciprocal relationship, Kaczynski has become a recurrent feature in eco-fascist discourse and propaganda.[41] Besides these three figures, Devi, Linkola, and Kaczynski, additional influential names include the Italian philosopher Julius Evola and the German philosopher

Martin Heidegger, who championed a dystopic understanding of techno-industrial civilization.[42]

Spearheads of the Movement

So, as we can see, the roots of eco-fascism long pre-date its recent manifestations. Having grasped its intellectual and historical origins, we must now turn to its role and place within the contemporary far-right milieu before we analyse its anti-technology stance and praxis. As mentioned, post-World War II Europe saw the proliferation of a myriad of small far-right groups. Many of these – for example, *Ordine Nero* (Black Order) and *Nuclei Armati Rivoluzionari* (Armed Revolutionary Nuclei) in Italy, the *Deutsche Aktionsgruppen* (German Action Groups) in Germany, and the *Fédération d'Action Nationale et Européenne* (Federation of National and European Action) in France – embraced terrorist violence and played a crucial role in the turbulent 1970s and 1980s, decades dense with political violence.[43] Across the Atlantic, the post-war period witnessed a resurgence in the United States of the Ku Klux Klan along with the emergence of additional groups, with Aryan Nations, the Order, and the National Alliance rising to prominence in the 1970s.[44] In particular, the National Alliance was led by William Luther Pierce – a central figure for the contemporary far right. Yet his centrality does not derive primarily from his leadership in the National Alliance but from a dystopian novel he wrote. Published in 1978, *The Turner Diaries* is set in the year 2099. It depicts a violent revolution led by white supremacists in the United States who ultimately start a global race war pursuing the establishment of a racially pure society.[45] *The Turner Diaries* has become the 'deadly bible' for all those who embrace anti-Semitic, white supremacist, and racist views and advocate for the resort to terrorism against non-white people. While far-right extremism appeared to wane towards the end of the 1980s, this phenomenon experienced a revival in the 1990s both in Europe and in the United States, where the 1992 Ruby Ridge and the 1993 Waco incidents reawakened the movement.[46] A few years later, on 19 April 1995 – the second anniversary of Waco – this reawakening led to violence when Timothy McVeigh detonated a truck bomb under a federal building in Oklahoma City, killing 168 and injuring hundreds.[47] By the end of the 1990s, far-right terrorism had also struck countries like the United Kingdom, where the 1999 nail bomb campaign left three dead and injured many more.[48] The movement has since grown in the last two decades.

The digital space was undoubtedly a crucial factor contributing to the resurgence and spread of far-right extremism. Back in the early 1990s, the far right had already established an online presence on the message board Stormfront. Then, the advent of social media and the increasing digitalization of society have revolutionized how extremist movements of different ideological backgrounds communicate, recruit, and operate. In the case of the far right, this has led to the emergence of a complex online ecosystem comprising four key elements: entities, communities, biotopes, and the whole network. The entities represent the individual platforms (websites, social media pages, forums, blogs, etc.). These are connected in communities through hyperlinks, content flows, and user base migration. Such communities are highly dynamic, rising and disappearing quickly. Depending on their thematic or ideological character, communities can then be categorized into a set of non-mutually exclusive biotopes: for example, white supremacy or anti-Islam.[49] Taken together, all these elements constitute the overarching network.

The far right's widespread online presence was facilitated by the advent of anonymous message boards, such as 4chan and 8chan, in 2003 and 2013, respectively. These websites soon became main hubs for far-right extremists and for terrorists to share their manifestos and videos. Indeed, it was on 8chan that Tarrant and Crusius published their manifestos before the attacks in 2019. Following the El Paso attack, 8chan was finally taken down, only to be replaced by a growing number of forums like 8kun, neinchan, endchan, and shitchan.[50] Other prominent platforms included Iron March – founded in 2011 by Alexander Slavros (pseudonym for Alisher Mukhitdinov, a man believed to be an Uzbek immigrant to Russia) and taken offline in 2017 – and Fascist Forge – Iron March's less popular successor, which was closed down in 2020.[51]

As 8chan and the other lax websites went offline, users started migrating to a different platform, Telegram – an app that allows end-to-end encrypted messaging and groups to host up to thousands of participants.[52] Starting in 2013, Telegram has seen more than two hundred public channels disseminating far-right material to users. Known as Terrorgram, this collective has been implicated in different cases of violent extremism and terrorism. In January 2021, a few days after the attacks on Capitol Hill, Telegram took down dozens of channels inciting violence.[53] This has favoured another wave of migration towards new online venues, such as videogames platforms like Discord, Steam, and Twitch. At the same time, mainstream social media sites like Facebook, X, Instagram, and YouTube retain high value.[54] Yet, despite the 2021 crackdown, Telegram remains a prime hub for far-right extremism, so much so that the UK government added the Terrorgram collective to the list of proscribed terrorist organizations in April 2024 – the first government to do so.[55]

Of course, the term 'organization' should be interpreted in its broad sense here. Terrorgram constitutes a loosely connected, transnational network. As was also the case with both insurrectionary anarchism and eco-extremism, the contemporary far-right movement has embraced leaderless resistance, a strategy whose adoption was discussed by Louis Beam – an American white supremacist also active in the Ku Klux Klan and Aryan Nations – in a famous 1992 essay. Beam was painfully aware of how vulnerable to infiltration and government disruption extremist organizations had become. To survive, he believed that the far-right movement had to break down into smaller units – lone actors or small, self-organized cells – that would carry on the struggle on their own initiative. Calling it 'a child of necessity', for Beam the adoption of leaderless resistance was an imposition dictated by the movement's predicament rather than an unconstrained choice.[56]

Beam's wasn't the only voice calling for leaderless resistance. James Mason, a long-standing American neo-Nazi, has similarly advocated for it. Unlike Beam's preoccupation with evading law enforcement, Mason's rationale for adopting leaderless resistance is more strategic. The idea is that a series of terrorist attacks initiated by lone attackers could heighten social tension to the point of triggering a race war. Widely popular among far-right extremists, this doctrine is known as accelerationism, though Macklin reminds us that Mason never used the term himself.⁵⁷ As we have seen, this strategy is also popular among insurrectionary anarchists and eco-extremists. After all, accelerationism is not a creation of the far right. Ironically, it originated within Marxism, and it was popularized as a strategy for a white supremacist revolution only in the 1980s in Mason's newsletter *Siege*.⁵⁸ This collection of almost seven hundred pages circulated among the various online platforms, paving the way to the emergence of the Siege Culture – a fringe set of beliefs underpinning several far-right terrorism cases in recent years. As a neo-Nazi current, Siege Culture supports an anti-democratic, anti-enlightenment, anti-government, racist, and white supremacist worldview based on the supposed superiority of Aryans – the race that, in a natural state, should dominate all others. Its supporters are hostile towards anyone who is not white, heterosexual, and male, although they unsurprisingly manifest a particular distaste for Jews. Central to Siege Culture is also the idea of 'the System' – a conspiracy of all the forces trying to undermine Aryans – such as the government and Jews. In an unexpected rush of sympathy for the contemporary jihadist movement, some far-right accelerationists have adopted jihadi narratives and aesthetics, advocating for a 'white jihad' against the System. For example, on the now-deleted channel of Rapewaffen Division – a neo-Nazi group that promoted sexual assaults as a form of political violence – a member shared a picture of a masked man holding a knife with the captioning 'behead the infidels and rape'.⁵⁹

A protean subculture, Siege does not display a single, coherent ideology – a characteristic that, as discussed, it shares with the broader far-right movement. Moreover, aesthetics and performativity are dear to Siege Culture supporters, who seem pretty conscious of their impression, with their online material making explicit references to militancy, hyper-masculinity, firearms, and neo-Nazi symbols.⁶⁰ The online Siege community also extensively resort to memes in their propaganda material. A Canadian militant known as Dark Foreigner appears largely responsible for Siege Culture's aesthetics and many of their now iconic symbols.⁶¹ One such symbol is the skull mask; initially a clothing item worn by members of the terrorist group Atomwaffen Division in 2016, it has since become a popular meme among online far-right circles.

Another popular feature in Siege-related propaganda is Theodore Kaczynski. Images of the Unabomber are, indeed, frequently used as calls for violence. On some occasions, Kaczynski's image has been blended with the skull mask. Another propaganda image depicts a masked armed figure holding a copy of Kaczynski's 2016 book *Anti-Tech Revolution*, in a trend that Michael Loadenthal has described as the 'Kaczynski-zation of the neo-Nazi'.[62] Siege Culture supporters revere Kaczynski in a quasi-religious fashion. He forms a 'holy trinity' alongside Timothy McVeigh (the Oklahoma City bomber) and Anders Breivik (the Norwegian neo-Nazi terrorist who murdered seventy-seven and injured more than three hundred in his 2011 attacks in Oslo and Utøya). This reflects a broader trend within the digital far-right space, where a range of far-right terrorists – including Tarrant and Crusius – are granted the status of 'saints'.[63]

Over the last few years, Siege Culture has constituted the cradle of many far-right terrorist organizations, including several that have displayed eco-fascist traits. This transformation into a clandestine terrorist network has also occurred as the ideology of the occultist and Satanist Order of Nine Angles has become increasingly influential among Siege's 'skull mask' network.[64] Prominent examples of organizations that have emerged from Siege Culture include Atomwaffen Division (AWD – German for Nuclear Weapons Division). Officially launched in 2015 by Brandon Russell and Devon Arthurs in the United States, Atomwaffen Division counted between sixty and eighty members as of 2019 and over 1,500 users on Iron March until the website went down that same year. Although AWD was a decentralized network, Russell played a crucial role until his arrest in 2018. Taking up Russell's baton was John Cameron Denton – a gentleman going by the alias 'Rape' – who was himself arrested in 2021. AWD set up training camps in rural locations to prepare its members for the 'Racial Holy War'.[65] Its followers also spread to other countries, including Canada and Germany, and were implicated in a series of murders.[66] Following AWD's demise, new organizations like the National Socialist Order arose. It is essential to understand that the far-right terrorism landscape is highly dynamic, with groups rising and falling within short periods. Emerging from the same milieu of AWD, another prominent organization, The Base, was established in 2018. The Base aligned with the Green Brigade to then incorporate it as its eco-fascist wing before they both met their demise.[67] On its now defunct Telegram account, the Green Brigade presented itself as '[an] organization consisting of openly accelerationist, Eco-Extremist members focused on tearing down the system that exploits our land, animals, and people. These individuals prioritize and practice an autonomous environmentalist lifestyle, with a fascist emphasis and with a hatred for modern civilization.'[68] Membership in these groups is not exclusive. There are cases of extremists being simultaneously members of The Base, AWD, and Feuerkrieg Division – a group founded in 2018 by a 13-year-old Estonian kid known as 'Commander'. Though shocking, such a young age is not necessarily exceptional. In September 2019, a 16-year-old British member of Feuerkrieg Division was arrested for planning to bomb a synagogue.[69]

Not all the organizations that declare themselves eco-fascist promote an anti-technology perspective – a testimony to the multifaceted nature of Siege Culture and the broader far-right movement. An example is the Nordic Resistance Movement, a pan-Nordic, neo-Nazi group, one of whose followers asked: 'Do we want to go back to the Stone Age and do away with all technology because nature did not supply us with these inventions from the beginning? No, because remember that nature has also given us the capacity to create all these innovations.'[70] On a post on Discord, Payton Gendron – responsible for a racially motivated mass shooting in Buffalo, New York, in 2022 – similarly argued that, while he had read the Unabomber's manifesto and agreed with many of its arguments, he did not believe 'that technological advancement harms humanity and that progression of science is useless'.[71] At the same time, other groups have taken a much more pronounced anti-technology stance.

One such group is the Pine Tree Party. Established on 3 November 2017 through an Instagram post shared by Mike Ma, the Pine Tree Party expanded into an online community before landing on the shores of Telegram in 2020. Members of this community find each other online by placing a pine tree emoji in their bio or usernames.[72] Mike Ma has also authored two accelerationist novels, *Harassment Architecture* and *Gothic Violence*. Ma used these works to share his worldview and instructions despite their fictional nature. In *Harassment Architecture*, he lamented how '[m]odem [sic] technology allows the weak to not just survive, but flourish'.[73] Almost mimicking the Unabomber, he then argues that '[t]he industrial revolution was a flicking disaster',[74] and that both 'the Industrial and Agricultural Revolutions and their consequences have been a disaster for the human race'.[75] Bringing the Divine into the fold, he argues that:

> God cannot be reached, nor can he reach us, so long as we surround ourselves in the unchecked technological expansion. From just around the industrial revolution forward, God has been rapidly phased out by the fruits of ill labor. It only gets worse every day. Another cell tower erected is another spot in which God becomes blind. At this point, with the amount we've built, it is safely assumed that He's unable to see our world at all.[76]

Then, Ma gives a few tips in the form of an ironic warning:

> [D]o not cover your face and destroy the many and largely unprotected power stations and cell towers. Electricity is a ghost, but one you can catch and kill. Do not do that. Do not become the sort of person who gets really good at blowing power stations up while never getting caught.[77]

Overall, through the co-option of Ted Kaczynski, Ma blends elements of anti-technology extremism with militant accelerationist white supremacy, advocating the resort to violence to safeguard nature, which will, in turn, promote the advancement of the white race.[78]

Between Anti-Technology Discourse and Praxis

As such, within eco-fascism, the critique of technology and techno-industrial civilization is inevitably and intimately related to racist views and an alleged mystical and harmonious relationship with nature. Urban, industrial life contributes to the decay of the white race and societal weakness by promoting racial mixing.[79] Adding to this, '[r]ampant urbanization and industrialization, ever expanding cities and shrinking forests' have led to 'a complete removal of man from nature' – which, in turn, has resulted in cultural decay and widespread degeneracy and depravity.[80] This is not an unintended consequence of modern life; it is by design that '[m]odernity aims to destroy human nature and its relation to nature'.[81] If – as mentioned above – nature is fascist, then bringing about the collapse of techno-industrial civilization will pave the way to a restoration of the imagined natural hierarchy that eco-fascism envisions.[82] To attack technology is, therefore, to promote a fascist 'natural' and ethno-pluralist order where white men sit at the top echelon of this 'natural' hierarchy. And yet the emergence of the anti-technological ideological current within the far right did not yield a significant tactical shift – or, at least, not until the last few years, as we will see shortly. Most of the focus of eco-fascist violence, as exemplified by the cases of Tarrant and Crusius, has initially lingered on the overpopulation and immigration problems. Their chosen targets (i.e. ethnic or religious minorities) were not so different from those of more 'traditional' far-right extremism. Indeed, in 2021, Kiernan Christ observed that '[r]ather than attacking oil pipelines or hydroelectric dams, self-professed "ecofascists" like Tarrant attack the same kinds of people and places as non-environmentalist right-wing terrorists'.[83] An exception was a 2020 arson attack against a Swedish mink farm which, while bearing all the hallmarks of classic animal rights activism, was actually perpetrated by the Green Brigade. No one was harmed in the attack, but it resulted in roughly 95,000 USD worth of damage.[84]

Thus, despite gaining traction at an ideological and narrative level, the anti-technology turn has initially had a lesser impact on the tactical and strategic domains. In other words, with the overpopulation and immigration issues retaining their primacy within the emerging eco-fascist discourse of the far right, the anti-technology revolution has been sidelined. A recent publication by the Terrorgram collective helps us to understand the rationale behind this dynamic. This document, titled 'Do it for the "Gram"', includes reflections on a few obstacles that need to be overcome.

One such obstacle is 'to realize that technology and industrial society are not to be completely abandoned until realistic, hyper-ecofascist solutions are implemented, [so] as to preserve the advancement of technology and the advantage it brings to combat enemies with that same technological advancement'.[85]

Eco-fascists acknowledge that their chances of victory against their enemies would be far lower if they renounced technology. Despite themselves, they realize that they must 'temporarily join and play the game of industrial society if we do not wish to become a colony of another hyper-industrial state like China, that can achieve more as an industrial society than scattered warlord tribes could'.[86] The harmonious society that eco-fascists yearn for will not be completely devoid of technology. The goal is to return 'to an age that is extremely advanced, yet entirely in harmony with our Mother Nature and, therefore, our Aryan essence'.[87] This incomplete rejection of modern technology was the target of harsh criticism by Kaczynski, who, besides disagreeing with their racist worldview, lamented the eco-fascists' goal of creating 'a society in which technology will be "limited and wisely" used in such a way as to ensure the ecological health of our planet'.[88]

Writing in 2022, Joshua Farrell-Molloy and Graham Macklin acknowledged the discrepancies between the anti-technology discourse and praxis within the eco-fascist fringes of the contemporary far right. At the same time, they argued that the increasing influence of Kaczynski and his anti-technology ideas might provide eco-fascists and other accelerationists with 'a potential template for effective target selection' and 'a green accelerationist pathway towards an idyllic vision of the "back-to-the-land" utopia that occupies the eco-fascist imaginary'.[89] Farrell-Molloy's and Macklin's analysis is not wrong here. Since 2020, far-right attacks on critical infrastructure across North America, Europe, and Australia have multiplied.[90] It is possible to group these attacks into two different categories. On the one hand, attacks on infrastructure are situated within the strategy of accelerationism. On the other hand, they form a more visceral expression of concerns about technology, one that is often linked to conspiracy theories.

It is not hard to grasp why the assault on critical infrastructure fits very well within the accelerationism strategy. As accelerationism advocates for hastening the collapse of society with the belief that a more desirable order will subsequently emerge, damaging or destroying key infrastructural components could kickstart this process. There is no need to minutely describe the consequences that a breakdown of communication, transport, or the electrical grid would have on everyday life in our contemporary hyperconnected society. This could undermine societal resilience and contribute to chaos and disorder if sufficiently widespread and prolonged, even more so considering how such dynamics would play out in social contexts that are already polarized. Attacks on infrastructure could also result in calls for stricter surveillance measures, which, in turn, could further radicalize those who have set out to destroy the existing order.

One of Terrorgram's latest publications discusses such considerations at length. Titled 'The Hard Reset', this 261-page document dedicates no fewer than forty-seven pages to attacks on infrastructure, outlining desirable targets and ideal courses of action.[91] 'The Hard Reset' opens with a conspiracy-infused statement: the elites have a vision for the future – they call it the 'Great Reset' of the system. This will entail 'an integration of all of the System's parts, all converging on top of your head'. Against this plan, far-right accelerationists promise to implement a competing vision, one which includes, among others, 'saboteurs' attacks on infrastructure crippling the System's ability to enforce its rules'.[92] From these pages, the centrality of the assault on critical infrastructure emerges as one of the backbones of the accelerationist strategy. This is also the case in another recent Terrorgram publication. Published in 2021, 'Militant Accelerationism: A Collective Handbook' similarly called for attacks on infrastructure – including highways and train tracks:

> Now, I've seen a lot of posts about power stations [...]. But I am here to tell you about the 140,490 miles of standard hauling gauge train track that exists across the USA. Imagine how much unguarded track there is out there? [...] Hurt a power station and hurt the area around you; hurt the tracks and hurt everyone.[93]

This quote highlights not only the crucial role of striking critical infrastructure to accelerate the demise of society but also the 'soft' nature of these targets. Often unguarded and defenceless, infrastructure presents critical and convenient targets. The proliferation of attacks against critical infrastructure has led different departments and agencies within the US government to voice growing concerns about these unsettling trends.[94] Between 2016 and 2022, white supremacist plots to target energy systems – which is just one type of crucial infrastructure – increased dramatically. While thirteen individuals were charged with planning such attacks in this period, eleven of them were charged after 2020.[95] Moreover, since 2014, there have been approximately six hundred cases of suspected and confirmed physical attacks against the electrical grid, with the number of attacks on the grid in the United States rising by 77% between 2021 and 2022.[96] In addition to such targets, far-right attackers have sought to derail trains, poison water supplies, and attack nuclear power plants.[97] This growing trend transcends US borders and hasn't spared Europe, with Europol's 2023 Terrorism Situation and Trend Report expressing concerns over the rising number of far-right attacks on critical infrastructure.[98]

While these attacks are part and parcel of the accelerationist doctrine, the increasing influence of conspiracy theories has also bolstered the anti-technology trend within the far right and eco-fascism. The COVID-19 pandemic was instrumental in popularizing conspiracy theory-related violence. As mentioned earlier, conspiracy theory-related attacks experienced an increase of 1,833% between 2019 and 2020. While they were nearly all non-lethal, 96% targeted telecommunication infrastructure, most notably 5G technology.[99] In a remarkable convergence of extremisms, the last few years have witnessed anarchist and far-right extremists aligning in their campaign against 5G. In the context of the pandemic, the far-right justification for striking 5G is akin to the anarchist one; these devices have been described as detrimental to people's health and as designed to control citizens.[100] In fact, unlike conspiracy theories like the 'Great Replacement', the conspiracies surrounding 5G technologies are exogenous to the far right, having been imported from outside circles, not least because they are compatible with the pre-existing far-right worldview and ideology about a Jewish-controlled totalitarian world order.[101] Threats to strike 5G technology multiplied in the early days of the pandemic, along with actual attacks. In October 2020, 221 arson attacks were reported across eighteen countries.[102] Although anarchists were responsible for many such attacks, some may have been perpetrated by far-right extremists. However, while far-right extremists claim 'innumerable instances of arson against 5G towers', there is little evidence for linking a high number of the cases to them.[103] Nonetheless, they were generally celebrated on far-right forums and platforms.[104] Soon enough, the online far-right space was populated by manuals providing specific technical details on how to take out 5G masts and cell towers – along with other infrastructure such as railways, bridges, and the electrical grid.[105] Moreover, the 5G conspiracies often intersect with different theories. For example, in June 2023, two UK conspiracy theorists, Christine Grayson and Darren Reynolds, were convicted of trying to blow up 5G masts. They saw 5G as part of an arsenal of measures for the vaccinated population.[106]

What emerges from all this is that the ongoing far-right assault on technology is not solely intended to cause the collapse of techno-industrial civilization, but it also aims at kickstarting a race war. Moreover, the escalation brought about by the intersection of conspiracy theories and anti-technology sentiments intensified the assault on the machines, giving renewed substance to the eco-fascist struggle against technology. In this conflict, far-right accelerationists display a rather selective approach and predominantly strike technologies that are strategic targets or are perceived as harmful or dangerous for ideological and idiosyncratic reasons. As such, the far right presents a curious case. In their narrative, white supremacist accelerationists and eco-fascists seem to embrace the eradication of technologies as a goal. Yet such a narrative may be exploited to accelerate the System's demise, in which case the fight against technology will assume more instrumental, rather than intrinsic, value. For the moment, more pressing concerns – such as immigration and overpopulation – have contributed to sidelining the technology issue. This could change. The preconditions for a further escalation are there: an extraordinary inclination for violence, an ever-increasing obsession with Kaczynski, a polarized context, and a worldview that is both multifaceted and flexible enough to accommodate ideological innovations. With the advancements of AI, robotics, and other emerging technologies, it is possible that, given time and enough momentum, this partial aversion could evolve into a full-fledged anti-technology assault.

5
The Fight to End Civilization

In the previous chapters, we have seen how technological advancement, celebrated by many as a beacon of progress, has engendered a plethora of dissenters. From the early Luddites, who destroyed machinery to protect their livelihood, to modern-day anti-technology extremists aiming to dismantle civilization, the struggle between technology and those who oppose it has been a recurring undercurrent in history, at least since the First Industrial Revolution – the period covered in this book. While it is important to note that not all those who resist technology have decided to take up arms against it, some fringe movements have chosen violence. Drawing together insights from the cases we've explored, this closing chapter presents the Anti-Technology Movement – a loose ensemble of actors who, drawing from different ideological wells, have set out to eradicate technology and destroy civilization – and discusses how this struggle to stop the machines could develop.

Contemporary manifestations of anti-technology sentiments – found within the insurrectionary anarchist, eco-extremist, and eco-fascist milieus – are built on legacies that span decades. This exploration has shown that, to fully grasp their contemporary expressions and future trajectories, we must understand their evolution through 'processes that take a long time to unfold'.[1] This historical approach tells us that anti-technology extremism possesses a remarkable quality: flexibility. This characteristic enables it to unite disparate actors – such as anarchists and white supremacists – under a common banner. Such flexibility is hardly surprising. Even if we took all other contextual variables out of the equation, a complex and multifaceted phenomenon such as technology cannot possibly elicit a monolithic reaction. Much like the opposition to capitalism, the fight against technology has developed within different intellectual and ideological traditions.

Rather than representing a barrier, the cross-cutting nature of anti-technology extremism encapsulates its potential as a catalyst for violence. As Manuel Torres-Soriano and Mario Toboso-Buezo have argued, both existing and future extremist groups 'will be able to adapt their respective agendas and priorities to include opposition to a technological society and identify targets best suited to their own interests as the enemy to be overcome'.[2] This might, in turn, trigger the emergence of seemingly implausible 'synergies' between different extremisms. Torres-Soriano and Toboso-Buezo are not wrong in this. Such synergies are already occurring. In the fight against technology, we have seen how antipodean movements found common ground. Sure enough, this does not necessarily signal a reconciliation or an alliance between such movements; neo-Nazis and anarchists will never be friends – of this, we can be sure. Yet, despite their historical and irreconcilable hostility, they display similar trends in their opposition to technology, signalling a convergence of contrasting worldviews.

This is not an isolated development. Quite the opposite: it epitomizes dynamics leading to increasingly blurred boundaries between different forms of extremisms. When studying violent extremism and terrorism, it is customary to use categories to capture the essential characteristics of the group(s) under scrutiny. However, traditional categories are no longer entirely useful when dealing with some of today's forms of violent extremism. Until recently, labels such as 'Marxist-Leninist', 'ethno-nationalist', 'neo-fascist', 'Christian extremist', or 'jihadist' would have painted a reductive yet specific picture of a given organization or actor. Reductive, because no organization or individual is so monolithic and monochromatic as to be reduced to a single label or category. Specific, because these labels could tell us something crucial about an organization's or actor's objective. Saying that the Italian Red Brigades were Marxist-Leninist or that the Basque ETA was ethno-nationalist does not give an exhaustive profile of these organizations. Still, it does not leave much to the imagination regarding their end goals. As imperfect as they were, these labels could usefully encapsulate a given actor's hallmarks.[3] By contrast, some of today's violent extremists often increasingly embrace worldviews that are composed of multiple – and, at times, conflicting –

ideological currents, sentiments, and grievances. This has led to a proliferation of concepts attempting to capture and explain these multifaceted worldviews. One such term was popularized in 2020 by FBI Director Christopher Wray, who referred to 'salad bar' extremism to indicate how extremist actors are picking and choosing aspects from different ideologies to construct their worldview.[4] Others assume less intentionality in this process and argue that such complex belief systems are constructed more haphazardly, proposing an alternative framework based on the concept of 'composite violent extremism'.[5]

From this perspective, it is possible to understand how anti-technology extremism functions as an ideological current. Rather than dominating the worldview of a specific group, it combines with other ideological traits to form amalgamations that lead to complex systems of belief. We have seen, for example, how the contemporary far right displays an array of trends and characteristics, from misogyny to antisemitism, Islamophobia, and anti-government extremism. The same goes for anarchism and its multi-focus struggle spanning issues such as migration, the environment, and the penitentiary system. Even the eco-extremists, despite their anti-technology zealotry, exhibit a multifaceted worldview encompassing animism, legacies of anarchism, and explorations into occultism and Satanism. Ironically, none of Kaczynski's disciples adopted their master's staunch and monolithic anti-technology extremism.

Naturally, the flexibility of anti-technology extremism means its expressions and forms depend on pre-existing values, norms, and principles – the differences in *modus operandi* between the blood-averse anarchists, the indiscriminate eco-extremists, and the mass casualty-seeking eco-fascists make a strong case in this regard. Anti-technology ideas need to manage the co-habitation with other ideologies currently making up the milieu's overarching worldview, resulting in diverging trends. Therefore, it is at the intersection of these different normative, cultural, and ideological traditions that the Anti-Technology Movement emerges as an informal collection of groups, organizations, and individuals based on and mobilized around the shared belief that technology is harmful and must be eradicated.

A clarification is needed here. When we speak of an Anti-Technology 'Movement', we must adopt a broad perspective. As with many other social science concepts, the definition of 'social movement' remains a contentious issue. Here, I draw on the work of Marco Diani and understand social movements as 'networks of informal interactions between a plurality of individuals, groups, or associations, engaged in a political or cultural conflict, on the basis of a shared collective identity'.[6] While the anti-technology milieus exhibit some of these characteristics, they lack a shared collective identity; a process that brings 'a sense of common purpose and shared commitment to a cause, which enables single activists and organizations to regard themselves as inextricably linked to other actors, not necessarily identical but surely compatible, in a broader collective mobilization'.[7] When we look at the current milieus displaying an anti-technology stance, we do see a shared commitment to the cause of taking down techno-industrial civilization. However, this commitment has not forged a collective identity robust enough to overcome the incompatibilities among these milieus. There are shared identities within the individual anti-tech milieus, but not across them. From the approach to violence to their end goals, there is no harmony within the Anti-Technology Movement. There are indeed many aspects on which insurrectionary anarchists, eco-extremists, and eco-fascists disagree. Despite some initial flirting and mutual declarations of support, insurrectionary anarchists and eco-extremists are at odds with one another over issues such as the possibility of revolution and the use of indiscriminate violence. Moreover, although a few individuals – such as Federico Buono or Kevin Garrido – are said to have migrated from the anarchist to the eco-extremist camp,[8] mutual contempt generally defines the relationship between these two milieus. Anarchists have also accused eco-extremists of eco-fascism, of which they are even less fond than they are of eco-extremists. For their part, eco-extremists weren't exactly torn up about this accusation. They arguably reacted more vehemently when associated with the insurrectionary anarchist universe – despite having originally been somewhat linked to it. And yet there are also substantial differences between eco-fascism and eco-extremism. While there might be some level of agreement on the role of indiscriminate violence, eco-extremists share neither the eco-fascist desire to return to the past – for that would negate their nihilism – nor their optimistic stance about the prospect of a race war and, therefore, a revolution. At the same time, eco-extremists do not make the same racial argument as eco-fascists; their identification is with Wild Nature, not a specific nation or race. They don't hate a particular ethnic or religious group; they hate hyper-civilized humans *per se*.

So, the Anti-Technology Movement constitutes a variegated ensemble of ideologically diverse groups and individuals rather than a monochromatic front intent on attacking technology. However, for all their differences and disagreements, there are also several commonalities among the three milieus, thus allowing us to speak of them, albeit broadly, as a movement. Indeed, the flexible nature of anti-technology extremism does not dilute its characteristics enough to prevent us from identifying what we could – paraphrasing Roger Eatwell – call an 'anti-technology minimum'.[9]

Towards an Anti-Technology Minimum

To begin with, we can identify an overarching theme emerging from the previous chapters: anti-technology extremism as a reaction to the epoch of human domination – the Anthropocene. Coined by atmospheric chemist Paul Crutzen in 2000, the Anthropocene refers to the geological epoch defined by the dominating presence that human activity has 'on multiple aspects of the natural world and the functioning of the Earth system'.[10] While scholars debate its exact onset, the prevailing perspective links it to the Industrial Revolution.[11] With its profound and far-reaching social and economic consequences, the Industrial Revolution(s) led to urbanization, technological advancements, division of labour, and globalization, contributing to environmental degradation and climate change, making the overlap with the Anthropocene relatively intuitive.[12]

From this perspective, anti-technology extremism emerges as a reaction to this, an attempt to violently undo the Anthropocene and revert to an era not defined by human domination. Naturally, such attempts vary across the Movement's ideological milieus. Yet we can identify four common elements: a perception of technology as an all-encompassing mega-machine; an effort to preserve nature and humanity; an apocalyptic millenarian mindset; and an accelerationist and leaderless approach. As will be argued, all this contributes to the Anti-Tech Movement's potential for escalation.

Against the Mega-Machine

As we have seen, the opposition to technology has emerged as a transversal phenomenon, cutting across different social actors and ideological milieus. At the end of this spectrum, extremist fringes pursue nothing short of the total eradication of technology and the dismantlement of civilization itself. While the specific manifestations of anti-technology extremism vary based on cultural and ideological contexts, the ultimate objective remains unchanged: technology must be destroyed. Whether it's anarchists rejecting technology as a conspiracy and project of the techno-elites, eco-extremists longing to avenge and defend Wild Nature, or eco-fascists planning to destroy 'everything we have developed over the last 100 years'[13] to reconnect with nature, they all converge on one goal: laying waste to techno-industrial civilization to do away with the Industrial Revolution and its consequences, to paraphrase Kaczynski. Yet such an opposition to the techno-world isn't merely about rejecting specific technologies. Sure, some, like 5G or nanotechnology, elicit more hatred. However, it is the whole technological system that must be eliminated. This perspective sees technology not as isolated devices but as a cohesive organization of humans and machines, forming the mega-machine. This concept is explicit in the anarchist and eco-extremist narratives, and it also permeates eco-fascism, which frames technology as the overwhelming force of modernity that severs the connection between race and land.

Additionally, conspiracy theories play a significant role in this context. As beliefs that help make sense of complex patterns in human affairs through oversimplification and reductionism, conspiracy theories have historically tended to gain strength in situations of societal crisis.[14] In the current one, they have contributed to identifying specific technologies, such as vaccines or 5G, as harmful. However, they have also added layers of narrative to the fight against the whole techno-industrial civilization: for example, the conspiracy mindset that emerged among insurrectionary anarchists during the COVID-19 pandemic or the way that conspiracy theories intersect with anti-technology and anti-modernity positions within the far right.

This recalls another crucial aspect: the genesis of the mega-machine is far from spontaneous. Instead, it is both a product and a producer of human domination in the Anthropocene. This epoch thus becomes synonymous with the mega-machine and its 'collective capacities of aggregate systems of regimented human beings, mechanized technologies and their environments, and the slow violence that the combination inflicts to produce what many believe are destabilizing environmental effects that will continue to escalate'.[15] Viewing technology as a mega-machine has a significant implication: it dismisses the idea of technology as neutral. Instead, it's seen as an all-encompassing system that reflects the moral values and power relations of the social and economic systems in which it is embedded.[16] Consequently, distinguishing between 'good' and 'bad' technologies is untenable. Hence the necessity to extirpate technology altogether. Yet the desire to eradicate technology doesn't prevent anti-technology extremists from resorting to it to fight the mega-machine. In other words, anti-technology extremists use technology to attack technology. This oxymoron is justified through different narratives across the Anti-Technology Movement, often pointing out the necessity of 'fighting fire with fire' or 'having to fight with what they got'. Such rhetorical artifices deal with an inconvenient fact: from the internet to explosives, even those who oppose technology rely on it.[17]

At the same time, the mega-machine concept incorporates humans as integral components – inseparable cogs within the broader interconnected system. Indeed, if the mega-machine is both a product and a producer of human domination in the Anthropocene, it follows that targeting only mechanical or structural parts won't suffice; the human element – the Anthropos – cannot be spared. This perspective provides an ideological and moral justification for violence against people. Who, then, are the humans who ought to be targeted? The targets vary across the milieus, but, as the next section shows, their construction of the target follows a comparable logic, identifying the 'enemy' with the Anthropos – or *Homo Anthropocenicus*: that is, those who contribute to and benefit from the Anthropocene.

Preserving Nature and Humanity

It becomes evident, then, that the opposition to technology is about more than dismantling the complex system of humans and mechanical components. Complementing the desire to destroy the mega-machine, anti-technology extremists seek to preserve what is fundamentally human and natural in the era of the Anthropocene. The understanding of nature and humanity varies considerably within the Anti-Technology Movement.

For insurrectionary anarchists, the expressions of the Anthropocene intertwine with an intersectional class struggle and environmental concerns. First, they challenge the simplistic understanding that attributes the Anthropocene to all human beings without regard for class, gender, and race, highlighting instead the disproportionate responsibility of a few privileged individuals, the techno-elites.[18] In this regard, technology is a cornerstone of the Anthropocene as it consolidates the grip on power of *Homo Anthropocenicus* (i.e. techno-elites) by enabling the ultimate form of social control: preventing dissent in the machine-led totalitarianism of the prison-society. At the same time, technology also blurs the boundaries between the artificial and the natural. In addition to causing environmental degradation, technology leads to the commodification and exploitation of nature, whereby the natural world becomes an artificial entity integrated into the system. This process won't spare humans, with transhumanism ultimately seeking to incorporate technology into human bodies. To fight technology thus becomes synonymous with fighting to liberate us from the yoke of the techno-elites and to save the natural world, re-establishing a genuine connection with it.

Moving on, the concept of Wild Nature represents the organizing principle of the milieu in eco-extremism. As such, it logically constitutes the antithesis of technology. By identifying themselves as an integral part of Wild Nature, eco-extremists place themselves outside techno-industrial civilization. Crucially, there is a zero-sum competition between technology and Wild Nature. One cannot flourish without degrading the other. Ultimately, they cannot coexist. Nature is inherently violent and tends to defend itself from the onslaught of technology. On its part, techno-industrial society relies on the domestication and subjugation of Wild Nature – a process which alters the very fabric and functioning of the natural world, propelling us into the Anthropocene. Rejecting the epoch of human domination means reclaiming one's feral status, thereby siding with nature in its cosmic war against technology. This comes with an imperative of attack. Whether they choose to live a nomadic life or embrace an urban lifestyle, eco-extremists must strike civilization. While such attacks may be undertaken to hasten the 'Days of Chaos', there is no grand scheme or plan for a post-Anthropocene. The rejection of the future that underlies the eco-extremist struggle places the focus on the present – the here-and-now of identifying with nature and fighting against technology. While eco-extremists do emphasize the role of white, Western people in the expansion of techno-industrial civilization – and, therefore, the rise of the Anthropocene – their fury is not directed solely at them. Instead, eco-extremists indiscriminately strike the hyper-civilized – all those who, consciously or not, do not side with Wild Nature. To these eco-extremists, these hyper-civilized individuals represent *Homo Anthropocenicus*. While a full-fledged colonial discourse is absent, eco-extremism has witnessed a revival of indigenous animism – a development which could be viewed as part of a broader rising trend of religious responses to the Anthropocene.[19]

Finally, eco-fascism attempts to establish a deep connection between humanity and nature, intertwining ideas of identity and territory within the latter. In particular, the 'custodian' branch of eco-fascism calls for protecting and conserving the environment, not for some materialistic purpose but for its intrinsic value. From this perspective, nature shapes and determines the nation and its spirit. Whereas eco-extremism praises the violence inherent in nature to justify indiscriminate use of force, eco-fascism promotes a fascist interpretation of nature whereby the natural world is – or should be – itself an expression of fascism and a reflection of a supposed 'natural hierarchy' where the 'superior' Aryan race occupies the highest ranks. The Anthropocene, with its processes of industrialization and urbanization, has weakened this connection. The agents of the Anthropocene include migrants, race traitors, and essentially any minority. In the eco-fascist mindset, all these actors constitute *Homo Anthropocenicus.* Whereas harsh Social Darwinism previously regulated the relationship between individuals and between races, technology has now created a world where the weak can thrive at the expense of the fittest. Of course, the environmental consequences of the Anthropocene have also intensified phenomena like displacement. Climate change, biodiversity loss, and changes to land, resources, and ecosystems all constitute drivers of migration.[20] For eco-fascists, these migration flows represent nothing short of a life-and-death crisis, as they further sever the connection between nation and land, thereby endangering the survival of the Aryan race.

What emerges from this is that the idea of technology as an existential threat is linked to its role as a primary force of the Anthropocene. As the cornerstone of techno-industrial civilization, technology is nature's nemesis, the agent undermining the foundation of our connection with the natural world. The manifestations of such an existential threat vary, with insurrectionary anarchists viewing technology in the Anthropocene as an existential threat to individual freedom. For eco-extremists, instead, nature and technology are trapped in a cosmic war. As such, the existential threat is to Wild Nature and life on Earth. Finally, eco-fascists perceive technology as an existential threat to race and nation. All these groups draw, therefore, on existing traditions within their respective communities in their struggle against technology.

At the same time, the past plays a vital role in the anti-tech imaginary, contributing to the construction of the worldview and praxis. The picture painted here is also one of nostalgia for times long gone: a yearning for a past that appears untainted by technology. It's a wistful gaze backwards: a vision of a romanticized past where technology didn't reign supreme, and humanity existed in harmony with nature. Naturally, this idealized version of the past glosses over the hardship and complexities that characterized the pre-industrial world. Such idyllic images project a nostalgic desire rather than an accurate depiction of the past. Whether we look at the anarchist celebration of the primitive, the eco-extremist praise of the indigenous, or the imagined pre-modern natural order praised by eco-fascists, the 'past' offers a narrative that depicts a world free from the shackles of technology. Despite the mismatches between the imagined and actual pasts, such narratives hold the potential to shape the present fight to stop the machines. In eco-fascism, for example, these imagined pasts can provide a blueprint for action or a vision on which to base the future. However, re-evaluating the past does not continually transmute into a desire to return to a preceding epoch. The past can inspire and inform but is not necessarily a blueprint for what's to come. In the futureless world of the eco-extremists, the lessons gleaned from indigenous resistance to colonialism serve as powerful sources of inspiration for the struggle against techno-industrial civilization. For insurrectionary anarchists, the past serves as a counterpoint to the present and the techno-elites' creeping project of domination, highlighting how new subtle forms of domination are taking hold.

An Apocalyptic Millenarian Mindset

Where the present is deprecated and the past re-evaluated, the future represents what is at stake. Unchecked technological progress casts a shadow over what lies ahead; the future becomes synonymous with visions of dystopia. Within anti-technology extremism, there is, therefore, a palpable element of apocalyptic millenarianism.

Millenarianism embodies an anticipation of radical shifts. Those who adopt this worldview look forward to – and hope to participate in – sudden and dramatic changes that will dismantle the current world, paving the way for a new thousand-year idyll.[21] Norman Cohn traced the original meaning of 'millenarianism' to the view held by some Christians that 'after his Second Coming Christ would establish a messianic kingdom on earth and would reign over it for a thousand years before the Last Judgement'.[22] Such millenarian beliefs manifest across several sects and movements as a process that is collective, terrestrial, imminent, total, and miraculous. All millenarians adopt a strict Manichaean view: good vs evil, in-groups vs out-groups.[23]

In simpler terms, apocalyptic millenarianism revolves around the imminent destruction of the corrupt and evil order that now exists. These events are expected to bring about widespread suffering and loss, but a select group will play a unique role throughout this process. Following the chaos, these chosen few will live in an earthly paradise, either bestowed upon them or created by their efforts.[24] The latter part of the twentieth century witnessed a notable revival of apocalyptic millenarianism. As humanity approached the end of the millennium, the belief that sudden and tremendous changes were about to occur began spreading, finding fertile ground among New Religious Movements. This led to a series of tragic incidents. Some involved rituals of collective suicides or murder-suicides.[25] As the Hale-Bopp comet visited the Earth in 1997, the members of Heaven's Gate took their lives to allow their spirits to leave their human shells behind and hop on the spaceship they believed was hiding behind the celestial body to 'evacuate planet Earth before it is recycled'.[26] In another instance, the Japanese cult Aum Shinrikyo sought instead to hasten the apocalypse by releasing sarin gas in the Tokyo subway in April 1995, killing fourteen and injuring over a thousand.[27] As the case of Aum Shinrikyo shows, despite its religious origins within Christianity, apocalyptic millenarianism has characterized several non-Western religious movements.[28] Similarly, other ideologies, including secular ones like communism, Nazism, and – as I will now argue – anti-technology extremism, have not been immune to it.

In the insurrectionary anarchist imaginary, the prison-society looms on the horizon. This dystopian vision of impending totalitarian doom will unfold fully once we reach the Singularity – the moment machine intelligence surpasses human intelligence. This shift will trigger a conflict between those who embrace technology and those who resist it. This will not just be about physical survival; it's also, and presumably mostly, about preserving what makes us human – our connection to nature and our freedom. As technology takes over, these traits could fade away, propelling us past the current era, the Anthropocene, and into a world ruled by machines. For insurrectionary anarchists, the fight to stop the machines means undoing the Anthropocene and, at the same time, preventing a hypothetical 'Mechanocene'.[29] It means creating a world where machines are not used to exploit humans and nature.

Inherited from the radical environmentalist movement that emerged in the 1970s, eco-extremists similarly display a firm apocalyptic millenarian mindset. Scattered reflections on the future barge through the thick nihilism pervading their worldview. As the relentless march of progress forces Wild Nature to retreat, eco-extremists are left contemplating the prospects of a total subjugation – and, therefore, destruction – of 'all that is wild and natural'.[30] At the same time, they believe in the eventual collapse of techno-industrial civilization. A system so bent on self-destruction cannot escape its demise, and recent events like the COVID-19 pandemic offer glimpses of this impending downfall. Despite their lack of interest in revolutions, eco-extremists have a role to play in the future of the planet. In the cosmic war between technology and nature, they do not just side with the latter, they are part of it. Thus, any victory of nature over technology is inherently theirs as well. Despite their stubborn nihilistic rhetoric, statements released during the pandemic acknowledge their potential role in hastening the 'Days of Chaos'.

As previously mentioned, apocalyptic millenarian beliefs permeated Nazi ideology, which left an indelible mark on the roots of eco-fascism and the broader far-right milieu.[31] With the rising forces of modernity severing the connection between nationhood and nature, eco-fascists are left facing a crippling sense of existential threat due to the pollution threatening the purity of their race and the sanctity of their land. The looming spectres of overpopulation, resource depletion, and mass migration all fuel the eco-fascist narrative of a dystopian future where the white race faces oppression and marginalization. The eco-fascist apocalyptic millenarian mindset springs from its pursuit of a 'cleansing' catastrophe. In this scenario, the breakdown of civilization will lead to a racial war destined to depopulate the planet, ultimately paving the way for the establishment of a white society. Once the dust has settled and the enemy is defeated, eco-fascists anticipate a return to a pristine world. Thanks to the rejection of modern technology and a renewed communion with nature, they believe the lifeblood of the white race will be revitalized.

Overall, within the Anti-Technology Movement, the apocalyptic millenarian mindset serves as a significant catalyst for violence. To understand this, we must first distinguish between passive and active apocalyptic millenarianism. As Jeffrey Bale delineates, passive apocalyptic millenarians believe the world's end will unfold due to forces beyond human intervention. They do not think 'they themselves must carry out certain actions, perform prescribed duties, or fulfil particular responsibilities'.[32] As opposed to this, active apocalyptic millenarianism refers to a spectrum of behaviours ranging from peaceful to violent actions. At the violent end, individuals or groups deem violence necessary to fulfil their apocalyptic visions. This violence can be directed either against themselves or against outsiders. The tragic fate of Heaven's Gate is a poignant example of violence directed inwardly towards the group's members. The case of Aum Shinrikyo, by contrast, epitomizes violence wielded against outsiders in pursuit of apocalyptic goals. The notion that a select group can precipitate the apocalypse through deliberate actions echoes a concept we have encountered across all milieus of the Anti-Technology Movement: accelerationism.

An Accelerationist and Leaderless Fight

The combination of an active apocalyptic millenarian mindset and viewing technology as a mega-machine has led to the widespread adoption of violence within the Anti-Technology Movement as a tool to heighten social tensions and hasten the collapse of civilization. This accelerationist stance drives the Movement in two intertwined directions.

On one front, anti-tech extremists from all milieus target the vital nerve centres of civilization. After all, not all machines have the same strategic value. For example, striking a refrigerator might offer fleeting satisfaction to an anti-technology extremist, but its impact will pale compared to targeting more vital technologies like the electrical grid. As such, violence has focused chiefly on critical infrastructure, research centres, and laboratories, hoping to destabilize what are perceived as the very foundations of civilization. Concurrently, anti-technology extremists have directed their rage towards the human components of the mega-machine. The underlying premise is that to win the fight against technology effectively, one must not limit the assault to its physical manifestations but should, instead, also target the individuals who perpetuate its existence and operation. Therefore, disrupting the mega-machine necessitates confronting and even neutralizing the human components – the Anthropos. As we have seen, the identification and targeting of specific groups as crucial components of the mega-machine vary and depend mainly on the ideological nuances across the different milieus. Anarchists often focus on challenging the 'techno-elites' – the mixture of conventional political and economic elites, scientists, and researchers. For eco-extremists, targets include all those who are not aligned with the principles of Wild Nature. Eco-fascists, meanwhile, target non-white individuals – Jews, Muslims, ethnic minorities – but also 'race traitors'. Notably, while eco-fascists strike infrastructure, their attacks on humans typically align with more conventional far-right targets, such as migrants and ethnic/religious minorities.

So, all three milieus adopt a two-pronged strategy consisting of strikes on the nerve centres of the system to hasten its collapse and attacks targeting the human components of the mega-machine. The fact that, in principle, all three milieus adopt an accelerationist strategy might sound surprising. How, after all, can blood-thirsty eco-fascists employ a strategic posture that is similar to that of insurrectionary anarchists – who generally tend, by contrast, to avoid lethal violence? There are two observations we can make in this regard. First, this underscores the complex interplay of ideological currents within the Anti-Technology Movement, where competing or complementary ideas share the narrative and praxis of extremist actions. Then, adopting a strategy that is, at least in name, similar doesn't imply similar tactics and targets. As a strategy that left- and right-wing revolutionaries have adopted across the decades, accelerationism will naturally assume different connotations depending on the specific cultural, ideological, and material context in which it is implemented. In theory, even a blood-averse accelerationist strategy can bear fruit if it succeeds in dismantling the established order. In other words, the underlying rationale of accelerationism is to destabilize the system to bring about its collapse. Whether that entails mass murder or a more discriminate approach to lethal violence depends on the extent to which that is deemed necessary – from a strategic, moral, and ideological standpoint – to create the conditions for societal collapse.

Different interpretations of accelerationism, therefore, constitute the backbone of the Anti-Technology Movement's strategies across its milieus. Who's responsible for devising and implementing these strategies? Typically, we expect leaders to oversee such a task; strategies are usually their prerogative. This is true in the case of business companies and states but also in the context of hierchical violent non-state actors like terrorist organizations.[33] From the Provisional IRA to al-Qaeda, history gives us plenty of examples of leaders playing crucial roles within such groups by performing two aggregated functions: to inspire the organization's members and to provide operational directions.[34] However, this is not the case in the Anti-Technology Movement. As we have seen, this is primarily characterized by leaderless resistance, defined as individuals or small cells resorting to violence entirely independent of any leadership hierarchy or support network.[35]

Leaderless resistance is not unique to the Anti-Technology Movement, nor to violent movements in general, for that matter. Contemporary social movements like Occupy or the Hong Kong Anti-Extradition Bill Movement similarly display a shift from traditional hierarchical leadership to leaderless approaches.[36] In the realm of violent non-state actors, leaderless resistance gained traction in the 1990s, although early examples include nineteenth-century anarchists and far-left movements in the 1970s.[37] Such a rise in popularity can be attributed mainly to the increase in resilience it affords. Whereas hierarchical organizations are more vulnerable to infiltration, dismantling a leaderless movement is no easy feat, thanks to its decentralized and horizontal structure.

However, leaderless resistance can be a double-edged sword. It positively impacts on resilience and operational security but decreases the movement's lethality. Lone attackers are generally less deadly than large, sophisticated organizations[38] – except for in the United States, where they tend to be more lethal.[39] Equally, the absence of a clear command-and-control structure poses significant issues in terms of coordination. Technology can alleviate organizational challenges, allowing movements to share propaganda, recruit, ensure minimal coordination, and provide a sense of community.[40] Admittedly, the idea that technology facilitates the leaderless nature of the Anti-Technology Movement is ironic, but, as we know, anti-tech extremists make vast use of different technological platforms.

How is the adoption of leaderless resistance justified throughout the Anti-Technology Movement? The multiple answers to this question underscore how similar trends have different origins within the Movement. For insurrectionary anarchists, leaderlessness is second nature, a trait inherent in their ideology.[41] Indeed, anarchists have traditionally condemned leadership-based approaches to the armed struggle.[42] A similar genesis underlies the adoption of leaderless resistance by eco-extremists. After all, they trace their origins back to the radical environmentalism tradition of the 1970s – a movement that displayed anarchist influences in their ideology and praxis. In addition to such a heritage, eco-extremists acknowledge the tactical advantages a leaderless struggle affords when it comes to anonymity. Regarding eco-fascism, the adoption of leaderless resistance is related to the prevalence of this strategy among the broader far-right movement. As we have seen, two prominent figures influenced this process: Louis Beam, who advocated for leaderless resistance as a last resort, and James Mason, who considered it functional to the accelerationist strategy.[43]

The leaderless nature of the anti-technology struggle doesn't mean that the Anti-Technology Movement is immune to the charm of its most prominent members. As it turns out, some forms of leadership are hard to do away with, so it would be foolish to think that 'any kind of group or organization can exist without' them.[44] As movements adopt horizontal and decentralized structures, leadership becomes informal, meaning it emerges spontaneously without being crystallized in any fixed role or form of governance.[45] Individuals like Alfredo Cospito and Toby Shone for the anarchists, MictlanTepetli, Xale, and Chahta-Ima for the eco-extremists, and James Mason, Mike Ma, Brenton Tarrant, and the other Terrorgram 'saints' for the eco-fascists have risen as influential figures, providing both ideological and operational guidance to fellow militants.

Normally, the influence of each informal leader is confined within the boundaries of their respective milieu. Theodore Kaczynski is, however, a whole different story. The Unabomber's message manages to cut across the Anti-Technology Movement, exerting a discernible influence despite its contrasting ideologies. As the father of contemporary anti-technology extremism, he must be dealt with in one way or another by all those who fight the machines. His legacy is too vast to ignore in terms of a blueprint for action and ideological influence. The relationship was not always amicable. Before passing away in June 2023, the Unabomber expressed contempt for contemporary anti-technology extremists. In some cases, he was equally treated with disdain. Many anarchists – in particular, those who reject violence – saw him as a reactionary and condemned his 'fascistic comments'.[46] By contrast, while acknowledging his many lessons, eco-extremists progressively distanced themselves from Kaczynski.[47] Despite such contradictions, his name is indelibly associated with anti-technology politics, and his influence is likely to endure, occupying a special place among the prominent figures who steer the struggle against technology without detracting from its fundamental leaderless nature. So, overall, leaderless resistance and accelerationism have different origins and expressions across the Movement, but they form an inseparable pair that underlies the fight to stop the machines.

A Potential for Escalation

All these elements concur in giving anti-technology extremism the potential to become a significant driver of political violence. Viewing technology as an all-encompassing mega-machine creates a sense of encirclement. Enemies – and, therefore, targets – are everywhere. Sure enough, specific categories of individuals (i.e. the Anthropos) might represent a more appealing target. The 'techno-elites', the 'hyper-civilized', and ethnic and religious minorities constitute, for now, the target of choice for, respectively, insurrectionary anarchists, eco-extremists, and eco-fascists. At the same time, as we have seen, critical infrastructure stands for another common target, along with research centres and tech companies. This perception of technology also frames the struggle as a battle against power structures and socio-economic systems, thereby portraying the resistance to techno-industrial civilization as a proactive attempt to challenge and dismantle its very foundations. As the saying goes, to break the suffocating siege of technology, the best defence is a good offence. If technology is everything and everywhere, then there is no escape, and the only solution is to fight it.

In this all-out war against technology, everything that stands for humanity and nature is at stake. The impulse to defend and preserve nature and humans fuels the anti-tech extremists with a sense of moral righteousness about their struggle. It becomes inseparable from the struggle against technology. As we have seen, the concepts of nature and humanity take on diverging meanings depending on the specific ideological milieu, and range from individual freedom to the idea of nation and race or life on Earth. Regardless of their differences, these interpretations all point to the existential threat the all-encompassing and omnipresent technology poses. In the fight against technology, the Anti-Technology Movement stands to lose everything. Much has already been lost. The past offers a constant reminder of this, along with inspiration on how to fight against techno-industrial civilization.

The apocalyptic millenarian mindset of the Anti-Tech Movement also contributes to its potential for escalation by fostering a sense of urgency in anticipation of impending radical shifts and cataclysmic events. As visions of dystopian futures loom large, inhibitions against taking extreme actions could wane, creating an environment where drastic measures are not only conceivable but also necessary. This could further imbue the anti-technology vanguards with a sense of moral righteousness. In the cosmic war against technology, an inescapable Manichaean perspective dominates the conflict, with the current technological civilization representing everything corrupt and evil. In this sense, resisting techno-industrial civilization becomes an essential and morally justified path.

Deeply intertwined with this is the adoption of an accelerationist posture. As a calculated approach to sow chaos and disruption, accelerationism is, by definition, an escalation-bound strategy that glorifies violence. In some cases, accelerationism could foster a competitive dynamic. For example, the 'saint' culture within eco-fascism could encourage extremists to outdo each other. Related to this, the leaderless nature of the Movement makes it harder to prevent and stop attacks, particularly when they are directed against soft yet crucial targets such as the electrical grid, while also creating the potential for a diverse and unpredictable array of actions. Leaving individual anti-tech extremists to their own devices, this lack of coordination can result in a fragmented but persistent and creative wave of attacks. Leaderless resistance might generally be less lethal than hierarchical organization. Yet, arguably, lethality is not a necessary factor in an accelerationist context as long as lone attackers strike crucial nodes of the system. At the same time, its decentralized nature would also make the Movement harder to dismantle and less vulnerable to decapitation strategies.

Glimpses of Future War: Towards Anti-Tech Escalation?

Ultimately, these elements create a considerable potential for escalation within the Anti-Technology Movement. The flexibility that characterizes anti-technology extremism contributes to making such escalation unpredictable. Which combinations of ideological currents will make anti-technology violence more prominent? Will we see the rise of a more single-minded, monochromatic Anti-Technology Movement, or will this remain a patchwork of different ideological milieus? Attempts to establish a more coherent Anti-Tech Movement are not lacking. In 2021, an entity known as Luddite Resistance started circulating online documents advocating for an anti-technology revolution and the establishment of an anti-technology movement. These documents adhere to a strict Kaczynskian interpretation and spend considerable efforts in demonstrating why and how they shouldn't be mistaken as anarchist, environmentalist, or right-wing in their orientation.[48] They often include a symbol resembling a Nordic rune in the shape of a tree and pursue 'as Kaczinsky defined it "the total collapse of the worldwide technological system"' employing a so-called 'tribal resistance'.[49] Interestingly, Luddite Resistance displays many of the above-mentioned characteristics, including a perception of technology as an all-encompassing essence, a leaderless approach, and the idea that inspiration for how to fight the superior technological enemy 'can be found all over History'.[50] The strategy of 'tribal resistance' consists, in a nutshell, of trying to expand in areas where the 'Tech System' is less strong and then attacking the state structures that support the System so that people lose faith in it.[51] However, Luddite Resistance – and its quasi-Maoist anti-tech strategy – remains an obscure entity. It is unclear if it is an organization, a small group, or just a disgruntled individual at odds with technology. I am unaware of any attacks it has claimed or other documents besides the seven already published – of which only three or four provide substantial discussion. I find it unlikely that this is the vanguard of the anti-technology revolution, though I could be wrong here.

Will we see a dramatic escalation in anti-technology violence? Will anti-technology extremism persist as an ideological current within broader milieus, or will the Anti-Technology Movement create a strong shared collective identity? For now, anti-technology extremism represents a rising trend within different ideological milieus. Yet, as the above discussion has shown, the preconditions exist for an escalation of anti-technology violence. Whether such an upgrade occurs will depend on the interactions among a few additional factors. Using available information and analysis, we can probe the future of anti-technology extremism in a process of 'informed speculation'.[52]

First, there are increasing signs of disaffection with technology, and the growing sense of alienation and disgruntlement with our current society could increase the popularity of anti-technology extremism. Potential economic displacement due to automation, loss of privacy, continuous environmental degradation, and a perceived erosion of human values could facilitate this. At the same time, more effective charismatic figures or opinion leaders could contribute to articulating anti-tech grievances and goals. Kaczynski's passing in June 2023 has not diminished his influence. Yet a new generation of anti-tech leaders could help cultivate a shared purpose. Then, if the accelerationist strategy of the current anti-tech milieus were to achieve some degree of success, this could build some momentum. However, escalation could also come as a response to further technological advancements. As technology advances rapidly, these developments could be interpreted as additional evidence of impending technological doom. Similarly, a triggering event or catalyst could accelerate the escalation. Building on the interactions among the above factors, such an event, which could range from technological failures in critical infrastructure to legislative actions favouring tech corporations or high-profile and controversial tech experiments involving emerging technologies, could lead to a new stage in the fight to stop the machines.

At the same time, it would be unwise to analyse the potential developments of anti-technology extremism without considering the bigger context. Undoubtedly, these dynamics are a product of their time, reflecting and contributing to today's complex political climate, which we could describe with one word: 'polycrisis' – a world 'where disparate crises interact such that the overall impact far exceeds the sum of each part'.[53] In the last twenty-five years, we have lived through a series of once-in-a-lifetime events: 9/11 and the Global War on Terror, the Global Financial Crisis, and the coronavirus pandemic. Add to this a growing polarization within and between states, the return of Great Power conflict, the looming catastrophe of climate change, and the future is not looking rosy. These are all complex issues, with multiple constituencies responsible for both generating and solving them.[54] Unfortunately, the situation is exacerbated by various factors, such as the urgency of addressing climate change, the lack of a strong central authority, and the tendency to delay decisions on tackling such issues.[55]

To accurately assess the potential future trajectory of antitechnology extremism, it is essential to consider the various dynamics and issues that may contribute to its evolution. In today's interconnected and complex world, technology has permeated every aspect of our lives, shaping how we communicate, work, and interact with the world around us. As a result, the – sometimes violent – rejection of technology can stem from different sectors of society, such as cultural, economic, or ideological domains. While a unified anti-technology movement could emerge, currently, anti-technology extremism takes the form of an increasing incorporation of anti-technology sentiments within different ideological groups, leading to a growing focus on the issue of technology in their narratives and actions. As these pages have demonstrated, this variegated Anti-Technology Movement could experience both a qualitative and quantitative upgrade, as anti-technology violence gains prominence and momentum and more ideological milieus join the fight to stop the machines.

Conclusion

Anti-technology extremism is a far more complex and multifaceted phenomenon than it initially appears. I didn't anticipate finding a monolithic resistance movement against technology when I started working on this book. Equally, I didn't expect anti-technology extremism to bring such different ideological milieus together. What I found was a flexible ideological current capable of operating within radically different historical, doctrinal, cultural, and operational environments. As we have seen, insurrectionary anarchists combine their anti-technology stance with class struggle and ecological concerns, viewing technology as an instrument of domination. Eco-extremists adopt a staunch nihilistic approach. Identifying with nature, they engage in indiscriminate violence to defend and avenge it. Meanwhile, eco-fascists see technology as a force that seeks to undermine their vision of a racially pure society where nature shapes the nation. Despite such differences, all three milieus share a commitment to eradicate technology. Such flexibility tells us one crucial thing about anti-technology extremism: it is here to remain. It could present a continuous challenge with the potential to evolve and persist in various forms. This book offers readers the tools to understand the roots and evolution of anti-technology extremism. By reading these pages, one gains an insight into the evolution of anti-technology feelings, the ideological justifications behind the rejection of technology, and the strategies employed to stop the machines. This knowledge is essential for anyone seeking to understand the broader implications of technological progress and the social reaction it provokes.

For now, anti-technology extremism remains on the fringes, a spectre haunting the future of civilization rather than an immediate threat. Yet it could escalate and become a more serious concern. This potential escalation, though not present now, should be considered. Anti-technology extremism could become a significant driver of political violence in the near future. While I maintain scepticism about the ability of anti-technology extremists to cause societal collapse, their actions can continue to harm individuals and inflict significant financial damage, thereby contributing to heightening tensions.

What are we to do about this impending threat? Much wiser scholars than I have already shown us how futile and, more importantly, counter-productive it is to try to eradicate political violence and terrorism. Sure enough, we can and should minimize their impact, but we must also learn to live with them 'as part of our political reality'.[1] Moreover, despite their best efforts, anti-technology extremists, although dangerous, are hardly existential threats, and we shouldn't fall into the recurrent fallacy of treating them as such.[2] While acknowledging the danger of anti-technology extremism, this book doesn't call for its securitization. Good intelligence and law enforcement work, in adherence to the rule of law, should suffice to keep it under control. At the same time, we should address its underlying causes and problems – if and where possible.[3]

Naturally, I condemn anti-technology violence. But this violence comes from somewhere, and for some reason, and we need to understand this. Whether we consider the grievances and concerns of anti-technology extremists legitimate or not, grasping them will help us address the issue effectively. Personally, when confronted with aberrations such as eco-fascism, I see nothing that even remotely resembles a legitimate grievance or concern. This doesn't mean that we can't work to turn people away from it. At the same time, I am sure that many people, including readers of this book, will find that some concerns about the impact of technology on working conditions and the planet are somewhat reasonable. We certainly disagree with the anti-tech extremists' diagnoses and solutions, but their concerns express a discomfort with technology that is increasingly widespread within society.[4] I often contemplate the impact of technology on society – I guess this is not shocking news, as I have written this book. I find myself worrying about my privacy; about technologies that I don't understand, such as blockchain, bitcoin, machine learning, and so on; about the consequences of progress on the environment; about my students and the impact of generative AI on learning; about the future of warfare and political violence. But when I do so, I am constantly reminded of two crucial imperatives: we cannot and should not halt progress, but we can and should work towards reducing the alienation that comes with it.

There's no need to describe how technology has improved our lives. As the short discussion provided in the first chapter highlighted, we experience and benefit from the wonders of technology daily. I definitely wouldn't want all this to disappear. Meanwhile, emerging technologies promise to afford us much more. It is estimated, for example, that AI could contribute up to 15.7 trillion USD to the global economy, which is more than the current combined output of countries like China and India.[5] In addition to economic gains, emerging technologies could lead to new medicines and treatments while also helping us deal with the transition to a more sustainable economy. We stand at the cusp of a Fifth Industrial Revolution – one that will see humans and machines work synchronously, with the latter being given tasks and decision-making capabilities, and that promises to improve humans' well-being dramatically.[6] Yet, for all the good it pledges to do, this revolution will predictably cause winners and losers. As with any revolution, it will, by definition, bring dramatic and wide-reaching changes in conditions or operations. Inevitably, the new system will favour some more than others.

Let us go back in time for a moment. Sure enough, the Luddites weren't happy when they saw the First Industrial Revolution questioning their role in the production process to then replace them often with child labour – in an act of exploitation that, E.P. Thompson argued, was, 'on this scale and with this intensity, [. . .] one of the most shameful events in our history'.[7] If Luddites and children did not benefit from the changes occurring at the turn of the eighteenth century, however, the same cannot be said about those factory owners seeing their profits skyrocketing. Decades of workers' and unions' struggles have improved working conditions in many parts of the globe, but exploitation, sadly, hasn't vanished. Are we going to make the same mistakes again and prioritize profit over human and workers' rights? Judging from reports of AI being used to monitor employees' robotic performances at the workplace, we're not off to a good start.[8] These contemporary forms of technology-enabled exploitation could further foment those feelings of 'mass alienation' and of 'technology as existential threat' that animate contemporary anti-technology extremists.[9]

Let me be clear here. I do not share the blind techno-optimism that market capitalism and technology will solve all the world's problems.[10] Nor am I anti-tech: I believe that ingenuity, intellect, and a desire to move forward are among the qualities that make us human. I admit it is not easy to reconcile these two positions: accepting progress as a constitutive element of humanity and acknowledging the inherent danger of an unchecked march of technology. While I think we need a radical change, this shouldn't be at the expense of progress. My disillusionment with the techno-optimist argument does not lie primarily with technology but with market capitalism. How do we protect people and the environment while ensuring technology moves forward in our contemporary hyper-capitalist society? To do so, we must work on the three dimensions of anti-technology feelings identified in the first chapter: the material, the ontological, and the existential. This will require a blend of measures and approaches; regulations to tackle and lessen the impact of material exploitation and a paradigm shift in the way we relate to technology, the world, and one another to address the growing ontological and existential crisis.

Let us, again, go back to the nineteenth century briefly. You will recall that the machine-breaking of the Luddites was not in opposition to technology as such. Instead, they were protesting against the *unmitigated* introduction of new technologies in the production process. You will also recall that when and where regulations were in place, we did not witness machine-breaking at a scale comparable to that of the Luddites. As we have seen, we are on the verge of an AI revolution, with many other emerging technologies promising to reshape society and the economy. By definition, emerging technologies have a prominent but also uncertain and ambiguous impact.[11] The aftershocks of these monumental and uncertain changes could reverberate across society, but regulations could help lessen such impact. Calls for regulation have been made for over a decade now, and they've come from scholars, governments, and people working in different tech industries.[12] They all seem to agree that the system we've employed up until now to regulate technology is obsolete. For one thing, technology now evolves much faster than regulations do.[13] For another, emerging technologies often cross traditional industry boundaries (shifting from one regulatory category to another) as well as national borders. Regulations should, therefore, be flexible, collaborative, and based on results and performances rather than rigid forms.[14]

Additionally, the top-down efforts to regulate emerging technologies should be complemented by an equally important bottom-up push to make such regulations just and effective in preserving and advancing workers' and human rights in an age of rapid technological changes. Unions and other labour associations should, then, be at the forefront of such efforts to mitigate the effects of emerging technology at both the domestic and international levels before we usher in the Fifth Industrial Revolution.[15] In the nineteenth century, being a Luddite didn't mean being anti-technology or against progress. It meant organizing to undo exploitation. Violence wasn't the first answer and was also a consequence of being ignored and unheard. In the twenty-first century, being a Luddite can have the same meaning, and if such concerns are not dismissed but addressed, then maybe reducing exploitation will decrease the chances of anti-technology violence escalating.[16]

Yet, while necessary, regulations won't be enough. They address concerns of material security but do little to tackle the alienation that fuels contemporary anti-technology extremism. This alienation can manifest in several ways. People may feel disconnected from the products of their labour as technologies, such as automation and AI, increasingly intervene in processes once carried out by human hands. The sense of craftsmanship, creativity, or ownership over one's work becomes diminished, replaced by a feeling of being a mere cog in an enormous and impersonal machine. This detachment can be exacerbated by surveillance technologies in the workplace, where human beings are monitored and evaluated as if they were themselves part of a machine – an approach that undermines dignity and further alienates individuals from meaningful participation in their labour.

Moreover, technology can create alienation through the social fragmentation it often fosters. While digital platforms connect us globally, they can paradoxically isolate us locally. The rise of social media and virtual interactions, while offering unprecedented levels of communication, can strip away the depth and authenticity of face-to-face interactions, contributing to feelings of loneliness and detachment from genuine human relationships. Alienation is not only from work or production but also from community.

Then, as our lives have become increasingly urbanized and mediated by digital technologies, we find ourselves physically and emotionally distanced from the natural world. The more reliant we become on technology, the less immediate and tangible our relationship with nature appears. This alienation is a matter of physical separation and perception: nature becomes something external, a resource to be managed or a backdrop to human activity rather than an integral part of our existence. This disconnection fosters a sense of loss and dislocation, as many people long for a deeper connection to the environment – a sentiment anti-technology extremists exploit in their rhetoric.

Finally, perhaps the most insidious form of alienation emerges from how technology redefines human agency. As advanced technologies make decisions on our behalf – whether through algorithms, machine learning, or automated systems – we become increasingly removed from the very processes that shape our lives. This alienation from decision-making can create a profound crisis of agency. When technology dictates the terms of our existence – deciding what content we see, how our data are used, or even how we navigate the world – we may begin to feel as though we have little control over our lives.

How can we alleviate alienation? How can we act meaningfully when our capacity to do so seems to be entangled in and constrained by vast technological systems? The anti-technology challenge invites us to reflect on what kind of world we are building and its costs. As scholars, policy-makers, and citizens, we shouldn't dismiss those concerns as reactionary nostalgia, fear of change, or irrational technophobia. Instead, we should reflect on the consequences that the current direction of technological progress has on nature and ourselves. I do not advocate for a rejection of technology or a retreat into primitivism but for reflection on how to balance progress with our collective sense of belonging, identity, and agency. By understanding the historical and ideological evolution of anti-technology extremism, we can develop more nuanced responses beyond regulation and address the existential and ontological concerns driving anti-technology movements and individuals.

While the risks of unchecked technological advancement are clear, we should also recognize that technology has immense potential to combat exploitation and alienation. It is not the technology itself that leads to these problems. It's how it is used within specific frameworks, particularly those driven by unregulated markets and power structures prioritizing profit over people. Instead, we should promote a paradigm shift – a new ethics of technology. As Mark Coeckelbergh argues, instead of thinking about what technologies can do, we should consider 'what *we* do in relation to the world and to others'.[17] Promoting this focus shift would allow us to evaluate new and old technologies depending on the skills and activities they promote rather than what the technologies themselves can do. This, in turn, would enable us to identify those technologies that can contribute to a better engagement with the world and one another instead of feeding growing alienation. In other words, it is not enough to say that 'this communication platform allows us to connect' or that 'this generative AI does this for us'. Instead, we should ask what skills and activities these technologies promote and how these shape our relation to the world and one another. 'Does this communication platform promote authentic and meaningful interaction or a superficial engagement driven by "likes" and "shares" for profit?' 'Does this generative AI encourage creative and fulfilling work, or does it replace the need for human originality and involvement in the workplace?' By reframing our understanding of technology in terms of the activities and skills it promotes, we can begin to prioritize those that deepen our connection with each other rather than those that both exacerbate our alienation from technology and fuel the existential crisis that underlies anti-technology extremism.

Now, I don't want to be naïve and attempt to convince you that this would be so straightforward. In the chapter on eco-fascism, we saw how Patrick Crusius was somewhat concerned about automation processes stealing his future job. Yet he also held beliefs that were fundamentally racist and white supremacist. Take his concerns about automation out of the equation and you still have an individual who holds extremist views and is ready to resort to violence. This is because, as mentioned in chapter 5, the landscape of political violence today is increasingly dominated by actors who defy traditional categories of extremism and who hold composite and variegated beliefs. Equally, regulations and paradigm shifts can lessen the impact of emerging technology but will not eliminate the possibility of disgruntled members of society who take up arms against technology. There's no silver bullet or one-size-fits-all solution. As mentioned above, addressing and countering violent extremism is important. Still, we must also learn to live with it and accept that a certain (hopefully minimal) degree of political violence will inevitably characterize our society.

Understanding the complex and multifaceted nature of anti-technology extremism represents a crucial first step towards addressing this challenging issue. We can develop more nuanced and effective responses by recognizing the diverse motivations and grievances driving the different – and prospective – factions within the Anti-Technology Movement. This knowledge not only helps mitigate the immediate threats posed by anti-technology extremists but also allows us to anticipate and prepare for future challenges. At the same time, as we stand on the brink of unprecedented and transformative technological advancements, we must balance progress with careful consideration of its societal impacts. To do so, we must work towards a paradigm shift in our relationship with technology, the world, and each other to be better equipped to handle the disruptions and transformations that lie ahead and avoid past and present mistakes of exploitation that further feed growing alienation. Let this book serve as a foundation for further research and dialogue on the increasingly dangerous interplay between anti-technology politics and violent extremism, and as a call to action for policy-makers, scholars, and citizens alike to engage with these important issues thoughtfully and proactively.

Notes

Introduction

1 A few weeks before, a document with the same title was published online. See Anonymous, 'Fall of AI: Ein Aufruf Zum Kampf gegen „Künstliche Intelligenz" als Teil der Technologischen Herrschaft', April 2019, https://anarchistischebibliothek.org/mirror/a/af/anonymous-fall-of-ai.a4.pdf.
2 For more information, see Victoria Turk, 'How a Berlin Neighbourhood Took on Google and Won', *Wired*, 26 October 2018; Josh O'Kane, 'When a Berlin Neighborhood Went to War With Google', Bloomberg UK, 25 October 2022.
3 I say this only to provide context as to why I was interested in political demonstrations against Google Campus. There is no intention to suggest that the anti-Google campaign had something to do with what we may call terrorism (a term that I will define shortly).
4 'Rise of AI Conference 2019', 2019, https://app.qwoted.com/opportunities/event-rise-of-ai-conference-2019.
5 Maria R. D'Angelo, Sentenza n. 6 del 11 luglio 2014 nel procedimento penale contro Alfredo Cospito e Nicola Gai, No. Verdict N. 6 (Corte d'Assise di Appello di Genova 11 July 2014).
6 EUROPOL, 'European Union: Terrorism Situation and Trend Report' (Luxembourg: Publications Office of the European Union, 2019), 57.
7 To name a few studies, see Audrey K. Cronin, *Power to the People: How Open Technological Innovation Is Arming Tomorrow's Terrorists* (Oxford: Oxford University Press, 2020); Gregory D. Koblentz, 'Emerging Technologies and the Future of CBRN Terrorism', *The Washington Quarterly* 43, no. 2 (2 April 2020): 177–96; Andrew Brown, 'Terror, Tech, and Transformation: Will Emerging Technologies Revolutionize Terrorism?', *Comparative Strategy* 42, no. 2 (4 March 2023): 308–20; Zachary Kallenborn

and Philipp C. Bleek, 'Swarming Destruction: Drone Swarms and Chemical, Biological, Radiological, and Nuclear Weapons', *The Nonproliferation Review* 25, no. 5–6 (2 September 2018): 523–43; Chelsea Daymon, Yannick Veilleux-Lepage, and Emil Archambault, 'Learning from Foes: How Racially and Ethnically Motivated Violent Extremists Embrace and Mimic Islamic State's Use of Emerging Technologies', GNET Report (London: International Centre for the Study of Radicalisation, 2022).

8 Ioana Petcu et al., 'Shaping the Future: Between Opportunities and Challenges of the Ongoing 4th and the Forthcoming 5th Industrial Revolution' (eLSE 2020, Bucharest, 2020), 91–7; Mary Doyle-Kent and Peter Kopacek, 'Industry 5.0: Is the Manufacturing Industry on the Cusp of a New Revolution?', in *Proceedings of the International Symposium for Production Research 2019*, ed. Numan M. Durakbasa and M. Güneş Gençyılmaz (Cham: Springer International Publishing, 2020), 432–41.

9 'Revealed: The 50 New Technologies That Could Shape the Future', UK Research and Innovation, 6 December 2023.

10 Anna Tong, 'AI Threatens Humanity's Future, 61% of Americans Say: Reuters/Ipsos Poll', *Reuters*, 17 May 2023.

11 Matthew Smith, 'Britons Lack Confidence That AI Can Be Developed and Regulated Responsibly', YouGov UK, 1 November 2023.

12 See, for example, Laurens Cerulus, 'EU Countries Sound Alarm about Growing Anti-5G Movement', *Politico*, 19 October 2020; Kelvin Chan, Beatrice Dupuy, and Arijeta Lajka, 'Conspiracy Theorists Burn 5G Towers Claiming Link to Virus', *AP News*, 21 April 2020; Michael Loadenthal, 'Anti-5G, Infrastructure Sabotage, and COVID-19' (Global Network on Extremism & Technology, 19 January 2021).

13 Astrid Bötticher, 'Towards Academic Consensus Definitions of Radicalism and Extremism', *Perspectives on Terrorism* 11, no. 4 (2017): 73–7.

14 This explains the lack of engagement with groups like the Amish in this book.

15 Stathis N. Kalyvas, 'The Landscape of Political Violence', in *The Oxford Handbook of Terrorism*, ed. Erica Chenoweth et al. (Oxford: Oxford University Press, 2019), 12.

16 This definition builds on Jeffrey M. Bale, *The Darkest Sides of Politics, I: Post-War Fascism, Covert Operations, and Terrorism* (New

York: Routledge, 2018), 4. See also Mauro Lubrano, 'Choosing What (Not) to Do Next: A Preliminary Theoretical Framework on Strategic Innovation in Terrorist Organizations', *Dynamics of Asymmetric Conflict* 17, no. 1 (2 January 2024): 3.

17 Anyone can use terrorism – be it state or non-state actors – regardless of their ideological background. This book focuses, however, on non-state actors.

18 Rodney L. Custer, 'Examining the Dimensions of Technology', *International Journal of Technology and Design Education* 5, no. 3 (1995): 219–44.

19 Bruce Mazlish, 'Civilization in a Historical and Global Perspective', *International Sociology* 16, no. 3 (September 2001): 293–300.

20 Wolf Schäfer, 'Global Civilization and Local Cultures: A Crude Look at the Whole', *International Sociology* 16, no. 3 (September 2001): 310.

21 Ibid., 312. Emphasis in original.

Chapter 1 Long Live King Ludd!

1 Robert A. Buchanan, *The Power of the Machine: The Impact of Technology from 1700 to the Present* (London: Penguin Books, 1992), 3–4.

2 The First Industrial Revolution occurred at the turn of the eighteenth century when, thanks also to a series of new developments such as coal extractions, steam engines, and railways, industry replaced agriculture as the backbone of society. The Second Industrial Revolution started around 1870 and brought several advancements in industries contributing to the emergence of new sources of energy, including electricity, gas, and oil. This period also saw a series of inventions, such as combustion engines, telegraphs, telephones, cars, and aeroplanes. The Third Industrial Revolution occurred in the second half of the twentieth century and saw the rise of electronics, telecommunications, computers, and nuclear energy. Finally, the Fourth Industrial Revolution started at the dawn of the new millennium and brought about a wave of digitalization. See Klaus Schwab, 'The Fourth Industrial Revolution', in *Encyclopedia Britannica*, 31 May 2023.

3 Gilbert Ramsay, 'Consuming the Jihad: An Enquiry into the Subculture of Internet Jihadism' (PhD thesis, University of St Andrews, 2011), 33.
4 An asymmetric conflict refers to a military engagement between parties that have significantly different capabilities and strategies. 'Propaganda of the deed' (or *by* the deed) refers to the idea that specific political direct actions – including violent ones – can set an example to other like-minded individuals and serve as a catalyst for revolution. Although this concept emerged from the anarchist tradition, it was embraced by radical and extremist groups of different ideological background in the nineteenth, twentieth, and twenty-first centuries.
5 An improvised explosive device, built by and named after Felice Orsini, who used it in an unsuccessful assassination attempt against France's Napoleon III on 14 January 1858.
6 This refers to the events of 4 May 1886 when a dynamite bomb was thrown at police as they broke up a rally in Haymarket Square, Chicago, in support of striking workers. The rally was called after six unarmed strikers were killed by police the previous day at the city's McCormick Reaper Works.
7 Richard Jensen, 'Daggers, Rifles and Dynamite: Anarchist Terrorism in Nineteenth-Century Europe', *Terrorism and Political Violence* 16, no. 1 (January 2004): 116–53.
8 On the relevance of dynamite for anarchists and non-state actor violence in the nineteenth century, see also Audrey K. Cronin, *Power to the People: How Open Technological Innovation Is Arming Tomorrow's Terrorists* (Oxford: Oxford University Press, 2020).
9 The techno-optimistic argument that technologies might help address and mitigate climate change should also be mentioned here.
10 See, for example, Coco Khan, 'Is My Phone Listening to Me? We Ask the Expert', *The Guardian*, 29 October 2021; Juliana Kenny, 'Does Your Phone Listen to You? Yes, and Here's What You Can Do About It', All About Cookies, 24 August 2023; Claudia Stouffer, 'Is My Phone Listening to Me? Yes, Here's Why and How to Stop It', Norton, 13 June 2023.
11 Shoshana Zuboff, *The Age of Surveillance Capitalism: The Fight for the Future at the New Frontier of Power* (London: Profile Books, 2019).

12 Aaron Mok and Jacob Zinkula, 'ChatGPT May Be Coming for Our Jobs. Here Are the 10 Roles That AI Is Most Likely to Replace.', *Business Insider*, 4 September 2023, sec. Economy.
13 Laurence Peter and Steven McIntosh, 'Hollywood Writers in Deal to End US Studio Strike', BBC News, 25 September 2023.
14 Steven E. Jones, *Against Technology: From the Luddites to Neo-Luddism* (New York: Routledge, 2006), 3–4.
15 David Linton, 'The Luddites: How Did They Get That Bad Reputation?', *Labor History* 33, no. 4 (October 1992): 1.
16 Jon Baggaley, 'The Luddite Revolt Continues', *Distance Education* 31, no. 3 (November 2010): 338.
17 Jones, *Against Technology*, 32.
18 George Gilder, 'Osama Bin Luddite', Discovery Institute, 1 October 2001. See also Jones, *Against Technology*, 32–4.
19 Gavin Mueller, *Breaking Things at Work: The Luddites Are Right About Why You Hate Your Job* (London: Verso, 2021), 15.
20 Kevin Hjortshøj O'Rourke, Ahmed S. Rahman, and Alan M. Taylor, 'Luddites, the Industrial Revolution, and the Demographic Transition', *Journal of Economic Growth* 18, no. 4 (December 2013): 373. The Malthusian trap refers to the idea that population growth will outpace agricultural production causing poverty, famine, conflict, and depopulation.
21 Jim Carlopio, 'A History of Social Psychological Reactions to New Technology', *Journal of Occupational Psychology* 61, no. 1 (March 1988): 69.
22 O'Rourke et al., 'Luddites, the Industrial Revolution, and the Demographic Transition', 373. See also E.P. Thompson, *The Making of the English Working Class*, reprint (Harmondsworth: Penguin Books, 1991).
23 Mueller, *Breaking Things at Work*, 16.
24 Carlopio, 'A History of Social Psychological Reactions to New Technology', 71–4; Brett Clancy, 'Rebel or Rioter? Luddites Then and Now', *Society* 54, no. 5 (October 2017): 392.
25 Joel Mokyr, *The Lever of Riches: Technological Creativity and Economic Progress* (New York: Oxford University Press, 1990). See also Klaus Desmet and Stephen L. Parente, 'Resistance to Technology Adoption: The Rise and Decline of Guilds', *Review of Economic Dynamics* 17, no. 3 (July 2014): 437.

26 In 1805, for example, French silk weavers attempted to assassinate the inventor of the Jacquart loom while also destroying the device publicly. Following the demise of the Luddites, machine-breaking riots erupted in France, the United States, Silesia, and Bavaria. See Mueller, *Breaking Things at Work*, 16–17.
27 David Linton, 'The Making of a Pariah: The Case of the Luddites', *ETC: A Review of General Semantics* 48, no. 4 (1991): 3; Maciej Kryszczuk and Michal Wenzel, 'Neo-Luddism: Contemporary Work and Beyond', *Przegląd Socjologiczny* 66, no. 4 (2017): 46.
28 Jones, *Against Technology*, 27.
29 O'Rourke et al., 'Luddites, the Industrial Revolution, and the Demographic Transition', 373.
30 C. Spencer Yost, 'Luddites', *ICU Director* 2, no. 3 (May 2011): 51.
31 Baggaley, 'The Luddite Revolt Continues', 337–9; Yost, 'Luddites', 51.
32 Adrian Randall, 'Reinterpreting "Luddism": Resistance to New Technology in the British Industrial Revolution', in *Resistance to New Technology: Nuclear Power, Information Technology and Biotechnology*, ed. Martin Bauer (Cambridge: Cambridge University Press, 1997), 60–1.
33 For example, the Plug Riots of the 1840s or the campaign against brick-making machines in the 1860s. See, respectively, Jones, *Against Technology*, 48–9; Randall, 'Reinterpreting "Luddism"', 60–1.
34 Clancy, 'Rebel or Rioter?', 393.
35 Baggaley, 'The Luddite Revolt Continues', 338.
36 E.J. Hobsbawm, 'The Machine Breakers', *Past and Present* 1, no. 1 (1952): 59.
37 Mueller, *Breaking Things at Work*, 18.
38 Jones, *Against Technology*, 3–4.
39 Mueller, *Breaking Things at Work*, 14; 'Handbill Issued by the Weavers and Townspeople of Royton, near Manchester, Lancashire in May 1808, after Parliament Rejected a Bill to Guarantee the Weavers a Minimum Wage', HO 42/95 f.375, The National Archive, https://www.nationalarchives.gov.uk/education/resources/why-did-the-luddites-protest/why-did-the-luddites-protest-source-5/.
40 For a comprehensive discussion on this, see Alessandro Nuvolari, 'The "Machine Breakers" and the Industrial Revolution', ECIS

Working Paper Series (Eindhoven: Eindhoven Centre for Innovation Studies, 2000).

41 Eric Schatzberg, *Technology: Critical History of a Concept* (Chicago: University of Chicago Press, 2018), 119.

42 Charles Bright and Michael Geyer, 'Benchmarks of Globalization: The Global Condition, 1850–2010', in *A Companion to World History*, ed. Douglas Northrop (Hoboken, NJ: Wiley-Blackwell, 2012), 285–300.

43 Haradhan Kumar Mohajan, 'The Second Industrial Revolution Has Brought Modern Social and Economic Developments', *Journal of Social Sciences and Humanities* 6, no. 1 (2020): 1–14; Mokyr, *The Lever of Riches*.

44 Jeffrey Wasserstrom, '"Civilization" and Its Discontents: The Boxers and Luddites as Heroes and Villains', *Theory and Society* 16, no. 5 (1987): 676.

45 George H.C. Wong, 'China's Opposition to Western Science during Late Ming and Early Ch'ing', *Isis* 54, no. 1 (March 1963): 42.

46 Lisa Mitchell, '"To Stop Train Pull Chain": Writing Histories of Contemporary Political Practice', *The Indian Economic & Social History Review* 48, no. 4 (December 2011): 491.

47 See David F. Lindenfeld, *The Transformation of Positivism: Alexius Meinong and European Thought, 1880–1920* (Berkeley: University of California Press, 1980); August Comte, *A General View of Positivism*, trans. J.H. Bridges (Cambridge: Cambridge University Press, 2009).

48 Schatzberg, *Technology*, 8.

49 Thomas Carlyle, *A Carlyle Reader: Selections from the Writings of Thomas Carlyle*, ed. G.B. Tennyson (Acton, MA: Copley Pub. Group, 1999), 34.

50 Ralf Haekel, 'Thomas Carlyle and the Emergence of the Concept of Romanticism: "Signs of the Times" and *Sartor Resartus*', *European Romantic Review* 35, no. 2 (2 April 2024): 422.

51 Charles H. Kegel, 'Carlyle and Ruskin: An Influential Friendship', *Brigham Young University Studies* 5, no. 3/4 (1964): 219–29.

52 Alan Davis, 'Technology', in *The Cambridge Companion to John Ruskin*, ed. Francis O'Gorman (Cambridge: Cambridge University Press, 2015), 170.

53 John Matteson, 'Constructing Ethics and the Ethics of Construction: John Ruskin and the Humanity of the Builder', *CrossCurrents* 52,

no. 4 (2002): 298; Jenny Fryman, 'William Morris and Edward Carpenter: Back to the Land and the Simple Life 1880–1910' (PhD thesis, University of Gloucestershire, 2002), 16.

54 John Ruskin, *The Storm-Cloud of the Nineteenth Century: Two Lectures Delivered at the London Institution, February 4th and 11th, 1884* (London: Wentworth Press, 2016); Brian J. Day, 'The Moral Intuition of Ruskin's "Storm-Cloud"', *Studies in English Literature, 1500–1900* 45, no. 4 (2005): 917–33; Jesse Oak Taylor, 'Storm-Clouds on the Horizon: John Ruskin and the Emergence of Anthropogenic Climate Change', *19: Interdisciplinary Studies in the Long Nineteenth Century* 26 (6 July 2018).

55 Fryman, 'William Morris and Edward Carpenter', 15.

56 Peter C. Gould, *Early Green Politics: Back to Nature, Back to the Land, and Socialism in Britain, 1880–1900* (Brighton: Harvester Press; New York: St Martin's Press, 1988), 21.

57 Other examples include Fritz Lang's 1927 film *Metropolis* or Karel Čapek's 1920 play *RUR*.

58 Daniel Dinello, *Technophobia! Science Fiction Visions of Posthuman Technology* (Austin: University of Texas Press, 2006), 2.

59 Lewis Mumford, *Technics and Civilization* (Chicago: University of Chicago Press, 2010).

60 Melvin Kranzberg, 'Man and Megamachine', *The Virginia Quarterly Review* 43 (1967): 687. See also Lewis Mumford, *The Myth of the Machine: Volume I, Technics and Human Development* (Boston, MA: Mariner Books, 1971).

61 Jones, *Against Technology*, 177.

62 Mario Savio, 'Sit-in Address on the Steps of Sproul Hall', 2 November 1964, https://www.americanrhetoric.com/speeches/mariosavioproulhallsitin.htm. See also John P. Williams, 'Rage Against the Machine: Berkeley 1964 and the Birth of the Free Speech Movement', *Perspectives on Global Development and Technology* 17, nos 1–2 (February 2018): 158–72.

63 Jones, *Against Technology*, 178.

64 Jacques Ellul, *The Technological Society*, trans. John Wilkinson, 7th edn (New York: Alfred A. Knopf, 1976).

65 Arne Næss, 'The Shallow and the Deep, Long-range Ecology Movement: A Summary', *Inquiry: An Interdisciplinary Journal of*

Philosophy 16, nos 1–4 (1973): 95–100; Arne Næss, 'The Basic Principles of Deep Ecology', *The Trumpeter* 3, no. 4 (1986): 14.

66 See, for example, Dave Foreman, *Man Swarm and the Killing of Wildlife* (Durango, CO: Raven's Eye Press, 2011); Christopher Manes, *Green Rage: Radical Environmentalism and the Unmaking of Civilization* (Boston: Little, Brown and Co, 1990).

67 Horacio R. Trujillo, 'The Radical Environmentalist Movement', in *Aptitude for Destruction Volume 2: Case Studies of Organizational Learning in Five Terrorist Groups*, ed. Brian A Jackson (Santa Monica, CA: RAND Corporation, 2005), 146.

68 Paul Watson, *Earthforce! An Earth Warrior's Guide to Strategy* (Los Angeles: Chaco Press, 1993), 18.

69 Sivan Hirsch-Hoefler and Cas Mudde, '"Ecoterrorism": Terrorist Threat or Political Ploy?', *Studies in Conflict & Terrorism* 37, no. 7 (3 July 2014): 590; Keith Tester and John Walls, 'The Ideology and Current Activities of the Animal Liberation Front', *Contemporary Politics* 2 (1996): 79–91.

70 Keith Makoto Woodhouse, *The Ecocentrists: A History of Radical Environmentalism* (New York: Columbia University Press, 2018), 105.

71 Martha F. Lee, *Earth First! Environmental Apocalypse* (Syracuse, NY: Syracuse University Press, 1995); Benjamin Seel and Alex Plows, 'Coming Live and Direct: Strategies of Earth First!', in *Direct Action in British Environmentalism*, ed. Brian Doherty, Matthew Paterson, and Benjamin Seel (London: Routledge, 2000); 'About Earth First!', https://www.earthfirst.uk/what-is-earth-first/.

72 Hirsch-Hoefler and Mudde, '"Ecoterrorism"', 591; Stefan H. Leader and Peter Probst, 'The Earth Liberation Front and Environmental Terrorism', *Terrorism and Political Violence* 15, no. 4 (2003): 37–58; Gary A. Ackerman, 'Beyond Arson? A Threat Assessment of the Earth Liberation Front', *Terrorism and Political Violence* 15, no. 4 (October 2003): 143–70; Paul Joosse, 'Leaderless Resistance and Ideological Inclusion: The Case of the Earth Liberation Front', *Terrorism and Political Violence* 19, no. 3 (4 July 2007): 351–68.

73 Donald D. Liddick, *Eco-Terrorism: Radical Environmental and Animal Liberation Movements* (London: Praeger, 2006), 20–1.

74 *Ecotage!*, published by Sam Love and David Obst in 1972 (New York: Pocket Books), performed a similar role in this regard.

75 Dave Foreman and Bill Haywood, eds, *Ecodefense: A Field Guide to Monkeywrenching* (Chico, CA: Abbzug Press, 1993). For the writings of the Earth First! movement, see 'Earth First! Movement Writings', Environment & Society Portal, https://www.environmentandsociety.org/mml/collection/11571.
76 Jones, *Against Technology*, 29.
77 Chellis Glendinning, 'Notes Toward a Neo-Luddite Manifesto', 1990, https://theanarchistlibrary.org/library/chellis-glendinning-notes-toward-a-neo-luddite-manifesto.pdf.
78 Ibid., 3. See also Mauro Lubrano, 'The EU Nuclear Option and the Potential for a Recrudescence of Anti-Nuclear Violence', *Insights* (Global Network on Extremism & Technology, 25 January 2022).
79 Kirkpatrick Sale, *Rebels Against the Future: The Luddites and Their War on the Industrial Revolution: Lessons for The Computer Age* (Wokingham: Addison-Welsey, 1995).
80 Monika Bauerstein, 'The Luddites Are Back', *Utne Reader*, 1 March 1996.
81 Jones, *Against Technology*, 24.
82 John Zerzan, *Future Primitive and Other Essays* (New York: Autonomedia, 1994). Anarcho-primitivism is a subset of anarchism that places strong emphasis on critiques of technology and civilization and basically advocates for a return to a pre-agricultural society to create a more equitable and ecologically sustainable world.
83 See John Zerzan, *Elements of Refusal* (Seattle, WA: Left Bank Books, 1988); Zerzan, *Future Primitive and Other Essays*; John Zerzan, ed., *Against Civilization: Readings and Reflections* (Eugene, OR: Uncivilized Books, 1999); John Zerzan, 'Against Technology: A Talk by John Zerzan (April 23, 1997)', 2006, https://theanarchistlibrary.org/library/john-zerzan-against-technology-a-talk-by-john-zerzan-april-23-1997.pdf.
84 Zerzan, *Future Primitive and Other Essays*, 59.
85 John Filiss, 'What Is Primitivism?', 2002, 1, https://theanarchistlibrary.org/library/john-filiss-what-is-primitivism.pdf.
86 Ron Grossman, 'Peaceful Anarchists Meet to Alter World', *Chicago Tribune*, 15 April 1996.
87 Kirkpatrick Sale, 'America's New Luddites', *Le Monde Diplomatique*, February 1997.

88 *Machines in Flames*, Documentary, 2022, https://machinesinflames.com/.
89 Alston Chase, *A Mind for Murder: The Education of the Unabomber and the Origins of Modern Terrorism* (New York: W.W. Norton & Company, 2004); Chris Waits and Dave Shors, *Unabomber: The Secret Life of Ted Kaczynski* (Helena, MT: Farcountry Press, 1999).
90 Carol M. Ostrom, 'Unabomber Suspect Is Charged – Montana Townsfolk Showed Tolerance for "The Hermit"', *The Seattle Times*, 4 April 1996.
91 Karl Stampfl, 'He Came Ted Kaczynski, He Left the Unabomber', *The Michigan Daily*, 16 March 2006.
92 Sean Fleming, 'The Unabomber and the Origins of Anti-Tech Radicalism', *Journal of Political Ideologies* 27, no. 2 (2022): 207–25.
93 Michael Safi, '"His Ideas Resonate": How the Unabomber's Dangerous Anti-Tech Manifesto Lives On', *The Guardian*, 19 June 2023; William Booth, 'Gender Confusion, Sex Change Idea Fueled Kaczynski's Rage, Report Says', *The Washington Post*, 12 September 1998; Bryan Pietsch, 'Before He Was the Unabomber, Ted Kaczynski Was a Mind-Control Test Subject', *The Washington Post*, 11 June 2023.
94 Sean Fleming, 'Searching for Ecoterrorism: The Crucial Case of the Unabomber', *American Political Science Review*, 6 February 2024, 4.
95 For the Unabomber manhunt, see Lis Wiehl, *Hunting the Unabomber: The FBI, Ted Kaczynski, and the Capture of America's Most Notorious Domestic Terrorist* (Nashville, TN: Nelson Books, 2021).
96 Fleming, 'The Unabomber'; Theodore J. Kaczynski, *Industrial Society and Its Future*, 1995, http://editions-hache.com/essais/pdf/kaczynski2.pdf.
97 Kaczynski, *Industrial Society and Its Future*, 24.
98 Ibid., 27.
99 Jones, *Against Technology*, 219.
100 John Zerzan, 'Whose Unabomber?', 1995, https://theanarchistlibrary.org/library/john-zerzan-whose-unabomber.pdf.
101 Fleming, 'The Unabomber', 218.
102 Roc Morin, 'The Anarcho-Primitivist Who Wants Us All to Give Up Technology', *Vice*, 25 April 2015; Theodore J. Kaczynski, 'The Truth About Primitive Life: A Critique of Anarchoprimitivism', 2008,

https://theanarchistlibrary.org/library/ted-kaczynski-the-truth-about-primitive-life-a-critique-of-anarchoprimitivism.pdf.
103 Theodore J. Kaczynski, *Anti-Tech Revolution: Why and How* (Scottsdale, AZ: Fitch & Madison Publishers, 2016), 4.
104 Jake Hanrahan, 'Inside the Unabomber's Odd and Furious Online Revival', *Wired*, 1 August 2018.
105 John Jacobi, 'Apostles and Heretics', in *Atassa: Readings in Eco-Extremism #1*, 2016, 15–34.
106 Fleming, 'The Unabomber', 218.
107 For the influence of Kaczynski in these milieus, see Mauro Lubrano, 'Stop the Machines: How Emerging Technologies Are Fomenting the War on Civilization', *Terrorism and Political Violence* 35, no. 2 (2023): 330; José Pedro Zúquete, 'Left-Wing Extremism and the War on Civilization', in *The Palgrave Handbook of Left-Wing Extremism, Volume 2*, ed. José Pedro Zúquete (Cham: Springer Nature Switzerland, 2023), 257–76; Joshua Farrell-Molloy and Graham Macklin, 'Ted Kaczynski, Anti-Technology Radicalism and Eco-Fascism', ICTT Perspectives (Leiden: The International Centre for Counter-Terrorism, 15 June 2022).
108 Theodore J. Kaczynski, 'Ted Kaczynski on Individualists Tending Toward Savagery (ITS)', 2017, https://theanarchistlibrary.org/library/ted-kaczynski-ted-kaczynski-on-individualists-tending-toward.pdf; Theodore J. Kaczynski, 'Ecofascism: An Aberrant Branch of Leftism', 29 September 2020, https://theanarchistlibrary.org/library/ted-kaczynski-ecofascism-an-aberrant-branch-of-leftism.pdf; Kaczynski, *Anti-Tech Revolution*, 167–8.
109 Edward Tenner, *Why Things Bite Back: Technology and the Revenge of Unintended Consequences* (New York: Vintage, 1997), 7.
110 For ontological security, see Anthony Giddens, *The Constitution of Society: Outline of the Theory of Structuration* (Cambridge: Polity, 1984); Anthony Giddens, *Modernity and Self-Identity* (Cambridge: Polity, 1991).
111 Zerzan, *Future Primitive and Other Essays*, 59.
112 Andrew Feenberg, *Transforming Technology: A Critical Theory Revisited* (New York: Oxford University Press, 2002).
113 Kaczynski, *Industrial Society and Its Future*, 1.
114 In my previous work on this topic, I used the two terms interchangeably. This proved unwise as anti-technology extremism pos-

sesses certain characteristics that, as I argue here, are absent in neo-Luddism and essentially incompatible with it. See Lubrano, 'Stop the Machines'.

115 Centre for Data Ethics and Innovation (now Responsible Technology Adoption Unit), 'Public Attitudes to Data and AI: Tracker Survey (Wave 3)' (Department for Science, Innovation and Technology, 12 February 2024); Giorgio Papavero, 'Molti Italiani non sono pronti all'impatto con l'intelligenza artificiale', *Wired*, 14 May 2024.

116 See, for example, Action Against 5G, 'About Us', https://actionagainst5g.org/.

117 Jeffrey M. Bale, *The Darkest Sides of Politics, I: Post-War Fascism, Covert Operations, and Terrorism* (New York: Routledge, 2018), 26.

Chapter 2 Smash the Prison-Society: Insurrectionary Anarchism

1 Thomas Latschan, 'Tesla Sabotage in Germany: Who Is the Volcano Group?', *Deutsche Welle*, 6 March 2024.
2 Agua de Pau, 'Vulkangruppe Tesla Abschalten!: Anschlag Auf Stromversorgung in Der Nähe von Steinfurt', 5 March 2024, https://kontrapolis.info/12465/.
3 Elon Musk @elonmusk, X, 5 March 2024.
4 C. Alexander McKinley, 'The French Revolution and 1848', in *The Palgrave Handbook of Anarchism*, ed. Carl Levy and Matthew S. Adams (Cham: Springer International Publishing, 2019), 307.
5 Nicholas Walter, 'About Anarchism', *Anarchy* 9, no. 6 (1969): 161–92.
6 McKinley, 'The French Revolution and 1848'.
7 See Robert Graham, *We Do Not Fear Anarchy, We Invoke It: The First International and the Origins of the Anarchist Movement* (Chico, CA: AK Press, 2015), 9; Robert Graham, 'Anarchism and the First International', in *The Palgrave Handbook of Anarchism*, ed. Carl Levy and Matthew S. Adams (Cham: Springer International Publishing, 2019), 325–42.
8 Murray Bookchin, 'Anarchism: Past and Present', in *Reinventing Anarchy, Again*, ed. Howard J. Ehrlich (Edinburgh: AK Press, 1996), 19.

9 Donald Rooum, *What Is Anarchism? An Introduction* (Oakland, CA: PM Press, 2016).
10 Among them, Russian Tsar Alexander II (1881), French President Carnot (1894), Spanish Premier Canovas (1897), Austrian Empress Elizabeth (1898), Italy's King Umberto I (1900), and US President McKinley (1901). See Richard Jensen, 'Daggers, Rifles and Dynamite: Anarchist Terrorism in Nineteenth-Century Europe', *Terrorism and Political Violence* 16, no. 1 (January 2004): 116–53.
11 David Berry, 'Anarchism and 1968', in *The Palgrave Handbook of Anarchism*, ed. Carl Levy and Matthew S. Adams (Cham: Springer International Publishing, 2019), 449–70; Dana M. Williams, 'Contemporary Anarchist and Anarchistic Movements', *Sociology Compass* 12, no. 6 (June 2018): e12582.
12 Williams, 'Contemporary Anarchist and Anarchistic Movements'; Dana M. Williams and Matthew T. Lee, 'Aiming to Overthrow the State (without Using the State): Political Opportunities for Anarchist Movements', *Comparative Sociology* 11, no. 4 (2012): 558–93.
13 Francis Dupuis-Déri, 'The Black Blocs Ten Years after Seattle: Anarchism, Direct Action, and Deliberative Practices', *Journal for the Study of Radicalism* 4, no. 2 (2010): 45–82. Originated within the German 'autonomous movements' during the 1970s and 1980s, 'black blocs' gained notoriety thanks to the 1999 Battle of Seattle. See David Van Deusen, 'Emergence of the Black Bloc & the Movement Towards Anarchism', 2002, https://mirror.anarhija.net/usa.anarchistlibraries.net/mirror/d/dv/david-van-deusen-green-mountain-anarchist-collective-emergence-of-the-black-bloc-the-movement-t.pdf. This term refers to an organizational tactic whereby protesters 'wear masks, bandanas, and head-to-toe black clothing to project strength and group uniformity while maintaining anonymity', thereby preventing 'identification from the authorities and political opponents'. See Daveed Gartenstein-Ross, Samuel Hodgson, and Austin Blair, *Behind the Black Bloc: An Overview of Militant Anarchism and Anti-Fascism* (Washington, DC: Foundation for Defense of Democracies, 2021), 23.
14 As Williams argues, these numbers are likely higher since the phenomenon was surely underreported. See Williams, 'Contemporary Anarchist and Anarchistic Movements', 3.

15 Leonard Williams, 'Anarchism Revived', *New Political Science* 29, no. 3 (September 2007): 300.
16 Williams, 'Contemporary Anarchist and Anarchistic Movements', 3.
17 Bob Black, 'My Anarchism Problem', 1994, https://theanarchistlibrary.org/library/bob-black-my-anarchism-problem.pdf.
18 Ibid.
19 Williams, 'Anarchism Revived', 299.
20 Francesco Marone, 'The Prisoner Dilemma: Insurrectionary Anarchism and the Cospito Affair', *CTC Sentinel* 16, no. 3 (2023): 21–6; Mauro Lubrano, 'Lone Leaders of Leaderless Resistors: A Theory of Informal Leadership in Contemporary Terrorism and Political Violence', *Studies in Conflict & Terrorism*, 29 June 2023, 1–24.
21 Subalternity is here conceived in the Gramscian sense as interpreted by Marcus E. Green – that is, subalternity refers to the 'intersectionality of the variations of race, class, gender, culture, religion, nationalism and colonialism functioning within an ensemble of socio-political and economic relations' and denotes a condition in which 'subaltern groups are subordinated to the power, will, influence, leadership, and direction of a dominant group or a "single combination" of dominant groups'. Marcus E. Green, 'Rethinking the Subaltern and the Question of Censorship in Gramsci's *Prison Notebooks*', *Postcolonial Studies* 14, no. 4 (December 2011): 340. See also Marcus E. Green, 'Gramsci Cannot Speak: Presentations and Interpretations of Gramsci's Concept of the Subaltern', *Rethinking Marxism* 14, no. 3 (September 2002): 1–24.
22 Williams, 'Contemporary Anarchist and Anarchistic Movements', 4.
23 Jeff Ferrell, 'An Anarchist Criminology for Uncertain Times', *Journal of Criminology* 54, no. 1 (March 2021): 97.
24 Paul Joosse, 'Leaderless Resistance and the Loneliness of Lone Wolves: Exploring the Rhetorical Dynamics of Lone Actor Violence', *Terrorism and Political Violence* 29, no. 1 (2 January 2017): 52.
25 Lubrano, 'Lone Leaders of Leaderless Resistors'; Phillip W. Gray, 'Leaderless Resistance, Networked Organization, and Ideological Hegemony', *Terrorism and Political Violence* 25, no. 5 (November 2013): 655–71.
26 CrimethInc., 'How to Form an Affinity Group. The Essential Building Block of Anarchist Organization', 6 February 2017, https://

crimethinc.com/2017/02/06/how-to-form-an-affinity-group-the-essential-building-block-of-anarchist-organization.

27 Francis Dupuis-Déri, 'Anarchism and the Politics of Affinity Groups', *Anarchist Studies* 18, no. 1 (2010): 41.

28 Anonymous, 'Do or Die. Insurrectionary Anarchism: Organising for Attack!', 2003, 13, https://theanarchistlibrary.org/library/do-or-die-insurrectionary-anarchy.

29 Randy Borum and Chuck Tilby, 'Anarchist Direct Actions: A Challenge for Law Enforcement', *Studies in Conflict & Terrorism* 28, no. 3 (May 2005): 203.

30 Vicente Ordóñez, 'Direct Action', in *Anarchism: A Conceptual Approach*, ed. Benjamin Franks, Nathan Jun, and Leonard Williams (New York: Routledge, 2018), 62.

31 Benjamin Franks, 'The Direct Action Ethic: From 59 Upwards', *Anarchist Studies* 11, no. 1 (2003): 13–41.

32 Constance Bantman, 'The Era of Propaganda by the Deed', in *The Palgrave Handbook of Anarchism*, ed. Carl Levy and Matthew S. Adams (Cham: Palgrave Macmillan, 2019), 371–88; Mark Shirk, 'The Universal Eye: Anarchist "Propaganda of the Deed" and Development of the Modern Surveillance State', *International Studies Quarterly* 63, no. 2 (1 June 2019): 334–45.

33 Benjamin J. Pauli, 'Pacifism, Nonviolence, and the Reinvention of Anarchist Tactics in the Twentieth Century', *Journal for the Study of Radicalism* 9, no. 1 (1 January 2015): 61–94; Andrew Fiala, 'Anarchism and Pacifism', in *Brill's Companion to Anarchism and Philosophy*, ed. Nathan J. Jun (Leiden: Brill, 2018), 152–70.

34 Borum and Tilby, 'Anarchist Direct Actions', 201–2.

35 Errico Malatesta, 'Anarchy and Violence', trans. Andy Carloff, *Liberty* 1, no. 9–10 (1894), https://www.marxists.org/archive/malatesta/1894/anarchy-and-violence.html.

36 Francesco Marone, 'The Rise of Insurrectionary Anarchist Terrorism in Italy', *Dynamics of Asymmetric Conflict* 8, no. 3 (2 September 2015): 196.

37 Lubrano, 'Lone Leaders of Leaderless Resistors', 6; Mauro Lubrano, 'Hidden in Plain Sight: Insurrectionary Anarchism in the Anti-Government Extremism Landscape', *Perspectives on Terrorism* 18, no. 1 (2024): 37–61.

38 Michael Loadenthal, *The Politics of Attack: Communiqués and Insurrectionary Violence* (Manchester: Manchester University Press, 2018), 32.
39 Alfredo Cospito, 'A Few Words of "Freedom": Interview by CCF – Imprisoned Members Cell with Alfredo Cospito', July 2014, https://theanarchistlibrary.org/library/a-few-words-of-freedom.pdf.
40 Williams, 'Anarchism Revived', 310.
41 The quote is taken from 325, '#11', 2014, 3 (no longer online). See also Alfredo Cospito, 'On the "Proposal For a New Anarchist Manifesto"', 19 April 2021, https://theanarchistlibrary.org/library/alfredo-cospito-on-the-proposal-for-a-new-anarchist-manifesto.pdf; Anonymous, 'Reflections on the Underlying Environment of Contemporary Informal, Insurrectional, International Anarchy (for a New Anarchic Manifesto)', April 2020, https://corrispondenzeanarchiche.files.wordpress.com/2020/11/manifesto-inglese.pdf.
42 Anonymous, 'On Anonymity, Claims and Reproducibility of Actions', 14 September 2017, https://theanarchistlibrary.org/library/anonymity-claims-and-reproducibility-of-actions.pdf.
43 Cospito, 'On the "Proposal"'.
44 Francesco Farinelli and Lorenzo Marinone, 'Contemporary Violent Left-Wing and Anarchist Extremism (VLWAE) in the EU: Analysing Threats and Potential for P/CVE' (Brussels: Publications Office of the European Union, 2021), 6–7.
45 Lubrano, 'Lone Leaders of Leaderless Resistors'; Lubrano, 'Hidden in Plain Sight'; Marone, 'The Rise of Insurrectionary Anarchist Terrorism in Italy'; Francesco Marone, 'A Profile of the Informal Anarchist Federation in Italy', *CTC Sentinel* 7, no. 3 (2014): 21–5; Francesco Marone, 'Left-Wing and Anarchist Extremism in Italy', in *The Palgrave Handbook of Left-Wing Extremism, Volume 1*, ed. José Pedro Zúquete (Cham: Palgrave Macmillan, 2023), 261–80.
46 Dipartimento delle Informazioni per la Sicurezza, 'Relazione al Parlamento 2014', Relazione Sulla Politica Dell'Informazione per La Sicurezza (Presidenza del Consiglio dei Ministri, 6 March 2015), 71.
47 José Pedro Zúquete, 'Left-Wing Extremism and the War on Civilization', in *The Palgrave Handbook of Left-Wing Extremism, Volume 2*, ed. José Pedro Zúquete (Cham: Springer Nature Switzerland, 2023), 264; ACRATES, 'Attacks Against 3 Mobile

Phone Towers', 15 November 2021, https://anarchistnews.org/content/attacks-against-3-mobile-phone-towers.

48 See, for example, Cospito, 'A Few Words of "Freedom"'.
49 Lubrano, 'Lone Leaders of Leaderless Resistors'.
50 Zúquete, 'Left-Wing Extremism and the War on Civilization', 265.
51 Tom Anderson, 'The Police Want to Impose a Chilling List of Conditions on a UK Anarchist Prisoner', *Canary*, 19 April 2022. See also Toby Shone, 'Toby Shone: The Subversive Written Word', 4 March 2024, https://lanemesi.noblogs.org/post/2024/03/15/toby-shone-the-subversive-written-word/.
52 Anti-Tech Collective, 'About Us', https://www.antitechcollective.com/about.
53 Randall Amster, *Anarchism Today* (Santa Barbara, CA: Praeger, 2012), 172.
54 T. Fulano, 'Against the Megamachine', *Fifth Estate*, no. 306 (July 1981); Fifth Estate Collective, 'Technology and the State', *Fifth Estate*, no. 290 (2 March 1978); Various Authors, 'Technology Debate Continues', *Fifth Estate*, no. 305 (18 March 1982).
55 Steve Millett, 'Technology Is Capital: Fifth Estate's Critique of the Megamachine', in *Changing Anarchism*, ed. Jonathan Purkis and James Bowen (Manchester: Manchester University Press, 2018), 73.
56 Ibid. See also Fulano, 'Against the Megamachine'.
57 Following the apprehension of Kaczynski, T. Fulano expressed solidarity with and adherence to the Unabomber's message. At the same time, he warned that '[u]nlike the Unabomber, who argues that the destruction of technology "must be [. . .] the single, overriding goal", we have many complex, interrelated aims that cannot be resolved by this mechanistic, monomaniacal determination alone'. See T. Fulano, 'The Unabomber and the Future of Industrial Society', 1996, 14, https://theanarchistlibrary.org/library/t-fulano-the-unabomber-and-the-future-of-industrial-society.pdf.
58 Fifth Estate Collective, 'Notes on "Soft Tech"', *Fifth Estate*, no. 312 (1983).
59 Fulano, 'Against the Megamachine', 10.
60 Pierleone Porcu, 'Against Technology', 1988, 1, http://theanarchistlibrary.org/library/pierleone-porcu-against-technology.pdf.

61. Anonymous, 'What Is Green Anarchy?', 8, https://theanarchistlibrary.org/library/anonymous-what-is-green-anarchy.pdf.
62. John Zerzan, *Future Primitive and Other Essays* (New York: Autonomedia, 1994), 59.
63. Anonymous, 'Antitechnology #0', 2009, https://theanarchistlibrary.org/library/anonymous-antitechnology-0.pdf.
64. Anonymous, *Journey Towards the Abyss: Scattered Reflections on the Technoworld* (n.p.: Hourriya, 2018), 10.
65. 325, '#11', 18.
66. John Moore, 'A Primitivist Primer', 2009, 4, https://theanarchistlibrary.org/library/john-moore-a-primitivist-primer.pdf.
67. Anonymous, 'What Is Green Anarchy?', 4.
68. Ibid., 8.
69. Fulano, 'Against the Megamachine', 5.
70. Anonymous, 'What Is Green Anarchy?', 8.
71. Porcu, 'Against Technology', 1.
72. Fulano, 'Against the Megamachine', 3.
73. Anonymous, 'What Is Green Anarchy?'
74. Porcu, 'Against Technology', 2. See also Anonymous, 'Antitechnology #0'; 325, '#12', 2020 (no longer online).
75. Anonymous, 'What Is Green Anarchy?', 7.
76. 325, '#12', 10.
77. Moore, 'A Primitivist Primer', 5.
78. 325, '#11', 23.
79. 325, '#12', 28.
80. Dipartimento delle Informazioni per la Sicurezza, 'Relazione al Parlamento 2020', Relazione Sulla Politica Dell'Informazione per La Sicurezza (Presidenza del Consiglio dei Ministri, 28 February 2022), 86.
81. 325, '#10', 2012, 7 (no longer online).
82. 325, '#12', 14.
83. Ibid., 28.
84. Jason Rodgers, 'The Control of Computerized Television', *Fifth Estate*, no. 394 (2015).
85. 325, '#11', 10.
86. 325, 30. See also 325, '#12', 17–18.
87. 325, '#10', 17–18.
88. 325, '#11', 30.

89 Anonymous, *Journey Towards the Abyss*, 9.
90 Dipartimento delle Informazioni per la Sicurezza, 'Relazione al Parlamento 2020', 86; 325, '#12', 14.
91 EUROPOL, 'European Union: Terrorism Situation and Trend Report' (Luxembourg: Publications Office of the European Union, 2010), 35.
92 325, '#11', 9.
93 325, 9; 325, 43; 325, '#12', 17–18.
94 For a discussion on the anthropocentric nature of Kaczynski's ideology, see Sean Fleming, 'The Unabomber and the Origins of Anti-Tech Radicalism', *Journal of Political Ideologies* 27, no. 2 (2022): 210.
95 325, '#11', 24.
96 Ibid., 10.
97 325, '#10', 9.
98 325, '#11', 25.
99 Ibid., 12.
100 325, '#12', 3.
101 Ibid., 17.
102 325, '#11', 9.
103 Theodore J. Kaczynski, *Industrial Society and Its Future*, 1995, 22, http://editions-hache.com/essais/pdf/kaczynski2.pdf.
104 Anonymous, *Journey Towards the Abyss*, 12.
105 Ibid., 77–9.
106 325, '#12', 49.
107 Theodore J. Kaczynski, *Anti-Tech Revolution: Why and How* (Scottsdale, AZ: Fitch & Madison Publishers, 2016), 174–5.
108 Anonymous, 'Antitechnology #0'.
109 EUROPOL, 'European Union: Terrorism Situation and Trend Report' (Luxembourg: Publications Office of the European Union, 2022), 62.
110 EUROPOL, 'European Union: Terrorism Situation and Trend Report' (Luxembourg: Publications Office of the European Union, 2023), 56–8; Anonymous, '3, 4, 5G... Bum!', 5 March 2021, https://www.rivoluzioneanarchica.it/3-4-5g-bum/; thecollective, 'Sabotage of Wind Measurement Mats in the Grand Est Regions', 14 November 2019, https://anarchistnews.org/content/sabotage-wind-measurement-mats-grand-est-regions.

111 EUROPOL, 'European Union: Terrorism Situation and Trend Report' (Luxembourg: Publications Office of the European Union, 2017), 42.
112 325, 'How to Destroy Cell Phone Towers', 13 February 2020, https://web.archive.org/web/20200925154545/https://325.nostate.net/2020/02/13/pdf-how-to-destroy-cell-phone-towers/.
113 EUROPOL, 'European Union: Terrorism Situation and Trend Report' (Luxembourg: Publications Office of the European Union, 2013), 33.
114 Lubrano, 'Hidden in Plain Sight'.
115 EUROPOL, 'European Union' (2023), 62.
116 Aurelien Breeden and Catherine Porter, 'After French Rail Sabotage, Some See Signs of a Murky "Ultraleft"', *The New York Times*, 7 August 2024; Sans Nom, 'JO: Le sabotage du réseau TGV revendiqué par une "délégation inattendue"', 28 July 2024, https://www.infolibertaire.net/jo-le-sabotage-du-reseau-tgv-revendique-par-une-delegation-inattendue/.
117 325, '#12', 54.
118 Ibid., 54.
119 325, '#11', 4.
120 325, '#12', 54; EUROPOL, 'European Union' (2023), 58; Anonymous, '3, 4, 5G... Bum!'
121 Kristy Campion, Jamie Ferrill, and Kristy Milligan, 'Extremist Exploitation of the Context Created by COVID-19 and the Implications for Australian Security', *Perspectives on Terrorism* 15, no. 6 (2021): 23–40.
122 Dark Nights, 'Italy: Fifth International Meeting 28–29–30 July 2023 Three Days Against Techno-Sciences', 11 July 2023, https://www.anarchistfederation.net/italy-fifth-international-meeting-28-29-30-july-2023-three-days-against-techno-sciences/.
123 Anonymous, 'Theses on Covid-1984', 2022, 19, https://theanarchistlibrary.org/library/anonymous-theses-on-covid-1984.pdf.
124 Lubrano, 'Hidden in Plain Sight'.
125 Dipartimento delle Informazioni per la Sicurezza, 'Relazione al Parlamento 2021', Relazione Sulla Politica Dell'Informazione per La Sicurezza (Presidenza del Consiglio dei Ministri, 28 February 2022), 100, https://www.sicurezzanazionale.gov.it/sisr.nsf/category/relazione-annuale.html.

126 thecollective, 'About an Attack on a Vaccination Centre', 8 August 2021, https://anarchistnews.org/content/about-attack-vaccination-centre; Anonymous, 'Roma – incendiato il portone dell'Istituto Superiore di Sanità', 18 March 2021, https://www.rivoluzioneanarchica.it/roma-incendiato-il-portone-dellistituto-superiore-di-sanita/.
127 325, '#12', 16.
128 Anonymous, *Journey Towards the Abyss*, 87.
129 CCF cited in Loadenthal, *The Politics of Attack*, 80.
130 Of course, exceptions exist and anarchists do sometimes kill people. See Lubrano, 'Hidden in Plain Sight'.
131 FAI, '"Do Not Say That We Are Few" – Statement from the Italian FAI', 2011, https://edmortimer.wordpress.com/2011/09/03/%E2%80%98do-not-say-that-we-are-few%E2%80%99-%E2%80%93-statement-from-the-italian-fai/; Leigh Phillips, 'Anarchists Attack Science: Armed Extremists Are Targeting Nuclear and Nanotechnology Workers.', *Nature* 485, no. 7400 (May 2012): 561.
132 Mauro Lubrano, 'Stop the Machines: How Emerging Technologies Are Fomenting the War on Civilization', *Terrorism and Political Violence* 35, no. 2 (2023): 325.
133 Phillips, 'Anarchists Attack Science'.
134 Mpalothia, 'Genoa, Italy: Attack Against the Italian Institute of Technology', 26 December 2018, https://mpalothia.net/genoa-italy-attack-against-the-italian-institute-of-technology-by-fai-fri-immediate-action-group. The attack in Gières was not claimed by anarchists but it followed a *modus operandi* similar to those of a series of other anarchist attacks in the same area and was reported on many anarchist websites. See 325, 'Gières, France: Fire against a Techno-Scientific Research Laboratory', 23 February 2020, https://web.archive.org/web/20200923203809/https://325.nostate.net/2020/03/06/gieres-france-fire-against-a-techno-scientific-research-laboratory/.
135 Farinelli and Marinone, 'Contemporary Violent Left-Wing and Anarchist Extremism (VLWAE) in the EU', 4.
136 Ariel Koch, 'The Non-Jihadi Foreign Fighters: Western Right-Wing and Left-Wing Extremists in Syria', *Terrorism and Political Violence* 33, no. 4 (19 May 2021): 669–96; Ariel Koch, 'Trends in Anti-Fascist and Anarchist Recruitment and Mobilization', *Journal for Deradicalization* 14 (2018): 1–51; Farinelli and Marinone,

'Contemporary Violent Left-Wing and Anarchist Extremism (VLWAE) in the EU'.
137 Farinelli and Marinone, 'Contemporary Violent Left-Wing and Anarchist Extremism (VLWAE) in the EU', 17.
138 Cospito, 'A Few Words of "Freedom"', 12.
139 Farinelli and Marinone, 'Contemporary Violent Left-Wing and Anarchist Extremism (VLWAE) in the EU', 11.
140 Anonymous, *Journey Towards the Abyss*, 87.

Chapter 3 Nature Fights Back: Eco-Extremism

1 'Chilean Eco Terrorist Group Claims Responsibility for Parcel Bomb against CEO of Largest Copper Corporation', *Merco Press*, 16 January 2017; Ross Brown, 'Chilean Eco Terrorist Group Claims Responsibility for Parcel Bomb Against CEO of Largest Copper Corporation', *The Santiago Times*, 17 January 2017.
2 Kóshmenk, ed., 'Bayaq: Communiqués of the Individualists Tending Towards the Wild from 16th to 30th', 2018, 14 Twenty-First Communiqué, Chile.
3 Ibid., 14–15.
4 'Chilean Eco Terrorist Group Claims Responsibility for Parcel Bomb against CEO of Largest Copper Corporation'.
5 Renato Javier Pinilla Garrido, Flavia María Inés Donoso Parada, and Gabriela Carreño Barros, 'Sexto TOP de Santiago condena a dos penas de 20 años de presidio a autor envío y colocación de artefactos explosivo y homicidios frustrados', No. RUC 1700047073-2 (Sexto Tribunal de Juicio Oral en lo Penal de Santiago, 19 October 2022).
6 Mauro Lubrano, 'Stop the Machines: How Emerging Technologies Are Fomenting the War on Civilization', *Terrorism and Political Violence* 35, no. 2 (2023): 321–37.
7 Rachel Monaghan, 'Not Quite Terrorism: Animal Rights Extremism in the United Kingdom', *Studies in Conflict & Terrorism* 36, no. 11 (November 2013): 935.
8 Bron Taylor, 'The Tributaries of Radical Environmentalism', *Journal for the Study of Radicalism* 2, no. 1 (2008): 46.
9 Teale Phelps Bondaroff, 'Throwing a Wrench into Things: The Strategy of Radical Environmentalism', *Journal of Military and Strategic Studies* 10, no. 4 (2008).

10 Arne Næss, 'The Shallow and the Deep, Long-Range Ecology Movement: A Summary', *Inquiry: An Interdisciplinary Journal of Philosophy* 16, no. 1–4 (1973): 95–100. The concept was then further developed in George Sessions, 'The Deep Ecology Movement: A Review', *Enrivonmental Review* 11, no. 2 (1987): 105–25; George Sessions, ed., *Deep Ecology for the Twenty-First Century* (Boston: Shambhala, 1995); Bill Devall and George Sessions, *Deep Ecology: Living as if Nature Mattered* (Salt Lake City, UT: Smith, 1999).
11 Taylor, 'The Tributaries of Radical Environmentalism', 46.
12 Stefan H. Leader and Peter Probst, 'The Earth Liberation Front and Environmental Terrorism', *Terrorism and Political Violence* 15, no. 4 (October 2003): 40–1.
13 Sean P. Eagan, 'From Spikes to Bombs: The Rise of Eco-Terrorism', *Studies in Conflict & Terrorism* 19, no. 1 (January 1996): 3.
14 Rachel Monaghan, 'Terrorism in the Name of Animal Rights', *Terrorism and Political Violence* 11, no. 4 (December 1999): 160.
15 Keith Mako to Woodhouse, *The Ecocentrists: A History of Radical Environmentalism* (New York: Columbia University Press, 2018), 105.
16 Monaghan, 'Terrorism in the Name of Animal Rights', 160; Monaghan, 'Not Quite Terrorism', 396; Paul Joosse, 'Leaderless Resistance and Ideological Inclusion: The Case of the Earth Liberation Front', *Terrorism and Political Violence* 19, no. 3 (4 July 2007): 354.
17 Paola Andrea Spadaro, 'Climate Change, Environmental Terrorism, Eco-Terrorism and Emerging Threats', *Journal of Strategic Security* 13, no. 4 (December 2020): 63; Leader and Probst, 'The Earth Liberation Front and Environmental Terrorism', 40; Liddick, *Eco-Terrorism*, 3.
18 Bondaroff, 'Throwing a Wrench into Things', 5; Donald D. Liddick, *Eco-Terrorism: Radical Environmental and Animal Liberation Movements* (London: Praeger, 2006), 3.
19 João Raphael da Silva, 'The Eco-Terrorist Wave', *Behavioral Sciences of Terrorism and Political Aggression* 12, no. 3 (2 July 2020): 209.
20 Michael Loadenthal, '"Eco-Terrorism": An Incident-Driven History of Attack (1973–2010)', *Journal for the Study of Radicalism* 11, no. 2 (1 July 2017): 17; Monaghan, 'Not Quite Terrorism', 395.

21 Rachel Monaghan, 'Animal Rights and Violent Protest', *Terrorism and Political Violence* 9, no. 4 (December 1997): 110.
22 Bron Taylor, 'Religion, Violence and Radical Environmentalism: From Earth First! To the Unabomber to the Earth Liberation Front', *Terrorism and Political Violence* 10, no. 4 (December 1998): 14. See also Sean Fleming, 'Searching for Ecoterrorism: The Crucial Case of the Unabomber', *American Political Science Review*, 6 February 2024.
23 Monaghan, 'Terrorism in the Name of Animal Rights', 162.
24 Jennifer Varriale Carson, Gary LaFree, and Laura Dugan, 'Terrorist and Non-Terrorist Criminal Attacks by Radical Environmental and Animal Rights Groups in the United States, 1970–2007', *Terrorism and Political Violence* 24, no. 2 (April 2012): 307.
25 Loadenthal, '"Eco-Terrorism"'. For a discussion on Kaczynski as an anti-technology extremist rather than an eco-radical, see Fleming, 'Searching for Ecoterrorism'.
26 Carson et al., 'Terrorist and Non-Terrorist Criminal Attacks by Radical Environmental and Animal Rights Groups'.
27 Sivan Hirsch-Hoefler and Cas Mudde, '"Ecoterrorism": Terrorist Threat or Political Ploy?', *Studies in Conflict & Terrorism* 37, no. 7 (3 July 2014): 590.
28 Rik Scarce, *Eco-Warriors: Understanding the Radical Environmental Movement*, updated edn (Walnut Creek, CA: Left Coast Press, Inc., 2006), 12.
29 Liddick, *Eco-Terrorism*, 20–1.
30 Fleming, 'Searching for Ecoterrorism', 4.
31 David Thomas Sumner and Lisa M. Weidman, 'Eco-Terrorism or Eco-Tage: An Argument for the Proper Frame', *Interdisciplinary Studies in Literature and Environment* 20, no. 4 (1 December 2013): 857.
32 Hirsch-Hoefler and Mudde, '"Ecoterrorism"', 589; Fleming, 'Searching for Ecoterrorism', 1.
33 Steve Vanderheiden, 'Eco-Terrorism or Justified Resistance? Radical Environmentalism and the "War on Terror"', *Politics & Society* 33, no. 3 (September 2005): 425–47.
34 See, for example, Joshua Newett, 'Prevent: Rise in Climate Activists Referred to Anti-Terror Scheme', BBC News, 23 December 2023.
35 Aric McBay, Lierre Keith, and Derrick Jensen, *Deep Green Resistance: Strategy to Save the Planet* (New York: Seven Stories Press, 2011). See

also Derrick Jensen, *Endgame, Volume 1: The Problem of Civilization* (New York: Seven Stories Press, 2006) and Derrick Jensen, *Endgame Volume 2: Resistance* (New York: Seven Stories Press, 2006).

36 Jensen, *Endgame, Volume 2*, 547.
37 Ben Warner, 'Industrial Technology Is a Death Cult', Deep Green Resistance News Service, 18 July 2020.
38 Deep Green Resistance, 'What Is Deep Green Resistance?', https://deepgreenresistance.org/about-us/.
39 Fleming, 'Searching for Ecoterrorism', 6.
40 The Dark Mountain Project, 'Uncivilisation: The Dark Mountain Manifesto', https://dark-mountain.net/about/manifesto/.
41 'Wilderness Front', https://www.wildernessfront.com/; 'For Wild Nature and Against Techno-Industrial Society', https://www.forwildnature.org/; '*Resistenze al Nanomondo*' (Resistance Against the Nano-World), https://www.resistenzealnanomondo.org/chi-siamo/. The latter organization also publishes a magazine called *L'Urlo della Terra* (Earth's Scream) which features several articles critiquing technology.
42 Anonymous, ed., 'Readings in Eco-Extremism #1', *Atassa* 1 (2016): 20.
43 Fleming, 'The Unabomber', 218.
44 'Introducing Hunter/Gatherer', *Hunter/Gatherer* 1, no. 1 (2016): 1.
45 Anonymous, ed., 'Atltlachinolli: Eco-Extremist Dialogues', *Regresión: Cuadernos Contra el Progreso Technoindustrial* (2016): 5.
46 Jeremy, 'An Update on The Wild Will Project', For Wild Nature, 27 December 2019, https://www.forwildnature.org/john-jacobi/an-update-on-the-wild-will-project/; 'Wild Will Project', Facebook, https://www.facebook.com/wildwillproject.
47 'The Foundations of Wildist Ethics', *Hunter/Gatherer* 1, no. 1 (2016): 6.
48 'Ideology and Revisionism', *Hunter/Gatherer* 1, no. 1 (2016): 29.
49 'The Foundations of Wildist Ethics', 7.
50 Anonymous, ed., 'Atltlachinolli', 21; John Jacobi, 'The Technology Problem', 31 August 2014, http://web.archive.org/web/201410060 85928/http://johnfjacobi.github.io/articles/2014/08/31/the-technology-problem/.
51 Anonymous, ed., 'Atltlachinolli', 32.
52 John Jacobi, *Repent to the Primitive* (N.C.: Wild Will Coalition, 2017), 87–8.

53 Jacobi, 'The Technology Problem'.
54 John Jacobi, 'We Fight for Life', 8 October 2014, https://www.thetedkarchive.com/library/j-j-we-fight-for-life.
55 Ibid.
56 Jacobi, *Repent to the Primitive*, 15.
57 Jacobi, 'The Technology Problem'.
58 Ibid.
59 Anonymous, ed., 'Atltlachinolli', 5.
60 Ibid., 22.
61 'Our Strategy, 2016', *Hunter/Gatherer* 1, no. 1 (2016): 2.
62 Anonymous, ed., 'Atltlachinolli', 23.
63 Anonymous, ed., 'Readings in Eco-Extremism #1', 33.
64 Anonymous, 'Eco-Extremism, Demonology, and the Birth of Criminality', 25, 5 November 2022, https://web.archive.org/web/20221105015737/https://www.thetedkarchive.com/library/anonymous-eco-extremism-demonology-and-the-birth-of-criminality.pdf.
65 Sometimes also translated as Individualists Tending Towards Savagery.
66 Individualists Tending Towards the Wild, 'Communiqués of ITS – 2011–2013', 2013, 38, https://theanarchistlibrary.org/library/individualists-tending-toward-the-wild-communiques.pdf.
67 Michael Loadenthal, 'Feral Fascists and Deep Green Guerrillas: Infrastructural Attack and Accelerationist Terror', *Critical Studies on Terrorism* 15, no. 1 (2 January 2022): 187.
68 Michael Loadenthal, *The Politics of Attack: Communiqués and Insurrectionary Violence*, (Manchester: Manchester University Press, 2018), 85.
69 Kóshmenk, ed., 'Bayaq: 16th to 30th', 2.
70 Wild Reaction, 'The Communiqués of Wild Reaction', 8 September 2014, 5, https://theanarchistlibrary.org/library/wild-reaction-the-communiques-of-wild-reaction.pdf.
71 Alfredo Cospito, 'A Few Words of "Freedom": Interview by CCF – Imprisoned Members Cell with Alfredo Cospito', July 2014, https://theanarchistlibrary.org/library/a-few-words-of-freedom.pdf.
72 Loadenthal, *The Politics of Attack*, 85.
73 Ibid., 84–6; Leigh Phillips, 'Armed Resistance: *Nature* Assesses the Aftermath of a Series of Nanotechnology-Lab Bombings in Mexico

and Asks How the Country Became a Target of Eco-Anarchists', *Nature* 488, no. 413 (2012): 576–9.
74 Lubrano, 'Stop the Machines', 328.
75 Ibid., 328.
76 Kóshmenk, ed., 'Bayaq: Communiqués of the Individualists Tending Towards the Wild from 1st to 15th', 2018, 4 Section I, First Communiqué, January 2016.
77 See, for example, Third, Eleventh, or Twelfth Communiqués in ibid. See also Anonymous, ed., 'Readings in Eco-Extremism #1', 4; Severin Carrell, '"Eco-Terrorist" Who Planted Bomb in Edinburgh Park Jailed', *The Guardian*, 16 February 2022.
78 Individualists Tending Towards the Wild, Interview of ITS with the Mexican press, interview by Por La Mañana – EPM, 1 July 2016, 8, https://anarchistnews.org/zines/ITS_interview.pdf; Anonymous, ed., 'Atltlachinolli', 17.
79 Polizia di Stato, 'Operazione Misantropia: terrorismo, la polizia di stato arresta anarchico', Ministero dell'Interno, 31 March 2022, https://www.poliziadistato.it/articolo/pdf/1526628f2555a513a5619 51123; 'Operazione "Misantropia": la digos di Milano Arresta un anarchico', Polizia di Stato, 31 March 2022, https://www.poliziadis tato.it/articolo/operazione-misantropia-la-digos-di-milano-arresta-un-anarchico; Sarah Martinenghi, '"Volevo colpire parchi e metrò": anarchico confessa e poi ritratta', *La Repubblica*, 9 January 2023.
80 Halputta Hadjo, 'The Calusa: A Savage Kingdom?', *Regresión: Cuadernos Contra el Progreso Technoindustrial* (2016): 6.
81 Anonymous, ed., 'Readings in Eco-Extremism #1', 5.
82 Ibid., 6.
83 Anonymous, ed., 'Readings in Eco-Extremism #2', *Atassa* 2 (2016): 103.
84 Anonymous, ed., 'Readings in Eco-Extremism #1', 7.
85 Edelweiss Pirates, 'Of Indiscriminate Attacks & Wild Reactions: An Anti-Civ Anarchist Engages with ITS and Atassa, Their Defenders and Their False Critics', 2017, https://itsgoingdown.org/of-indiscriminate-attacks-and-wild-reactions-an-anti-civ-anarchist-engages-with-its-and-atassa-their-defenders-and-their-false-critics/.
86 Anonymous, 'Ash and Ruin: Notes on Individual Revolt, Eco-Extremism and Misanthropy', *Subversive Nihilist Periodical* Volume 1 (2016): 16.

87 Anonymous, ed., 'Readings in Eco-Extremism #1', 8.
88 Kóshmenk, ed., 'Bayaq: 1st to 15th', 6 First Communiqué, Sec. VII, January 2016.
89 Anonymous, ed., 'Readings in Eco-Extremism #2', 150.
90 Individualists Tending Towards the Wild, 'Communiqués of ITS', 2013, 6 Communiqué One, 27 April 2011.
91 Individualists Tending Towards the Wild, 24 Communiqué Four, 21 September 2011; Individualists Tending Towards the Wild, 'Interview with Individualists Tending Towards the Wild (ITS)', 2014, 4, https://theanarchistlibrary.org/library/individualists-tending-toward-the-wild-interview-with-individualists-tending-toward-the-wild.pdf.
92 Anonymous, ed., 'Readings in Eco-Extremism #1', 26.
93 Individualists Tending Towards the Wild, 'Communiqués of ITS', 2013, 12 Communiqué Two, 11 May 2011.
94 Lubrano, 'Stop the Machines', 328.
95 Individualists Tending Towards the Wild, '94 Comunicado de ITS', 6 July 2020, Section 2 (no longer online).
96 Ibid., Section 4.
97 Anonymous, ed., 'Readings in Eco-Extremism #1', 8.
98 Individualists Tending Towards the Wild, Interview of ITS with the Mexican press.
99 See John Jacobi's discussion on this in 'Briefly Noted: Letters and Reviews', *Hunter/Gatherer* 1, no. 3 (2016): 47.
100 Individualists Tending Towards the Wild, 'Interviews with ITS' (no longer online). See also Anonymous, 'Regresión Magazine 4', *Regresión: Cuadernos Contra el Progreso Technoindustrial* (2015).
101 Anonymous, ed., 'Readings in Eco-Extremism #1', 5.
102 Anonymous, ed., 'Atltlachinolli', 11; Anonymous, 'Readings in Eco-Extremism #1', 25.
103 Individualists Tending Towards the Wild, 'Communiqués of ITS – 2016–2020', Ninety-Third Communiqué, Section II, 10 May 2020 (no longer online); Wild Reaction, 'Communiqués', 5 First Communiqué, Section IV, 14 August 2014.
104 Anonymous, 'Eco-Extremism, Demonology, and the Birth of Criminality', 25.
105 Anonymous, ed., 'Readings in Eco-Extremism #1', 26.
106 Ibid., 9.

107 Anonymous, ed., 'Readings in Eco-Extremism #2', 149; Anonymous, 'Regresión Magazine 4', 15.
108 Kóshmenk, ed., 'Bayaq: 16th to 30th', 16 Twenty-Second Communiqué, February 2017.
109 Anonymous, ed., 'Readings in Eco-Extremism #1', 9.
110 Hadjo, 'The Calusa: A Savage Kingdom?', 5.
111 Kóshmenk, ed., 'Bayaq: 1st to 15th', 5 First Communiqué, Section IV, January 2016.
112 Chahta-Ima, 'Ishi and the War Against Civilization', *Regresión: Cuadernos Contra el Progreso Technoindustrial* (2016): 3.
113 Anonymous, ed., 'Atltlachinolli', 28.
114 Ibid., 19.
115 Anonymous, 'Regresión Magazine 1', *Regresión: Cuadernos Contra el Progreso Technoindustrial* (2014): 3.
116 Anti-Humanist Editions – Taguatuhu, ed., *Eco-Extremist Reflections* No. 5 (2020): 12–13.
117 Individualists Tending Towards the Wild, 'Interview with Individualists Tending Towards the Wild (ITS)', 2.
118 Anonymous, ed., 'Readings in Eco-Extremism #2', 171.
119 Ibid., 166–70.
120 Anti-Humanist Editions – Taguatuhu, ed., *Eco-Extremist Reflections* No. 1 (2013): 3.
121 Ibid., 4.
122 Individualists Tending Towards the Wild, 'Communiqués of ITS', 2013, 4 Communiqué One, 27 April 2011.
123 Ibid., 49, Note 1, Communiqué Seven, 18 February 2013.
124 Anonymous, ed., 'Readings in Eco-Extremism #2', 141.
125 Anonymous, 'Regresión Magazine 5', *Regresión: Cuadernos Contra el Progreso Technoindustrial* (2016): 6.
126 Anonymous, ed., 'Readings in Eco-Extremism #2', 147.
127 Ibid., 48.
128 Anonymous, 'Eco-Extremism, Demonology, and the Birth of Criminality', 27.
129 Individualists Tending Towards the Wild, 'Communiqués of ITS', 2013, 33 Section VII, Communiqué Four, 21 September 2011.
130 Anonymous, ed., 'Atltlachinolli', 6.
131 Ibid., 32.

132 Kóshmenk, ed., 'Bayaq: 16th to 30th', 16 Twenty-Second Communiqué, February 2017.
133 Ibid., 16 Twenty-Second Communiqué, February 2017.
134 Anonymous, 'A Text Dump on the 325 Collective', 11, https://web.archive.org/web/20230116061947/https://www.thetedkarchive.com/library/a-text-dump-on-the-325-collective.pdf.
135 Kóshmenk, ed., 'Bayaq: 1st to 15th', 16 Seventh Communiqué.
136 Individualists Tending Towards the Wild, 'Communiqués of ITS', 2013, 6.
137 Individualists Tending Towards the Wild, 'Interview with Individualists Tending Towards the Wild (ITS)', 2.
138 Anonymous, ed., 'Readings in Eco-Extremism #2', 106–8.
139 Anonymous, 'Regresión Magazine 3', *Regresión: Cuadernos Contra el Progreso Technoindustrial* (2015): 17.
140 Anonymous, ed., 'Readings in Eco-Extremism #2', 53.
141 Anonymous, ed., 'Atltlachinolli', 29; Anonymous, 'Action and Response', 2015, https://www.thetedkarchive.com/library/anonymous-action-and-response.pdf.
142 Kóshmenk, ed., 'Bayaq: 1st to 15th', 16 Seventh Communiqué.
143 Anonymous, ed., 'Readings in Eco-Extremism #1', 41; Anonymous, 'Mictlanxochitl: The Flower from the Underworld That Grew in Our Time', *Regresión: Cuadernos Contra el Progreso Technoindustrial* (2016): 10; Anonymous, 'A Text Dump on the 325 Collective', 11.
144 Anonymous, 'Mictlanxochitl', 21; Anonymous, 'Regresión Magazine 5', 23; Anonymous, ed., 'Readings in Eco-Extremism #1', 39.
145 Anonymous, ed., 'Readings in Eco-Extremism #1', 146.
146 Anonymous, 'Regresión Magazine 3', 39.
147 Anonymous, ed., 'Atltlachinolli', 29.
148 Los hijos del Mencho, 'Against the World-Builders: Eco-Extremists Respond to Critics', 2018, https://theanarchistlibrary.org/library/los-hijos-del-mencho-against-the-world-builders-eco-extremists-respond-to-critics.pdf.
149 Scott Campbell, 'There's Nothing Anarchist about Eco-Fascism: A Condemnation of ITS', 12 May 2017, https://theanarchistlibrary.org/library/scott-campbell-there-s-nothing-anarchist-about-eco-fascism.pdf.
150 Juliana Fregoso, 'Más violencia en México: reaparecen los grupos eco-terroristas', *Infobae*, 17 June 2017.

151 Nidia Bautista, 'Justice for Lesvy: Indifference and Outrage in Response to Gender Violence in Mexico City', *Nacla*, 31 July 2017.
152 See, for example, Kóshmenk, ed., 'Bayaq: 16th to 30th', 4, 16th Communiqué; Wild Reaction, 'Communiqués', 1410th Communiqué, June 2015.
153 Theodore J. Kaczynski, 'Ted Kaczynski on Individualists Tending Toward Savagery (ITS)', 2017, https://theanarchistlibrary.org/library/ted-kaczynski-ted-kaczynski-on-individualists-tending-toward.pdf.
154 Último Reducto, 'Comments on the Communiques from Individualists Tending Toward the Wild', 2015, https://theanarchistlibrary.org/library/ultimo-reducto-comments-on-the-communiques-from-individualists-tending-toward-the-wild.pdf.
155 Alexander Reid Ross and Emmi Bevensee, 'Confronting the Rise of Eco-Fascism Means Grappling with Complex Systems', CARR Research Insight (London, UK: Centre for the Analysis of the Radical Right, March 2020), 23; Campbell, 'There's Nothing Anarchist about Eco-Fascism'.
156 Individualist Network, Palang Hitam Indonesia, 'Seek and Destroy Eco-Extremism Everywhere: A Joint Statement of Individualist Network and Indonesian Anarchist Black Cross', 24 November 2018, https://tinyurl.com/3nbha54v.
157 Kóshmenk, ed., 'Bayaq: 1st to 15th', 5 Section VI, First Communiqué, January 2016; Kóshmenk, ed., 'Bayaq: 16th to 30th', 20 Twenty-Third Communiqué.
158 Anonymous, ed., 'Readings in Eco-Extremism #2', 111.
159 Individualists Tending Towards the Wild, 'Communiqués of ITS', 2013, 61 Section V, Communiqué Seven, 18 February 2013.
160 Individualists Tending Towards the Wild, '9 Interview', 12 March 2021, https://web.archive.org/web/20211102005303/http://maldicionecoextremista.altervista.org/9-interview/#more-5446. See also Daveed Gartenstein-Ross, Emelie Chace-Donahue, and Thomas Plant, 'The Order of Nine Angles: Its Worldview and Connection to Violent Extremism', research memo (Washington, DC: Foundation for Defense of Democracies, 25 July 2023), 11.
161 Individualists Tending Towards the Wild, 'Communiqué 77', 3 April 2019 (no longer online).
162 Loadenthal, 'Feral Fascists and Deep Green Guerrillas', 188.
163 Anonymous, 'Action and Response', 5.

164 START (National Consortium for the Study of Terrorism and Responses to Terrorism), 'Global Terrorism Database – Individualists Tending Towards Savagery', 2024, https://www.start.umd.edu/gtd/search/Results.aspx?search=Individuals+Tending+Toward+Savagery&sa.x=13&sa.y=13. See also Spadaro, 'Climate Change, Environmental Terrorism, Eco-Terrorism and Emerging Threats', 65.

165 '"Explosive Mix" Caused Blast at Mexico Oil Firm Pemex', BBC News, 3 August 2013.

166 Loadenthal, *The Politics of Attack*, 86.

167 Attacks perpetrated by lone actors tend to be less lethal than those carried out by organizations, with the exception of the United States, where the opposite is true. See Brian J. Phillips, 'Deadlier in the US? On Lone Wolves, Terrorist Groups, and Attack Lethality', *Terrorism and Political Violence* 29, no. 3 (4 May 2017): 533–49.

168 Individualists Tending Towards the Wild, '9 Interview'.

169 Individualists Tending Towards the Wild, 'Communiqué 90', 11 November 2019, 90 (no longer online).

170 Jessica A. York, 'Santa Cruz Judge Rejects Challenges in Atre Case', *Santa Cruz Sentinel*, 7 December 2023; Melia Russell, 'A Cause of Death Has Been Identified in the Case of the 33-Year-Old Tech Founder Who Went to Silicon Valley on Business and Was Found Dead in Her Car a Week Later', *Business Insider*, 7 February 2020.

171 Jorge Poblete, 'La historia del "lobo solitario" acusado de enviar 6 bombas, una de ellas a la casa de Oscar Landerretche', *Ex-Ante*, 20 March 2021.

172 'Villa Urquiza: allanaron a un padre y a su hijo por vínculos con un grupo terrorista internacional especializado en bombas', *Infobae*, 16 March 2022.

173 Individualists Tendings Toward the Wild, 'Communiqué 94', 8 July 2020 (no longer online).

Chapter 4 Anti-Tech to Accelerate: Eco-Fascism

1 The Great Replacement theory was first coined by French writer Renaud Camus in 2010 and argues that there is a secret plot to destroy the ethnic character of Western countries by replacing it through immigration of non-white people and a drop in birth rates among white people. Institute for Strategic Dialogue, '"The

Great Replacement": A Conspiracy Claiming White Europeans Are Under Threat' (London: Institute for Strategic Dialogue, 2022). See also Jacob Davey and Julia Ebner, 'The "Great Replacement": The Violent Consequences of Mainstreamed Extremism' (Institute for Strategic Dialogue, 2019).

2 Patrick Crusius, 'The Inconvenient Truth', 3 August 2019, https://read.expert/documents/the-inconvenient-truth/.

3 Jacob Ware, 'Siege: The Atomwaffen Division and Rising Far-Right Terrorism in the United States', ICCT Policy Brief (The Hague: International Centre for Counter-Terrorism, 2019), 4.

4 UN Counter-Terrorism Committee Executive Directorate, 'Member States Concerned by the Growing and Increasingly Transnational Threat of Extreme Right-Wing Terrorism', CTED Trends Report (United Nations, April 2020), 3.

5 Crusius, 'The Inconvenient Truth'. Tarrant was also mentioned as an inspirational figure by John Earnest, a 19-year-old who entered the Chabad of Poway Synagogue on the last day of Passover in April 2019, killing one and injuring an additional three. John Earnest, 'Manifesto', 2019, https://read.expert/documents/manifesto-3/.

6 Brenton Tarrant, 'The Great Replacement', 15 March 2019, https://read.expert/documents/the-great-replacement/.

7 Kristy Campion, 'Defining Ecofascism: Historical Foundations and Contemporary Interpretations in the Extreme Right', *Terrorism and Political Violence*, 1 November 2021, 2. Original emphasis.

8 For example, Campion (ibid.) and Evangelos D. Protopapadakis ('Environmental Ethics and Linkola's Ecofascism: An Ethics Beyond Humanism', *Frontiers of Philosophy in China* 9, no. 4 (2014): 586–601) consider eco-fascism an ideology. By contrast, Graham Macklin ('The Extreme Right, Climate Change and Terrorism', *Terrorism and Political Violence* 34, no. 5 (4 July 2022): 982) calls it a 'state of mind', whereas Imogen Richards, Callum Jones, and Gearóid Brinn ('Eco-Fascism Online: Conceptualizing Far-Right Actors' Response to Climate Change on Stormfront', *Studies in Conflict & Terrorism*, 18 December 2022: 4) call it a belief system or trope.

9 Balša Lubarda, 'Beyond Ecofascism? Far-Right Ecologism (FRE) as a Framework for Future Inquiries', *Environmental Values* 29, no. 6 (December 2020): 716.

10 Chetan Bhatt, 'White Extinction: Metaphysical Elements of Contemporary Western Fascism', *Theory, Culture & Society* 38, no. 1 (January 2021): 27–52.
11 See, for example, Payton Gendron, 'Payton Gendron Manifesto', 14 May 2022, https://read.expert/documents/payton-gendron-manifesto/.
12 See, for example, Ware, 'Siege', 5; Amarnath Amarasingam and Marc-André Argentino, 'The QAnon Conspiracy Theory: A Security Threat in the Making?', *CTC Sentinel* 13, no. 7 (2020): 37–44; Institute for Strategic Dialogue, '"The Great Replacement"'; Davey and Ebner, 'The "Great Replacement"'.
13 Liam Farrell, 'Conspiracy Theories Fueled More Terror Attacks in 2020', UMD Report (College Park, MD: National Consortium for the Study of Terrorism and Responses to Terrorism, 7 July 2020).
14 Campion, 'Defining Ecofascism', 2.
15 Sam Moore and Alex Roberts, *The Rise of Ecofascism: Climate Change and the Far Right* (Cambridge: Polity, 2022), 97.
16 Campion, 'Defining Ecofascism', 10.
17 Ibid., 6.
18 Moore and Roberts, *The Rise of Ecofascism*, 26.
19 Protopapadakis, 'Environmental Ethics and Linkola's Ecofascism', 588.
20 Sadi Shanaah, Immo Fritsche, and Mathias Osmundsen, 'Support for Pro-Climate and Ecofascist Extremism: Correlates and Intersections', *Democracy and Security* 20, no. 1 (2 January 2024): 50.
21 David Lawrence, 'The Regrowth of Eco-Fascism', Hope Not Hate, 2 October 2019.
22 Janet Biehl and Peter Staudenmaier, *Ecofascism: Lessons from the German Experience* (Edinburgh: AK Press, 1995).
23 Lawrence, 'The Regrowth of Eco-Fascism'.
24 Campion, 'Defining Ecofascism', 7.
25 Marco Armiero, 'Introduction: Fascism and Nature', *Modern Italy* 19, no. 3 (August 2014): 241.
26 Campion, 'Defining Ecofascism', 8.
27 Jeffrey M. Bale, *The Darkest Sides of Politics, I: Post-War Fascism, Covert Operations, and Terrorism* (New York: Routledge, 2018), 61–211.

28 Brian Hughes, Dave Jones, and Amarnath Amarasingam, 'Ecofascism: An Examination of the Far-Right/Ecology Nexus in the Online Space', *Terrorism and Political Violence* 34, no. 5 (4 July 2022): 1006.
29 Campion, 'Defining Ecofascism', 8.
30 Savitri Devi, *Impeachment of Man* (Calcutta: Noontide Press, 1959), 145. Emphasis in original.
31 Macklin, 'The Extreme Right, Climate Change and Terrorism'.
32 Protopapadakis, 'Environmental Ethics and Linkola's Ecofascism', 592.
33 Moore and Roberts, *The Rise of Ecofascism*, 40.
34 Pentti Linkola, *Can Life Prevail?*, trans. Eetu Rautio (Wewelsburg Archives, 2009), 98, https://read.expert/documents/can-life-prevail/.
35 Protopapadakis, 'Environmental Ethics and Linkola's Ecofascism', 592.
36 Linkola, *Can Life Prevail?*, 99.
37 Ibid., 99.
38 Pentti Linkola, 'Pentti Linkola: Ideas', https://www.penttilinkola.com/pentti_linkola/ecofascism/.
39 Joshua Farrell-Molloy and Graham Macklin, 'Ted Kaczynski, Anti-Technology Radicalism and Eco-Fascism', ICCT Perspectives (Leiden: International Centre for Counter-Terrorism, 15 June 2022).
40 Theodore J. Kaczynski, 'Ecofascism: An Aberrant Branch of Leftism', 29 September 2020, https://theanarchistlibrary.org/library/ted-kaczynski-ecofascism-an-aberrant-branch-of-leftism.pdf.
41 Farrell-Molloy and Macklin, 'Ted Kaczynski'; Michael Loadenthal, 'Feral Fascists and Deep Green Guerrillas: Infrastructural Attack and Accelerationist Terror', *Critical Studies on Terrorism* 15, no. 1 (2 January 2022): 169–208.
42 Campion, 'Defining Ecofascism', 8; Hughes et al., 'Ecofascism', 1007; Martin Heidegger, *The Question Concerning Technology*, trans. William Lovitt (New York: Garland Publishing, 1977).
43 Bruce Hoffman, 'Right-Wing Terrorism in Europe', A RAND Note (Santa Monica, CA: RAND Corporation, March 1982).
44 Ware, 'Siege'.
45 William Luther Pierce, *The Turner Diaries*, 1978, https://read.expert/documents/the-turner-diaries/; J.M. Berger, 'The Turner Legacy: The Storied Origins and Enduring Impact of White Nationalism's

Deadly Bible' (International Centre for Counter-Terrorism Research Paper, September 2016).

46 Peter H. Merkl and Leonard Weinberg, eds, *The Revival of Right-Wing Extremism in the Nineties* (London: Frank Cass, 1997); Ware, 'Siege'.

47 Lou Michel and Dan Herbeck, *American Terrorist: Timothy McVeigh and the Tragedy at Oklahoma City* (New York: Avon Books, 2002).

48 Graham Macklin, 'The Evolution of Extreme-Right Terrorism and Efforts to Counter It in the United Kingdom', *CTC Sentinel* 12, no. 1 (2019): 15.

49 Stephane J. Baele, Lewys Brace, and Travis G. Coan, 'Uncovering the Far-Right Online Ecosystem: An Analytical Framework and Research Agenda', *Studies in Conflict & Terrorism* 46, no. 9 (2 September 2023): 1599–623.

50 Stephane J. Baele, Lewys Brace, and Travis G. Coan, 'The "Tarrant Effect": What Impact Did Far-Right Attacks Have on the 8chan Forum?', *Behavioral Sciences of Terrorism and Political Aggression* 15, no. 1 (2 January 2023): 3–4.

51 Hughes et al., 'Ecofascism', 1002.

52 Ayushman Kaul, 'Terrorgram: A Community Built on Hate', *Medium*, 20 April 2020.

53 'Telegram Blocks "Dozens" of Hardcore Hate Channels Threatening Violence', *Tech Crunch*, 13 January 2021.

54 Matthew Kriner et al., 'Behind the Skull Mask: An Overview of Militant Accelerationism' (Global Network on Extremism & Technology, March 2024).

55 'Terrorgram Added to List of Proscribed Terrorist Organisations', Gov.UK, 22 April 2024.

56 Louis Beam, 'Leaderless Resistance', *The Seditionist* 12 (1992).

57 Macklin, 'The Extreme Right, Climate Change and Terrorism', 988. See also James Mason, *Siege* (IronMarch Publications, 2018), https://read.expert/documents/siege-fourth-edition/.

58 Bruce Hoffman and Jacob Ware, *God, Guns, and Sedition: Far-Right Terrorism in America* (New York: Columbia University Press, 2024), 3.

59 Rapewaffen Division (2019), cited in Ariel Koch, Karine Nahon, and Assaf Moghadam, 'White Jihad: How White Supremacists Adopt Jihadi Narratives, Aesthetics, and Tactics', *Terrorism and Political Violence* 36, no. 7 (2024): 931.

60 Benjamin Lee, 'Siege Culture and Accelerationism in the UK' (Lancaster: Centre for Research and Evidence on Security Threats, 2021); Benjamin Lee, 'What Is Siege Culture?', *CREST Security Review* (Lancaster: Centre for Research and Evidence on Security Threats, 2022).
61 Kriner et al., 'Behind the Skull Mask', 28.
62 Loadenthal, 'Feral Fascists and Deep Green Guerrillas', 186.
63 Matthew Kriner and Bjørn Ihler, 'Analysing Terrorgram Publications: A New Digital Zine' (Global Network on Extremism & Technology, 12 September 2022) .
64 H.E. Upchurch, 'The Iron March Forum and the Evolution of the "Skull Mask" Neo-Fascist Network', *CTC Sentinel* 14, no. 10 (2021): 33.
65 Ware, 'Siege'; Press Office, 'Former Atomwaffen Division Leader Sentenced for Swatting Conspiracy' (US Attorney's Office, Eastern District of Virginia, 4 May 2021).
66 John Hendry and Anthony F. Lemieux, 'The Visual and Rhetorical Styles of Atomwaffen Division and Their Implications', *Dynamics of Asymmetric Conflict* 14, no. 2 (4 May 2021): 138.
67 Alex Newhouse, 'The Threat Is the Network: The Multi-Node Structure of Neo-Fascist Accelerationism', *CTC Sentinel* 14, no. 5 (2021): 22.
68 The Green Brigade (2019) cited in Michael Loadenthal, Samantha Hausseman, and Matthew Thierry, 'Accelerating Hate: Atomwaffen Division, Contemporary Digital Fascism, and Insurrectionary Accelerationism', in *Cyber Hate: Examining the Functions and Impact of White Supremacy in Cyberspace*, ed. Robin Maria Valeri and Kevin Borgeson (Lanham, MD: Lexington Books/Rowman & Littlefield, 2020), 105.
69 Upchurch, 'The Iron March Forum', 34–5.
70 Simon Lindberg, 'National Socialism and the Laws of Nature', Nordic Resistance Movement, 13 February 2020.
71 Payton Gendron, 'Payton Gendron April 29 and before Discord Transcript', 14 May 2022, 213, https://read.expert/documents/payton-gendron-april-29-and-before-discord-transcript/.
72 Ardian Shajkovci, 'Eco-Fascist "Pine Tree Party" Growing as a Violent Extremism Threat', *Homeland Security Today*, 27 September 2020;

Brian Hughes, '"Pine Tree" Twitter and the Shifting Ideological Foundations of Eco-Extremism', *Interventionen: Zeitschrift für Verantwortungspädagogik* 14 (2019): 20.
73 Mike Ma, *Harassment Architecture*, 74, https://read.expert/documents/a-scattered-look-at-harassment-architecture/.
74 Ibid., 85.
75 Ibid., 22.
76 Ibid., 45.
77 Ibid., 28.
78 Saddiq Basha, '"Death to the Grid": Ideological Narratives and Online Community Dynamics in Encouraging Far-Right Extremist Attacks on Critical Infrastructure', *Counter Terrorist Trends and Analyses* 15, no. 4 (2024): 19.
79 Campion, 'Defining Ecofascism', 7.
80 Tarrant, 'The Great Replacement', 36.
81 Bhatt, 'White Extinction', 38.
82 Farrell-Molloy and Macklin, 'Ted Kaczynski'.
83 Kiernan Christ, 'Why Right-Wing Extremists Love the Unabomber', *Lawfare*, 17 October 2021.
84 Zachary Kamel, Mack Lamoureux, and Ben Makuch, '"Eco-Fascist" Arm of Neo-Nazi Terror Group, the Base, Linked to Swedish Arson', *Vice*, 29 January 2020.
85 Terrorgram, 'Do It for the "Gram"', 201, https://read.expert/documents/do-it-for-the-gram/.
86 Ibid., 202.
87 Ibid., 201.
88 Kaczynski, 'Ecofascism'.
89 Farrell-Molloy and Macklin, 'Ted Kaczynski'.
90 Basha, '"Death to the Grid"', 18.
91 Kriner and Ihler, 'Analysing Terrorgram Publications'.
92 Terrorgram, 'The Hard Reset', 14 July 2022, 8, https://read.expert/documents/the-hard-reset/.
93 Terrorgram, 'Militant Accelerationism: A Collective Handbook', 2021, 44, https://read.expert/documents/militant-accelerationism-a-collective-handbook/.
94 Alejandro Beutel and Daryl Johnson, 'Domestic Violent Extremist Targeting of the US Electrical Transmission Grid', New Lines Institute, 16 November 2023.

95 Ilana Krill and Bennett Clifford, 'Mayhem, Murder, and Misdirection: Violent Extremist Attack Plots Against Critical Infrastructure in the United States, 2016–2022', Reports, Projects, and Research (Omaha, NE: National Counterterrorism Innovation, Technology, and Education Center, September 2022), 2.
96 See, respectively, Colin P. Clarke et al., 'The Targeting of Infrastructure by America's Violent Far-Right', *CTC Sentinel* 16, no. 5 (2023): 28; Basha, '"Death to the Grid"', 18.
97 Michael Loadenthal, 'Infrastructure, Sabotage, and Accelerationism' (Global Network on Extremism & Technology, 15 February 2021).
98 EUROPOL, 'European Union: Terrorism Situation and Trend Report' (Luxembourg: Publications Office of the European Union, 2023), 22.
99 Farrell, 'Conspiracy Theories Fueled More Terror Attacks in 2020'.
100 EUROPOL, 'European Union' (2023), 22.
101 Alexander Meleagrou-Hitchens and Blyth Crawford, '5G and the Far Right: How Extremists Capitalise on Coronavirus Conspiracies' (Global Network on Extremism & Technology, 21 April 2020).
102 Laurens Cerulus, 'EU Countries Sound Alarm about Growing Anti-5G Movement', *Politico*, 19 October 2020.
103 See, respectively, Terrorgram, 'Do It for the "Gram"', 239 and Michael Loadenthal, 'Anti-5G, Infrastructure Sabotage, and COVID-19' (Global Network on Extremism & Technology, 18 January 2021).
104 Clarke et al., 'The Targeting of Infrastructure by America's Violent Far-Right', 29.
105 See, for example, Terrorgram, 'The Hard Reset', 94–6.
106 Chloe Laversuch, 'Covid: Anti-Vaccine Conspiracy Theorists Guilty of 5G Mast Plot', BBC News, 1 June 2023.

Chapter 5 The Fight to End Civilization

1 Jo Guldi and David Armitage, *The History Manifesto* (Cambridge: Cambridge University Press, 2014), 12. On the importance of a historical analysis, see also Richard English, 'History and the Study of Terrorism', in *The Cambridge History of Terrorism*, ed. Richard English (Cambridge: Cambridge University Press, 2021), 3–28.

2 Manuel R. Torres-Soriano and Mario Toboso-Buezo, 'Five Terrorist Dystopias', *The International Journal of Intelligence, Security, and Public Affairs* 21, no. 1 (2 January 2019): 62.

3 The imperfection of these labels did not only stem from the fact that they were reductive but also from their misuse and abuse. Moreover, recent works argue that some of these labels reflect a colonial mindset, see, for example, Rabea M. Khan, 'The Coloniality of the Religious Terrorism Thesis', *Review of International Studies*, 25 October 2023, 1–20.

4 'Threats to the Homeland' (Washington, DC: U.S. Government Publishing Office, 24 September 2020).

5 Daveed Gartenstein-Ross et al., 'Composite Violent Extremism: Conceptualizing Attackers Who Increasingly Challenge Traditional Categories of Terrorism', *Studies in Conflict & Terrorism*, 29 March 2023, 1–27. Additional concepts and labels that have emerged recently include 'mixed, unstable, unclear' ideologies, 'fused extremism', 'idiosyncratic terrorism', or 'ideology à la carte'. See Ariel Koch, 'The ONA Network and the Transnationalization of Neo-Nazi-Satanism', *Studies in Conflict & Terrorism* 47, no. 10 (2024): 1172–99; Paige Pascarelli, 'Ideology à la Carte: Why Lone Actor Terrorists Choose and Fuse Ideologies', *Lawfare*, 2 October 2016; Jesse J. Norris, 'Idiosyncratic Terrorism', *Perspectives on Terrorism* 14, no. 3 (2024): 2–18; Lewys Brace, Stephane J. Baele, and Debbie Ging, 'Where Do 'Mixed, Unclear, and Unstable' Ideologies Come from? A Data-Driven Answer Centred on the Incelosphere', *Journal of Policing, Intelligence and Counter Terrorism* 19, no. 2 (2024): 103–24.

6 Mario Diani, 'The Concept of Social Movement', *The Sociological Review* 40, no. 1 (February 1992): 12. See also Donatella Della Porta and Mario Diani, *Social Movements: An Introduction* (Chichester: Wiley-Blackwell, 1996), 16.

7 Mario Diani and Ivano Bison, 'Organizations, Coalitions, and Movements', *Theory and Society* 33, no. 3/4 (June 2004): 284.

8 Instinto Salvaje, 'Regarding the Death of Kevin Garrido – Clarifications and Positioning', https://www.thetedkarchive.com/library/regarding-the-death-of-kevin-garrido-clarifications-and-positioning.pdf; Various, 'A Text Dump on Kevin Garrido', https://www.thetedkarchive.com/library/a-text-dump-on-kevin-garrido

.pdf; Sarah Martinenghi, 'Progettava attentati, condannato per terrorismo l'anarchico misantropo Federico Buono', *La Repubblica*, 11 May 2023; Polizia di Stato, 'Operazione Misantropia: terrorismo, la polizia di stato arresta anarchico' (Ministero dell'Interno, 31 March 2022).
9 Robert Eatwell, 'On Defining the "Fascist Minimum"': The Centrality of Ideology', *Journal of Political Ideologies* 1, no. 3 (1996): 303–19.
10 Yadvinder Malhi, 'The Concept of the Anthropocene', *Annual Review of Environment and Resources* 42, no. 1 (17 October 2017): 78.
11 Alternative possible start dates include the Columbian Exchange: a period of intense flow and movement of peoples, technologies as well as flora and fauna between Europe, Africa, and the Americas during the fifteenth and sixteenth century. The period's claim as the start of the Anthropocene comes from what geologists have called the 'Orbis spike' (1610), a human-made global drop in carbon emissions caused by the death of millions of Indigeneous people during the European conquest of the 'New World'. The 'Great Acceleration' is also often mentioned as a possible start date. This term refers to the post-World War II era with its spike in global carbon emissions and the beginning of the nuclear era. See Nicolás Juárez, 'The World Is Burning: Racialized Regimes of Eco-Terror and the Anthropocene as Eurocene', in *The Anthropocene: Approaches and Contexts for Literature and the Humanities*, ed. Seth Reno (New York: Routledge, 2022), 64–75; Will Steffen, 'Introducing the Anthropocene: The Human Epoch', *Ambio* 50, no. 10 (October 2021): 1784–7. Others, by contrast, argue that the seeds of the Anthropocene were planted during the Agricultural Revolution some eight thousand years ago. See John Gowdy and Lisi Krall, 'The Ultrasocial Origin of the Anthropocene', *Ecological Economics* 95 (November 2013): 137–47.
12 For a discussion on how these dynamics characterize the Anthropocene, see Gowdy and Krall, 'The Ultrasocial Origin of the Anthropocene'.
13 Pentti Linkola, 'Pentti Linkola: Ideas', https://www.penttilinkola.com/pentti_linkola/ecofascism/.
14 Jeffrey M. Bale, *The Darkest Sides of Politics, I: Post-War Fascism, Covert Operations, and Terrorism.* New York: Routledge, 2018),

50; Jan-Willem Van Prooijen and Karen M. Douglas, 'Conspiracy Theories as Part of History: The Role of Societal Crisis Situations', *Memory Studies* 10, no. 3 (July 2017): 323–33.

15 Gretchen Gano, 'The Soft Megamachine: Lewis Mumford's Metaphor of Technological Society and Implications for (Participatory) Technology Assessment' (Doctoral Thesis, Tempe, AZ, Arizona State University, 2014), 197.

16 See, for example, Michael Klenk, 'How Do Technological Artefacts Embody Moral Values?', *Philosophy & Technology* 34, no. 3 (September 2021): 525–44; Philip Brey, 'The Technological Construction of Social Power', *Social Epistemology* 22, no. 1 (January 2008): 71–95; Langdon Winner, 'Do Artifacts Have Politics?', *Daedalus* 109, no. 1 (1980): 121–36.

17 Daniel Akst, 'Ludd's Choosy Children', *MIT Technology Review*, 1 January 1999, 83.

18 Such a perspective has also been discussed among scholars. See, for example, Timothy W. Luke, 'Tracing Race, Ethnicity, and Civilization in the Anthropocene', *Environment and Planning D: Society and Space* 38, no. 1 (February 2020): 129–46.

19 For the trend of religious responses to the Anthropocene, see Arianne Françoise Conty, 'Religion in the Age of the Anthropocene', *Environmental Values* 30, no. 2 (April 2021): 215–34.

20 Richard Black et al., 'The Effect of Environmental Change on Human Migration', *Global Environmental Change* 21 (December 2011): S3–11; Kathleen Neumann et al., 'Environmental Drivers of Human Migration in Drylands – A Spatial Picture', *Applied Geography* 56 (January 2015): 116–26; Elizabeth Lunstrum and Pablo S. Bose, 'Environmental Displacement in the Anthropocene', *Annals of the American Association of Geographers* 112, no. 3 (3 April 2022): 644–53.

21 John R. Hall, 'Apocalyptic and Millenarian Movements', in *The Wiley-Blackwell Encyclopedia of Social and Political Movements*, ed. David A. Snow et al. (Oxford: Wiley, 2013), 1–6.

22 Norman Cohn, *The Pursuit of the Millennium: Revolutionary Millenarians and Mystical Anarchists of the Middle Ages* (London: Pimlico, 2004), 13.

23 James F. Rinehart, *Apocalyptic Faith and Political Violence* (New York: Palgrave Macmillan US, 2006), 143–61.

24 Jeffrey M. Bale, *The Darkest Sides of Politics, II: State Terrorism, 'Weapons of Mass Destruction', Religious Extremism, and Organized Crime* (New York: Routledge, 2018), 108–53.
25 John Walliss, 'Understanding Contemporary Millenarian Violence', *Religion Compass* 1, no. 4 (July 2007): 498–99.
26 Marshall Applewhite, 'Last Chance to Evacuate Earth Before It's Recycled – Edited Transcript of Videotape', 29 September 1996, https://www.heavensgate.com/misc/vt092996.htm.
27 Daniel A. Metraux, 'Religious Terrorism in Japan: The Fatal Appeal of Aum Shinrikyo', *Asian Survey* 35, no. 2 (1995): 1153.
28 Hall, 'Apocalyptic and Millenarian Movements'; Richard Allen Landes, *Heaven on Earth: The Varieties of the Millennial Experience* (New York: Oxford University Press, 2011).
29 The term 'Mechanocene' appeared in a recently published book. See Eddie Knight, *Nix: Records of the Mechanocene, Volume One* (independently published, 2023).
30 Anonymous, 'Readings in Eco-Extremism #2', *Atassa* 2 (2016): 147.
31 For the wider white supremacist and neo-Nazi milieu, see Michael Barkun, 'Racist Apocalypse: Millennialism on the Far Right', *American Studies* 31, no. 2 (1990): 121–40.
32 Bale, *The Darkest Sides of Politics, II*, 115.
33 Mauro Lubrano, 'Choosing What (Not) to Do Next: A Preliminary Theoretical Framework on Strategic Innovation in Terrorist Organizations', *Dynamics of Asymmetric Conflict* 17, no. 1 (2 January 2024): 5.
34 Michael Freeman, 'A Theory of Terrorist Leadership (and Its Consequences for Leadership Targeting)', *Terrorism and Political Violence* 26, no. 4 (September 2014): 666–87.
35 Paul Joosse, 'Leaderless Resistance and the Loneliness of Lone Wolves: Exploring the Rhetorical Dynamics of Lone Actor Violence', *Terrorism and Political Violence* 29, no. 1 (2 January 2017): 52.
36 Brian C.H. Fong, 'Leaderless Movements? Rethinking Leaders, Spontaneity, and Organisation-Ness', *Political Science* 75, no. 2 (4 May 2023): 105–21; Thomas Decreus, Matthias Lievens, and Antoon Braeckman, 'Building Collective Identities: How New Social Movements Try to Overcome Post-Politics', *Parallax* 20, no. 2 (3 April 2014): 136–48; Neil Sutherland, Christopher Land, and Steffen Böhm, 'Anti-Leaders(hip) in Social Movement Organizations:

The Case of Autonomous Grassroots Groups', *Organization* 21, no. 6 (November 2014): 759–81.

37 Jean-Marc Flükiger, 'The Radical Animal Liberation Movement: Some Reflections on Its Future', *Journal for the Study of Radicalism* 2, no. 2 (2008): 112–13; Kristy Campion, '"Unstructured Terrorism"? Assessing Left Wing Extremism in Australia', *Critical Studies on Terrorism* 13, no. 4 (1 October 2020): 545–67; Mauro Lubrano, 'Lone Leaders of Leaderless Resistors: A Theory of Informal Leadership in Contemporary Terrorism and Political Violence', *Studies in Conflict & Terrorism*, 29 June 2023, 1–24; Mauro Lubrano, 'Hidden in Plain Sight: Insurrectionary Anarchism in the Anti-Government Extremism Landscape', *Perspectives on Terrorism* 18, no. 1 (2024): 37–61.

38 Victor Asal and R. Karl Rethemeyer, 'The Nature of the Beast: Organizational Structures and the Lethality of Terrorist Attacks', *The Journal of Politics* 70, no. 2 (April 2008): 437–49.

39 Brian J. Phillips, 'Deadlier in the US? On Lone Wolves, Terrorist Groups, and Attack Lethality', *Terrorism and Political Violence* 29, no. 3 (4 May 2017): 533–49. See also Asal and Rethemeyer, 'The Nature of the Beast'.

40 On the notion of online communities, see Inger Storm Sandboe and Milan Obaidi, 'Imagined Extremist Communities: The Paradox of the Community-Driven Lone-Actor Terrorist', *Perspectives on Terrorism* 17, no. 4 (2024): 19–41.

41 Lubrano, 'Lone Leaders of Leaderless Resistors', 2.

42 Ibid., 15. See also Alfredo M. Bonanno, *Armed Joy* (*La gioia armata*), trans. Jean Weir (London: Elephant Editions, 1998), http://the anarchistlibrary.org/library/alfredo-m-bonanno-armed-joy.pdf.

43 Louis Beam, 'Leaderless Resistance', *The Seditionist* 12 (1992); James Mason, *Siege* (IronMarch Publications, 2018), https://read.ex pert/documents/siege-fourth-edition/.

44 Chaz Bufe, *A Future Worth Living: Thoughts on Getting There* (Tucson, AZ: Sharp Press, 1988). Cited in Simon Western, 'Autonomist Leadership in Leaderless Movements: Anarchists Leading the Way', *Ephemera: Theory & Politics in Organization* 14, no. 4 (2014): 679.

45 Hai Liang and Francis L.F. Lee, 'Opinion Leadership in a Leaderless Movement: Discussion of the Anti-Extradition Bill Movement in the "LIHKG" Web Forum', *Social Movement Studies*, 16 October

2021, 1–19; Western, 'Autonomist Leadership'; Phillip W. Gray, 'Leaderless Resistance, Networked Organization, and Ideological Hegemony', *Terrorism and Political Violence* 25, no. 5 (November 2013): 655–71; Lubrano, 'Lone Leaders of Leaderless Resistors'.

46 Fifth Estate Collective, 'Happy Birthday to the Unabomber?', 2016, https://fifthestate.anarchistlibraries.net/library/396-summer-2016-happy-birthday-to-the-unabomber.pdf. See also Sean Fleming, 'Searching for Ecoterrorism: The Crucial Case of the Unabomber', *American Political Science Review*, 6 February 2024, 9.

47 Kóshmenk, ed., 'Bayaq: Communiqués of the Individualists Tending Towards the Wild from 1st to 15th', 2018, 5 Section VI, First Communiqué, January 2016.

48 Luddite Resistance, 'Tribal Resistance: A Potential Strategy for the Anti-Tech Movement', n.d., 4, https://read.expert/documents/tribal-resistance-a-potential-strategy-for-the-anti-tech-movement/; Luddite Resistance, 'Generation 0: A Comment on Anti-Tech Revolution: Why and How by Ted Kackynski', 16 March 2021, 26–32, https://read.expert/documents/generation-0-a-comment-on-anti-tech-revolution-why-and-how-by-ted-kackynski/.

49 Luddite Resistance, 'Tribal Resistance', 4.

50 Ibid., 4, see also 9–11. See also Luddite Resistance, 'Generation 0', 6.

51 Luddite Resistance, 'Tribal Resistance', 9.

52 For a discussion of 'informed speculation', see Zachary Kallenborn and Philipp C. Bleek, 'Avatars of the Earth: Radical Environmentalism and Chemical, Biological, Radiological, and Nuclear (CBRN) Weapons', *Studies in Conflict & Terrorism* 43, no. 5 (3 May 2020): 355.

53 Kate Withing and HyoJin Park, 'This Is Why "Polycrisis" Is a Useful Way of Looking at the World Right Now', World Economic Forum, 7 March 2023.

54 Donna M. Mertens, 'Mixed Methods and Wicked Problems', *Journal of Mixed Methods Research* 9, no. 1 (January 2015): 3–6.

55 Kelly Levin et al., 'Overcoming the Tragedy of Super Wicked Problems: Constraining Our Future Selves to Ameliorate Global Climate Change', *Policy Sciences* 45, no. 2 (June 2012): 123–52.

Conclusion

1 Richard English, *Terrorism: How to Respond* (Oxford: Oxford University Press, 2009), 120.
2 For a discussion on the depiction of terrorism as an existential threat, see Jessica Wolfendale, 'The Narrative of Terrorism as an Existential Threat', in *Routledge Handbook of Critical Terrorism Studies*, ed. Richard Jackson (New York: Routledge, 2016), 114–23.
3 The inspiration here is, again, English, *Terrorism: How to Respond*.
4 See Anastasia Siapka, 'Rage Against the Machine: From Luddism to Anti-AI Resistance', KU Leuven, 28 March 2023, for a discussion on how technology keeps affecting working conditions, thereby keeping alive the Luddite ethos of dissent. And see also Jathan Sadowski, 'I'm a Luddite. You Should Be One Too', The Conversation, 9 August 2021, on the importance of being a Luddite today.
5 Digital Regulation Platform, 'Transformative Technologies (AI) Challenges and Principles of Regulation', 8 May 2024, https://digital regulation.org/3004297-2/.
6 Rushan Ziatdinov, Madhu Sudhan Atteraya, and Rifkat Nabiyev, 'The Fifth Industrial Revolution as a Transformative Step Towards Society 5.0', *Societies* 14, no. 2 (2 February 2024): 2.
7 E.P. Thompson, *The Making of the English Working Class*, reprint (Harmondsworth: Penguin Books, 1991), 349. See also Clark Nardinelli, 'Child Labor and the Factory Acts', *The Journal of Economic History* 40, no. 4 (December 1980): 739–55.
8 Steven Greenhouse, '"Constantly Monitored": The Pushback against AI Surveillance at Work', *The Guardian*, 7 January 2024; Wendi S. Lazar and Cody York, 'Watched While Working: Use of Monitoring and AI in the Workplace Increases', Reuters, 25 April 2024.
9 On technology and 'mass alienation', see Karam Adibifar, 'Technology and Alienation in Modern-Day Societies', *International Journal of Social Science Studies* 4, no. 9 (9 August 2016): 61–8.
10 For two different positions regarding techno-optimism, see Marc Andreessen, 'The Techno-Optimist Manifesto', Andreessen Horowitz, 16 October 2023; Tristan Bove, 'Techno-Optimism: Why Money and Technology Won't Save Us', Earth.org, 8 June 2021.

11 Daniele Rotolo, Diana Hicks, and Ben R. Martin, 'What Is an Emerging Technology?', *Research Policy* 44, no. 10 (December 2015): 1827–43.
12 Gregory N. Mandel, 'Regulating Emerging Technologies', *Law, Innovation & Technology* 1, no. 75 (2009): 1–14; Digital Regulation Platform, 'Transformative Technologies (AI) Challenges and Principles of Regulation'; Mike Turley, William D. Eggers, and Pankaj Kamleshkumar Kishnani, 'The Future of Regulation: Principles for Regulating Emerging Technologies', Deloitte Insights, 19 June 2018; John P. Holdren, Cass R. Sunstein, and Islam A. Siddiqui, 'Principles for Regulation and Oversight of Emerging Technologies', 11 March 2011, https://obamawhitehouse.archives.gov/sites/default/files/omb/inforeg/for-agencies/Principles-for-Regulation-and-Oversight-of-Emerging-Technologies-new.pdf.
13 Andy Pasztor and Robert Wall, 'Drone Regulators Struggle to Keep Up With the Rapidly Growing Technology', *The Wall Street Journal*, 10 July 2016.
14 Turley et al., 'The Future of Regulation'; Holdren et al., 'Principles for Regulation and Oversight of Emerging Technologies'; Digital Regulation Platform, 'Transformative Technologies (AI) Challenges and Principles of Regulation'.
15 For a discussion on a top-down struggle to regulate AI, see Dan McQuillan, *Resisting AI: An Anti-Fascist Approach to Artificial Intelligence* (Bristol: Bristol University Press, 2022).
16 For the importance of the Luddite lessons to counter contemporary forms of exploitation, see Brian Merchant, *Blood in the Machine: The Origins of the Rebellion Against Big Tech* (New York: Little, Brown and Company, 2023).
17 Mark Coeckelbergh, 'Technology as Skill and Activity: Revisiting the Problem of Alienation', *Techné: Research in Philosophy and Technology* 16, no. 3 (2012): 225. Original emphasis.

Selected Bibliography

Adibifar, Karam. 'Technology and Alienation in Modern-Day Societies'. *International Journal of Social Science Studies* 4, no. 9 (9 August 2016): 61–8.

Akst, Daniel. 'Ludd's Choosy Children'. *Technology Review*, 1 January 1999, 81–3.

Amarasingam, Amarnath, and Marc-André Argentino. 'The QAnon Conspiracy Theory: A Security Threat in the Making?' *CTC Sentinel* 13, no. 7 (2020): 37–44.

Armiero, Marco. 'Introduction: Fascism and Nature'. *Modern Italy* 19, no. 3 (August 2014): 241–5.

Baele, Stephane J., Lewys Brace, and Travis G. Coan. 'Uncovering the Far-Right Online Ecosystem: An Analytical Framework and Research Agenda'. *Studies in Conflict & Terrorism* 46, no. 9 (2 September 2023): 1599–623.

Baggaley, Jon. 'The Luddite Revolt Continues'. *Distance Education* 31, no. 3 (November 2010): 337–43.

Bale, Jeffrey M. *The Darkest Sides of Politics, I: Post-War Fascism, Covert Operations, and Terrorism*. New York: Routledge, 2018.

Bale, Jeffrey M. *The Darkest Sides of Politics, II: State Terrorism, 'Weapons of Mass Destruction', Religious Extremism, and Organized Crime*. New York: Routledge, 2018.

Barkun, Michael. 'Racist Apocalypse: Millennialism on the Far Right'. *American Studies* 31, no. 2 (1990): 121–40.

Basha, Saddiq. '"Death to the Grid": Ideological Narratives and Online Community Dynamics in Encouraging Far-Right Extremist Attacks on Critical Infrastructure'. *Counter Terrorist Trends and Analyses* 15, no. 4 (2024): 17–24.

Berry, David. 'Anarchism and 1968'. In *The Palgrave Handbook of Anarchism*, ed. Carl Levy and Matthew S. Adams. Cham: Springer International Publishing, 2019, 449–70.

Bhatt, Chetan. 'White Extinction: Metaphysical Elements of Contemporary Western Fascism'. *Theory, Culture & Society* 38, no. 1 (January 2021): 27–52.

Biehl, Janet, and Peter Staudenmaier. *Ecofascism: Lessons from the German Experience*. Edinburgh: AK Press, 1995.

Black, Richard, W. Neil Adger, Nigel W. Arnell, Stefan Dercon, Andrew Geddes, and David Thomas. 'The Effect of Environmental Change on Human Migration'. *Global Environmental Change* 21 (December 2011): S3–11.

Bondaroff, Teale Phelps. 'Throwing a Wrench into Things: The Strategy of Radical Environmentalism'. *Journal of Military and Strategic Studies* 10, no. 4 (2008).

Borum, Randy, and Chuck Tilby. 'Anarchist Direct Actions: A Challenge for Law Enforcement'. *Studies in Conflict & Terrorism* 28, no. 3 (May 2005): 201–23.

Bötticher, Astrid. 'Towards Academic Consensus Definitions of Radicalism and Extremism'. *Perspectives on Terrorism* 11, no. 4 (2017): 73–7.

Buchanan, Robert A. *The Power of the Machine: The Impact of Technology from 1700 to the Present*. London: Penguin Books, 1992.

Campion, Kristy. 'Defining Ecofascism: Historical Foundations and Contemporary Interpretations in the Extreme Right'. *Terrorism and Political Violence*, 1 November 2021, 1–19.

Campion, Kristy. '"Unstructured Terrorism"? Assessing Left-Wing Extremism in Australia'. *Critical Studies on Terrorism* 13, no. 4 (1 October 2020): 545–67.

Campion, Kristy, Jamie Ferrill, and Kristy Milligan. 'Extremist Exploitation of the Context Created by COVID-19 and the Implications for Australian Security'. *Perspectives on Terrorism* 15, no. 6 (2021): 23–40.

Carlopio, Jim. 'A History of Social Psychological Reactions to New Technology'. *Journal of Occupational Psychology* 61, no. 1 (March 1988): 67–77.

Carlyle, Thomas. *A Carlyle Reader: Selections from the Writings of Thomas Carlyle*. Ed. G.B. Tennyson. Acton, MA: Copley Pub. Group, 1999.

Carson, Jennifer Varriale, Gary LaFree, and Laura Dugan. 'Terrorist and Non-Terrorist Criminal Attacks by Radical Environmental and

Animal Rights Groups in the United States, 1970–2007'. *Terrorism and Political Violence* 24, no. 2 (April 2012): 295–319.

Clancy, Brett. 'Rebel or Rioter? Luddites Then and Now'. *Society* 54, no. 5 (October 2017): 392–98.

Clarke, Colin P., Mollie Saltskog, Michaela Millender, and Naureen C. Fink. 'The Targeting of Infrastructure by America's Violent Far-Right'. *CTC Sentinel* 16, no. 5 (2023): 26–32.

Coeckelbergh, Mark. 'Technology as Skill and Activity: Revisiting the Problem of Alienation'. *Techné: Research in Philosophy and Technology* 16, no. 3 (2012): 208–30.

Cohn, Norman. *The Pursuit of the Millennium: Revolutionary Millenarians and Mystical Anarchists of the Middle Ages*. London: Pimlico, 2004.

Conty, Arianne Françoise. 'Religion in the Age of the Anthropocene'. *Environmental Values* 30, no. 2 (April 2021): 215–34.

Cronin, Audrey K. *Power to the People: How Open Technological Innovation Is Arming Tomorrow's Terrorists*. Oxford: Oxford University Press, 2020.

Custer, Rodney L. 'Examining the Dimensions of Technology'. *International Journal of Technology and Design Education* 5, no. 3 (1995): 219–44.

da Silva, João Raphael. 'The Eco-Terrorist Wave'. *Behavioral Sciences of Terrorism and Political Aggression* 12, no. 3 (2 July 2020): 203–16.

Davis, Alan. 'Technology'. In *The Cambridge Companion to John Ruskin*, ed. Francis O'Gorman. Cambridge: Cambridge University Press, 2015, 170–86.

Day, Brian J. 'The Moral Intuition of Ruskin's "Storm-Cloud"'. *Studies in English Literature, 1500–1900* 45, no. 4 (2005): 917–33.

Devall, Bill, and George Sessions. *Deep Ecology: Living as if Nature Mattered*. Salt Lake City, UT: Smith, 1999.

Diani, Mario. 'The Concept of Social Movement'. *The Sociological Review* 40, no. 1 (February 1992): 1–25.

Diani, Mario, and Ivano Bison. 'Organizations, Coalitions, and Movements'. *Theory and Society* 33, no. 3/4 (June 2004): 281–309.

Dinello, Daniel. *Technophobia! Science Fiction Visions of Posthuman Technology*. Austin: University of Texas Press, 2006.

Dupuis-Déri, Francis. 'Anarchism and the Politics of Affinity Groups'. *Anarchist Studies* 18, no. 1 (2010): 40–61.

Dupuis-Déri, Francis. 'The Black Blocs Ten Years after Seattle: Anarchism, Direct Action, and Deliberative Practices'. *Journal for the Study of Radicalism* 4, no. 2 (2010): 45–82.

Eagan, Sean P. 'From Spikes to Bombs: The Rise of Eco-Terrorism'. *Studies in Conflict & Terrorism* 19, no. 1 (January 1996): 1–18.

Ellul, Jacques. *The Technological Society*. Trans. John Wilkinson. 7th edn. New York: Alfred A. Knopf, 1976.

English, Richard. 'History and the Study of Terrorism'. In *The Cambridge History of Terrorism*, ed. Richard English. Cambridge: Cambridge University Press, 2021, 3–28.

English, Richard. *Terrorism: How to Respond*. Oxford: Oxford University Press, 2009.

Feenberg, Andrew. *Transforming Technology: A Critical Theory Revisited*. New York: Oxford University Press, 2002.

Fleming, Sean. 'Searching for Ecoterrorism: The Crucial Case of the Unabomber'. *American Political Science Review*, 6 February 2024, 1–14.

Fleming, Sean. 'The Unabomber and the Origins of Anti-Tech Radicalism'. *Journal of Political Ideologies* 27, no. 2 (2022): 207–25.

Foreman, Dave. *Man Swarm and the Killing of Wildlife*. Durango, CO: Raven's Eye Press, 2011.

Foreman, Dave, and Bill Haywood, eds. *Ecodefense: A Field Guide to Monkeywrenching*. Chico, CA: Abbzug Press, 1993.

Gartenstein-Ross, Daveed, Andrew Zammit, Emelie Chace-Donahue, and Madison Urban. 'Composite Violent Extremism: Conceptualizing Attackers Who Increasingly Challenge Traditional Categories of Terrorism'. *Studies in Conflict & Terrorism*, 29 March 2023, 1–27.

Gowdy, John, and Lisi Krall. 'The Ultrasocial Origin of the Anthropocene'. *Ecological Economics* 95 (November 2013): 137–47.

Graham, Robert. 'Anarchism and the First International'. In *The Palgrave Handbook of Anarchism*, ed. Carl Levy and Matthew S. Adams. Cham: Springer International Publishing, 2019, 325–42.

Graham, Robert. *We Do Not Fear Anarchy, We Invoke It. The First International and the Origins of the Anarchist Movement*. Chico, CA: AK Press, 2015.

Guldi, Jo, and David Armitage. *The History Manifesto*. Cambridge: Cambridge University Press, 2014.

Haekel, Ralf. 'Thomas Carlyle and the Emergence of the Concept of Romanticism: "Signs of the Times" and *Sartor Resartus*'. *European Romantic Review* 35, no. 2 (2 April 2024): 417–34.

Hall, John R. 'Apocalyptic and Millenarian Movements'. In *The Wiley-Blackwell Encyclopedia of Social and Political Movements*, ed. David A. Snow, Donatella Della Porta, Bert Klandermans, and Doug McAdam. Oxford: Wiley, 2013, 1–6.

Hendry, John, and Anthony F. Lemieux. 'The Visual and Rhetorical Styles of Atomwaffen Division and Their Implications'. *Dynamics of Asymmetric Conflict* 14, no. 2 (4 May 2021): 138–59.

Hirsch-Hoefler, Sivan, and Cas Mudde. '"Ecoterrorism": Terrorist Threat or Political Ploy?' *Studies in Conflict & Terrorism* 37, no. 7 (3 July 2014): 586–603.

Hobsbawm, E.J. 'The Machine Breakers'. *Past and Present* 1, no. 1 (1952): 57–70.

Hoffman, Bruce, and Jacob Ware. *God, Guns, and Sedition: Far-Right Terrorism in America*. New York: Columbia University Press, 2024.

Hughes, Brian. '"Pine Tree" Twitter and the Shifting Ideological Foundations of Eco-Extremism'. *Interventionen: Zeitschrift für Verantwortungspädagogik* 14 (2019): 18–25.

Hughes, Brian, Dave Jones, and Amarnath Amarasingam. 'Ecofascism: An Examination of the Far-Right/Ecology Nexus in the Online Space'. *Terrorism and Political Violence* 34, no. 5 (4 July 2022): 997–1023.

Jensen, Derrick. *Endgame, Volume 1: The Problem of Civilization*. New York: Seven Stories Press, 2006.

Jensen, Derrick. *Endgame, Volume 2: Resistance*. New York: Seven Stories Press, 2006.

Jensen, Richard. 'Daggers, Rifles and Dynamite: Anarchist Terrorism in Nineteenth-Century Europe'. *Terrorism and Political Violence* 16, no. 1 (January 2004): 116–53.

Jones, Steven E. *Against Technology: From the Luddites to Neo-Luddism*. New York: Routledge, 2006.

Joosse, Paul. 'Leaderless Resistance and Ideological Inclusion: The Case of the Earth Liberation Front'. *Terrorism and Political Violence* 19, no. 3 (4 July 2007): 351–68.

Joosse, Paul. 'Leaderless Resistance and the Loneliness of Lone Wolves: Exploring the Rhetorical Dynamics of Lone Actor Violence'. *Terrorism and Political Violence* 29, no. 1 (2 January 2017): 52–78.

Koch, Ariel. 'The ONA Network and the Transnationalization of Neo-Nazi-Satanism'. *Studies in Conflict & Terrorism* 47, no. 10 (2024): 1172–99.

Koch, Ariel. 'Trends in Anti-Fascist and Anarchist Recruitment and Mobilization'. *Journal for Deradicalization*, no. 14 (2018): 1–51.

Koch, Ariel, Karine Nahon, and Assaf Moghadam. 'White Jihad: How White Supremacists Adopt Jihadi Narratives, Aesthetics, and Tactics'. *Terrorism and Political Violence* 36, no. 7 (2024): 919–43.

Landes, Richard Allen. *Heaven on Earth: The Varieties of the Millennial Experience*. New York: Oxford University Press, 2011.

Leader, Stefan H., and Peter Probst. 'The Earth Liberation Front and Environmental Terrorism'. *Terrorism and Political Violence* 15, no. 4 (October 2003): 37–58.

Lee, Martha F. *Earth First! Environmental Apocalypse*. Syracuse, NY: Syracuse University Press, 1995.

Liddick, Donald D. *Eco-Terrorism: Radical Environmental and Animal Liberation Movements*. London: Praeger, 2006.

Linton, David. 'The Luddites: How Did They Get That Bad Reputation?' *Labor History* 33, no. 4 (October 1992): 529–37.

Linton, David. 'The Making of a Pariah: The Case of the Luddites'. *ETC: A Review of General Semantics* 48, no. 4 (1991): 404–13.

Loadenthal, Michael. '"Eco-Terrorism": An Incident-Driven History of Attack (1973–2010)'. *Journal for the Study of Radicalism* 11, no. 2 (1 July 2017): 1–34.

Loadenthal, Michael. 'Feral Fascists and Deep Green Guerrillas: Infrastructural Attack and Accelerationist Terror'. *Critical Studies on Terrorism* 15, no. 1 (2 January 2022): 169–208.

Loadenthal, Michael. *The Politics of Attack: Communiqués and Insurrectionary Violence*. Manchester: Manchester University Press, 2018.

Love, Sam, and David Obst. *Ecotage!* New York: Pocket Books, 1972.

Lubrano, Mauro. 'Choosing What (Not) to Do Next: A Preliminary Theoretical Framework on Strategic Innovation in Terrorist Organizations', *Dynamics of Asymmetric Conflict* 17, no. 1 (2 January 2024): 1–22.

Lubrano, Mauro. 'Hidden in Plain Sight: Insurrectionary Anarchism in the Anti-Government Extremism Landscape'. *Perspectives on Terrorism* 18, no. 1 (2024): 37–61.

Lubrano, Mauro. 'Lone Leaders of Leaderless Resistors: A Theory of Informal Leadership in Contemporary Terrorism and Political Violence'. *Studies in Conflict & Terrorism*, 29 June 2023, 1–24.

Lubrano, Mauro. 'Stop the Machines: How Emerging Technologies Are Fomenting the War on Civilization', *Terrorism and Political Violence* 35, no. 2 (2023): 321–37.

Luke, Timothy W. 'Tracing Race, Ethnicity, and Civilization in the Anthropocene'. *Environment and Planning D: Society and Space* 38, no. 1 (February 2020): 129–46.

Macklin, Graham. 'The Evolution of Extreme-Right Terrorism and Efforts to Counter It in the United Kingdom'. *CTC Sentinel* 12, no. 1 (2019): 15–20.

Macklin, Graham. 'The Extreme Right, Climate Change and Terrorism'. *Terrorism and Political Violence* 34, no. 5 (4 July 2022): 979–96.

Malhi, Yadvinder. 'The Concept of the Anthropocene'. *Annual Review of Environment and Resources* 42, no. 1 (17 October 2017): 77–104.

Manes, Christopher. *Green Rage: Radical Environmentalism and the Unmaking of Civilization*. Boston: Little, Brown and Co., 1990.

Marone, Francesco. 'A Profile of the Informal Anarchist Federation in Italy'. *CTC Sentinel* 7, no. 3 (2014): 21–5.

Marone, Francesco. 'Left-Wing and Anarchist Extremism in Italy'. In *The Palgrave Handbook of Left-Wing Extremism, Volume 1*, ed. José Pedro Zúquete. Cham: Palgrave Macmillan, 2023, 261–80.

Marone, Francesco. 'The Prisoner Dilemma: Insurrectionary Anarchism and the Cospito Affair'. *CTC Sentinel* 16, no. 3 (2023): 21–6.

Marone, Francesco. 'The Rise of Insurrectionary Anarchist Terrorism in Italy'. *Dynamics of Asymmetric Conflict* 8, no. 3 (2 September 2015): 194–214.

McBay, Aric, Lierre Keith, and Derrick Jensen. *Deep Green Resistance: Strategy to Save the Planet*. New York: Seven Stories Press, 2011.

Merchant, Brian. *Blood in the Machine: The Origins of the Rebellion Against Big Tech*. New York: Little, Brown and Company, 2023.

Millett, Steve. 'Technology Is Capital: *Fifth Estate*'s Critique of the Megamachine'. In *Changing Anarchism*, ed. Jonathan Purkis and James Bowen. Manchester: Manchester University Press, 2018, 73–98.

Mokyr, Joel. *The Lever of Riches: Technological Creativity and Economic Progress*. New York: Oxford University Press, 1990.

Monaghan, Rachel. 'Animal Rights and Violent Protest'. *Terrorism and Political Violence* 9, no. 4 (December 1997): 106–16.

Monaghan, Rachel. 'Not Quite Terrorism: Animal Rights Extremism in the United Kingdom'. *Studies in Conflict & Terrorism* 36, no. 11 (November 2013): 933–51.

Monaghan, Rachel. 'Terrorism in the Name of Animal Rights'. *Terrorism and Political Violence* 11, no. 4 (December 1999): 159–69.

Moore, Sam, and Alex Roberts. *The Rise of Ecofascism: Climate Change and the Far Right*. Cambridge: Polity, 2022.

Mueller, Gavin. *Breaking Things at Work: The Luddites Are Right About Why You Hate Your Job*. London: Verso, 2021.

Mumford, Lewis. *Technics and Civilization*. Chicago: University of Chicago Press, 2010.

Mumford, Lewis. *The Myth of the Machine: Volume I, Technics and Human Development*. Illustrated edn. Boston, MA: Mariner Books, 1971.

Næss, Arne. 'The Basic Principles of Deep Ecology'. *The Trumpeter* 3, no. 4 (1986): 14.

Næss, Arne. 'The Shallow and the Deep, Long-Range Ecology Movement. A Summary'. *Inquiry: An Interdisciplinary Journal of Philosophy* 16, no. 1–4 (1973): 95–100.

Newhouse, Alex. 'The Threat Is the Network: The Multi-Node Structure of Neo-Fascist Accelerationism'. *CTC Sentinel* 14, no. 5 (2021): 17–25.

O'Rourke, Kevin Hjortshøj, Ahmed S. Rahman, and Alan M. Taylor. 'Luddites, the Industrial Revolution, and the Demographic Transition'. *Journal of Economic Growth* 18, no. 4 (December 2013): 373–409.

Phillips, Leigh. 'Anarchists Attack Science: Armed Extremists Are Targeting Nuclear and Nanotechnology Workers.', *Nature* 485, no. 7400 (May 2012): 561.

Phillips, Leigh. 'Armed Resistance: *Nature* Assesses the Aftermath of a Series of Nanotechnology-Lab Bombings in Mexico and Asks How the Country Became a Target of Eco-Anarchists'. *Nature* 488, no. 413 (2012): 576–9.

Protopapadakis, Evangelos D. 'Environmental Ethics and Linkola's Ecofascism: An Ethics Beyond Humanism'. *Frontiers of Philosophy in China* 9, no. 4 (2014): 586–601.

Randall, Adrian. 'Reinterpreting "Luddism": Resistance to New Technology in the British Industrial Revolution'. In *Resistance to New*

Technology: Nuclear Power, Information Technology and Biotechnology, ed. Martin Bauer. Cambridge: Cambridge University Press, 1997, 57–80.

Richards, Imogen, Callum Jones, and Gearóid Brinn. 'Eco-Fascism Online: Conceptualizing Far-Right Actors' Response to Climate Change on Stormfront'. *Studies in Conflict & Terrorism*, 18 December 2022, 1–27.

Ruskin, John. *The Storm Cloud of the Nineteenth Century: Two Lectures Delivered at the London Institution, February 4th and 11th, 1884*. London: Wentworth Press, 2016.

Sale, Kirkpatrick. *Rebels Against the Future: The Luddites and Their War on the Industrial Revolution: Lessons for the Computer Age*. Wokingham: Addison-Welsey, 1995.

Scarce, Rik. *Eco-Warriors: Understanding the Radical Environmental Movement*. Updated edn. Walnut Creek, CA: Left Coast Press, Inc., 2006.

Schäfer, Wolf. 'Global Civilization and Local Cultures: A Crude Look at the Whole'. *International Sociology* 16, no. 3 (September 2001): 301–19.

Schatzberg, Eric. *Technology: Critical History of a Concept*. Chicago: University of Chicago Press, 2018.

Sessions, George, ed. *Deep Ecology for the Twenty-First Century*. Boston: Shambhala, 1995.

Sessions, George. 'The Deep Ecology Movement: A Review', *Environmental Review* 11, no. 2 (1987): 105–25.

Spadaro, Paola Andrea. 'Climate Change, Environmental Terrorism, Eco-Terrorism and Emerging Threats'. *Journal of Strategic Security* 13, no. 4 (December 2020): 58–80.

Taylor, Bron. 'Religion, Violence and Radical Environmentalism: From Earth First! to the Unabomber to the Earth Liberation Front'. *Terrorism and Political Violence* 10, no. 4 (December 1998): 1–42.

Taylor, Bron. 'The Tributaries of Radical Environmentalism'. *Journal for the Study of Radicalism* 2, no. 1 (2008): 27–61.

Taylor, Jesse Oak. 'Storm-Clouds on the Horizon: John Ruskin and the Emergence of Anthropogenic Climate Change', *19: Interdisciplinary Studies in the Long Nineteenth Century* 26 (6 July 2018).

Thompson, E.P. *The Making of the English Working Class*. Harmondsworth: Penguin Books, 1991.

Trujillo, Horacio R. 'The Radical Environmentalist Movement'. In *Aptitude for Destruction Volume 2: Case Studies of Organizational Learning in Five Terrorist Groups*, ed. Brian A Jackson. Santa Monica, CA: RAND Corporation, 2005, 141–80.

Upchurch, H.E. 'The Iron March Forum and the Evolution of the "Skull Mask" Neo-Fascist Network'. *CTC Sentinel* 14, no. 10 (2021): 27–37.

Wasserstrom, Jeffrey. '"Civilization" and Its Discontents: The Boxers and Luddites as Heroes and Villains'. *Theory and Society* 16, no. 5 (1987): 675–707.

Watson, Paul. *Earthforce!: An Earth Warrior's Guide to Strategy*. Los Angeles: Chaco Press, 1993.

Western, Simon. 'Autonomist Leadership in Leaderless Movements: Anarchists Leading the Way'. *Ephemera: Theory & Politics in Organization* 14, no. 4 (2014): 673–98.

Williams, Dana M. 'Contemporary Anarchist and Anarchistic Movements'. *Sociology Compass* 12, no. 6 (June 2018): 1–17.

Williams, Leonard. 'Anarchism Revived'. *New Political Science* 29, no. 3 (September 2007): 297–312.

Wong, George H.C. 'China's Opposition to Western Science during Late Ming and Early Ch'ing'. *Isis* 54, no. 1 (March 1963): 29–49.

Woodhouse, Keith Makoto. *The Ecocentrists: A History of Radical Environmentalism*. New York: Columbia University Press, 2018.

Yost, C. Spencer. 'Luddites'. *ICU Director* 2, no. 3 (May 2011): 51–2.

Zerzan, John, ed. *Against Civilization: Readings and Reflections*. Eugene, OR: Uncivilized Books, 1999.

Zerzan, John. *Future Primitive and Other Essays*. New York: Autonomedia, 1994.

Zuboff, Shoshana. *The Age of Surveillance Capitalism: The Fight for the Future at the New Frontier of Power*. London: Profile Books, 2019.

Zúquete, José Pedro. 'Left-Wing Extremism and the War on Civilization'. In *The Palgrave Handbook of Left-Wing Extremism, Volume 2*, ed. José Pedro Zúquete. Cham: Springer Nature Switzerland, 2023, 257–76.

Index

5G, 4, 33, 53–4, 98–9, 106–7

Abbey, Edward, 22, 60
accelerationism, 5, 52, 76, 83,
    90–1, 94, 96–7, 99, 106,
    114–17, 118, 120, 122
Adinolfi, Roberto, 42, 55
al-Qaeda, 13, 80, 116
anarchism, 36–40 (*see also*
    anarcho-primitivism;
    insurrectionary anarchism)
anarcho-primitivism, 24, 31, 38,
    49, 72
Animal Liberation Front (ALF),
    21, 25, 60
animal liberationism, 22, 61, 66
Animal Rights Militia (ARM),
    60–1
Anthropocene, 6, 105–10, 113
Anthropos, 108 (*see also Homo
    Antropocenicus*)
Anti-Tech Collective, 42
Anti-Technology Movement, 103,
    105, 107–8, 114–18, 120–1,
    123, 131
Arthurs, Devon, 92
artificial intelligence (AI), 1–4, 11,
    12, 100, 126–8, 130
    ChatGPT, 11
Atomwaffen Division (AWD),
    91–3

Aum Shinrikyo, 112, 114
Autonomous Revolutionary
    Squads, 54

Bakunin, Mikhail, 39
Bale, Jeffrey, 33, 114
Bari, Judy, 28
Base, The, 93
Beam, Louis, 90, 117
Bhatt, Chetan, 83
Biehl, Janet, 85
Black, Bob, 37–8
Bookchin, Murray, 18, 36
Breivik, Anders, 93
Buchanan, Robert, 9
Buono, Federico, 67, 79, 104
Bythell, Shaun, 15

Campbell, Scott, 77
Campion, Kristy, 82
Carlyle, Thomas, 17
Carpenter, Edward, 18
Chahta-Ima, 71, 117
Christ, Kiernan, 95
Coeckelbergh, Mark, 130
Cohn, Norman, 111
Committee for Liquidation or
    Subversion of Computers
    – *Comité Liquidant pour
    Détournant les Ordinateurs*
    (CLODO), 25

Index

Conspiracy of Cells of Fire (CCF), 41–2, 55, 67
Coordinated Associations for the Anti-Tech Revolt and Eco-Sabotage (ACRATES), 42
Cospito, Alfredo, 42–3, 55–6, 117
COVID-19, 49–50, 54, 56, 69, 76, 98, 107, 113
Crusius, Patrick, 81–2, 89, 92, 95, 130
Crutzen, Paul, 105

Dark Foreigner, 91
Darré, Richard Walter, 85
Days of Chaos, 70, 76, 109, 113
deep ecology, 21–2, 49, 59–61
Deep Green Resistance (DGR), 62
Devi, Savitri, 86–7
Diani, Marco, 104
direct action, 13, 22, 39, 60

Earth First! (EF!), 23–4, 28, 60
Earth Liberation Front, 22, 25, 28, 60
eco-extremism, 4–6, 29, 58–9, 63, 65–80, 90–1, 93, 103–6, 108–11, 113, 115, 117–19, 124
  eco-extremist mafia, 67–8, 75, 77
eco-fascism, 4–6, 29, 77–9, 82–6, 88, 92–6, 98–9, 101, 103–6, 109–11, 113, 115, 118–19, 124–5, 130
ecotage, 59–60
Ellul, Jacques, 19–20, 26, 44, 50

Farrell-Molloy, Joshua, 96
Feenberg, Andrew, 31–2
Feuerkrieg Division, 93
Fifth Estate (FE), 44–6
Fifth Industrial Revolution, 3, 126, 128
Filiss, John, 24
Fleming, Sean, 27
For Wild Nature, 63
Foreman, Dave, 21–2, 60
Forster, E.M., 18–19, 52
Fulano, T., 45, 47

Gai, Nicola, 55
Gajardo Escalona, Camilo Eduardo, 59, 79
Garrido, Kevin, 104
Gendron, Payton, 93
Gilder, George, 13
Glendinning, Chellis, 23–4, 31
Graham, Robert, 36
Great Replacement, 81–3, 98
Green Brigade, 93, 95

Haeckel, Ernst, 85
Haymarket Massacre, 10
Haywood, Bill, 60
Heaven's Gate, 114
Heidegger, Martin, 20, 88
Hobsbawm, Eric, 15
Homo Antropocenicus, 108–10

Individualists Tending Towards the Wild (ITS), 58, 66–71, 76–80
indomitistas, 29, 63
Informal Anarchist Federation (FAI), 41–2, 66–7

Informal Anarchist Federation
(FAI) (*cont.*)
  Informal Anarchist Federation
  – International Revolutionary
  Front (FAI-FRI), 41–3,
  54–5
insurrectionary anarchism, 2,
  5–6, 29, 35–6, 38, 40–4, 46,
  49–50, 55, 59, 66, 78, 91,
  101, 104, 108, 111–13,
  117
International Conspiracy for
  Revenge, 54
International Revolutionary
  Front (*see* Informal Anarchist
  Federation – International
  Revolutionary Front)
IRA, 80, 116

Jacobi, John, 63–5
Jensen, Derrick, 62
Justice Department (JD), 60–1

Kaczynski, David, 27
Kaczynski, Theodore J., 2, 25–9,
  32, 46, 50–1, 59, 61, 63, 65,
  69–70, 77, 86–7, 92, 94, 96,
  99, 103, 106, 118, 120–1

Landerrechte Moreno, Óscar, 58
leaderless resistance, 38, 42, 68,
  90, 116–18, 120
Linkola, Pentti, 86–7
Loadenthal, Michael, 61, 78, 92
Lubarda, Balša, 83
Luddism, 12–17, 20, 23–4, 28–31,
  34, 101, 126–8
Luddite Resistance, 120–1

Ma, Mike, 93–4, 118
machine-breaking, 12–14, 18, 25,
  34, 127
Macklin, Graham, 86, 90–1, 96
Malatesta, Errico, 39–40
Marx, Karl, 13, 44
  Marxism, 84, 91
  Marxism-Leninism, 37, 102
Mason, James, 90–1, 117–18
McVeigh, Timothy, 88, 92
mega-machine, 5, 19, 44, 46, 49,
  52–3, 56, 73, 76, 106–8,
  114–15, 118
MictlanTepetli, 71, 117
millenarianism, 111–14
Millett, Steve, 44
Mokyr, Joel, 13
monkeywrenching, 26, 65
Mumford, Lewis, 19–20, 44, 46,
  50
Murray, Henry, 26
Musk, Elon, 35

Næss, Arne, 21, 59
neo-Luddism, 16, 23–4, 28–34, 43
Nobel, Alfred, 10, 36
Nordic Resistance Movement, 93

Offspring of Disaster, 54
Order of Nine Angles (O9A), 77,
  80, 92
Orwell, George, 19

Pierce, William Luther, 88
Pine Tree Party, 94
Piranian, George, 25
Porcu, Pierleone, 45
primitivism, 24, 129

prison-society, 6, 35, 44, 47–51, 108, 112
propaganda of the deed, 10, 39, 52

radical environmentalism, 4, 20, 22–3, 59–62, 66, 68, 178, 113, 117
Ramsay, Gilbert, 10
Randall, Adrian, 15
Rapewaffen Division, 91
Rivera Osorio, Lesvy Berlín, 77
Rule, John, 15
Ruskin, John, 17–18
Russell, Brandon, 92

Sale, Kirkpatrick, 23–4, 30
Savio, Mario, 20
Schäfer, Wolf, 8
Sea Shepherd Conservation Society, 21
Second Luddite Congress, 24, 28
Shields, Allen, 25–6
Shone, Toby, 43, 117
Siege Culture, 91–3
Singularity, 51, 112
Slavros, Alexander, 89
small-scale technology, 27–8
Staudenmeier, Peter, 85
Swing Riots, 14

Tarrant, Brenton, 82, 89, 92, 95, 118
Taylor, Bron, 59
techno-elites, 43, 47–50, 106, 108, 111, 115, 118
techno-industrial civilization, 5, 8, 20, 27, 32–4, 36, 45, 52, 56, 60, 62, 65, 69–70, 73–6, 80, 88, 94–5, 99, 106–7, 109, 119
techno-industrial society, 32, 34, 44, 46, 73, 109
Tempel ov Blood, 77, 80
Terrorgram, 90, 95, 97, 118
Tesla, 35
Thomis, Malcom Ian, 15
Thompson, E.P., 126
Toboso-Buezo, Mario, 102
Torres-Soriano, Manuel, 102
totalitarianism of the machines, 36, 49–50
totalitarianism of the prison-society, 108
transhumanism, 38, 50, 64, 74, 108

Último Reducto, 29, 63
Unabomber, 2, 25–9, 45, 52, 59, 63, 65–6, 71, 77, 87, 92–4, 118 (see also Kaczynski, Theodore J.)

Valenti, Eric, 79
völkisch movement, 84–5
Vulkangruppe Tesla abschalten, 35, 42

War on the Nerves, 75–6, 78–9
Watson, David (*see* Fulano, T.)
Watson, Paul, 21
Wild Nature, 64–5, 68–70, 73–4, 76, 105–6, 108–9, 113, 115
Wild Reaction (RS), 67, 69–71
Wildism, 63–5, 69–70, 74
Wong, George, 16

Woodhouse, Keith Makoto, 21–2
Woods, Percy, 26
Wray, Christopher, 103

Xale, 71, 79, 117

Zerzan, John, 24, 28–9, 31, 77
Zuboff, Shoshana, 11